NATIONS OF THE MODERN WORLD

ARGENTINA
H. S. Ferns
Professor of Political Science,
University of Birmingham

AUSTRALIA
O. H. K. Spate
Director, Research School of Pacific Studies,
Australian National University, Canberra

AUSTRIA
Karl R. Stadler
Professor of Modern and Contemporary History,
University of Linz

BELGIUM
Vernon Mallinson
Professor of Comparative Education,
University of Reading

BURMA
F. S. V. Donnison, C.B.E.
Formerly Chief Secretary to the Government of Burma
Historian, Cabinet Office, Historical Section 1949–66

CHINA
Victor Purcell, C.M.G.
Late Lecturer in Far Eastern History, Cambridge

CYPRUS
H. D. Purcell
Professor of English,
University of Libya, Benghazi

DENMARK
W. Glyn Jones
Reader in Danish, University College London

MODERN EGYPT Tom Little, M.B.E.
Former Managing Director and General Manager of
Regional News Services (Middle East), Ltd, London

ENGLAND
A Portrait
John Bowle
Formerly Professor of Political Theory, Collège d'Europe
Bruges 1950–67

FINLAND
W. R. Mead
Professor of Geography, University College London

SUDAN REPUBLIC	K. D. D. Henderson, C.M.G. *Formerly of the Sudan Political Service and Governor of Darfur Province, 1949–53*
SWEDEN	Irene Scobbie *Senior Lecturer in Swedish, University of Aberdeen*
SYRIA	Tabitha Petran
TURKEY	Geoffrey Lewis *Senior Lecturer in Islamic Studies, Oxford*
YUGOSLAVIA	Stevan K. Pavlowitch *Lecturer in Balkan History, University of Southampton*

NATIONS OF THE MODERN WORLD

SWEDEN

SWEDEN

By

IRENE SCOBBIE

LONDON
ERNEST BENN LIMITED

First published 1972 by Ernest Benn Limited
25 New Street Square, Fleet Street, London, EC4A 3JA

Distributed in Canada by
The General Publishing Company Limited, Toronto

© *Irene Scobbie 1972*

Printed in Great Britain

ISBN 0 510-39103-6

Preface

FOR MUCH OF her history Sweden has been a relatively unknown country tucked away in a northern backwater, seemingly outside main developments in Europe and only slowly absorbing influences from more advanced cultures to the south and west. Occasionally she would burst her way into the mainstream of European history, but this would be through the actions (usually warlike) of a few dynamic Swedes (the Swedish Vikings, Gustavus Adolphus, Karl XII, for example), the impetus would soon be spent, and the culture newly acquired by close direct contact with leading European powers would be too narrowly based within the country to lead to any rapid or universal changes.

This century, however, has seen a remarkable reversal of this situation. Sweden has become one of the most advanced modern states in Europe, and has gained her new reputation not by the military genius of exceptional Swedes but by the creative ability of her people, and by the whole nation assiduously avoiding war. The economic advantages of this new attitude have been more widely and evenly spread than in previous periods of Swedish history and have wrought great changes in the lives of the people as a whole.

Not many decades ago Sweden to the average Anglo-Saxon meant forests, polar bears, and the Arctic Circle. The forests and the Arctic Circle are still there (polar bears can best be viewed at Skansen in Stockholm), but now Sweden conjures up a different picture. To some, admittedly, she has become the country with a high incidence of alcoholism, suicide, and of beautiful but licentious women, but more deservedly she is also thought of as a model welfare state, a well-ordered democracy to which sociologists, designers, architects, and scientists from the most sophisticated nations in the world pay study visits. This book traces the remarkable development that has taken place in Sweden, gives a picture of the modern state as it has emerged, but also shows that modern Sweden is still rooted in her past.

In my attempt to present Swedish history, politics, culture, and general view of life in one volume I have inevitably produced an

9

eclectic study. To put it more crudely, I have run the risk of falling between not just two but several stools. However, I hope that the selective bibliography will assist those who require fuller information on issues which I have treated summarily.

Readers may like to know that in March 1972 the rate of exchange was 12·49 Swedish *kronor* to the pound sterling and 5·17 to the U.S. dollar.

I should like to take this opportunity of acknowledging my indebtedness to the Carnegie Trust for the Universities of Scotland for a grant which enabled me to spend a sabbatical term collecting much of the material necessary for this book.

I should also like to express my gratitude to Dr Nils-Gustav Hildeman and Miss Norma Nutt for their kindness in reading my manuscript and making many valuable suggestions, and to Professor Gunnar Ahlström and his colleagues at the Swedish Institute in Stockholm for their personal and professional guidance and generosity. I am greatly indebted too to my colleague Dr E. Alistair Smith of the Geography Department, Aberdeen University, for producing drafts for my two maps and several photographs and to the Swedish Institute in London for help in acquiring further illustrations.

Aberdeen   I.S.
24 March 1972

Contents

List of Illustrations

Maps

Acknowledgements

ACKNOWLEDGEMENT for kind permission to reproduce illustrations is made to the following, to whom the copyright of the illustrations belongs:

Camera Press Limited: 4, 5, 10, 13, 16, 17
Foto-Hernried, Bromma, Sweden: 23
Paul Popper Limited: 3, 9, 11, 15, 18
Reportagebild, Stockholm: 12, 14, 19
Dr E. Alistair Smith: 20, 21, 22, 24, 25, 26
The Swedish Institute, Stockholm: 1, 2, 6, 7, 8
The Swedish International Press Bureau, Stockholm: 27

List of Common Swedish Abbreviations

AB = Aktiebolag = limited company

ABF = Arbetarnas Bildningsförbund = Workers' Educational Association

AGA = Svensk AB Gasaccumulator

AMS = Arbetsmarknadsstyrelsen = Labour Market Board

ASEA = Allmänna svenska elektriska aktiebolaget

ASSI = AB Statens Skogsindustrier = National Forest Industries

JO = Justitieombudsman = the *Ombudsman*

KF = Kooperativa Förbundet = Co-operative Societies

LKAB = Luossavaara-Kiirunavaara AB

LO = Landsorganisationen = Swedish Confederation of Trade Unions

RFSU = Riksförbundet för sexuell upplysning = National Association for Sex Education

SAAB = Svenska aeroplan AB

SACO = Sveriges akademikers centralorganisation = Central Organization of Swedish Professional Workers

SAF = Svenska arbetsgivareföreningen = Swedish Federation of Employers

SJ = Statens järnvägar = Swedish Railways

SKF = AB Svenska kullagerfabriken = Swedish Ball Bearing Company

SR = Statstjänstemännens riksförbund = Federation of Government Employees

TCO = Tjänstemännens centralorganisation = Central Organization of Salaried Employees

TT = Tidningarnas Telegrambyrå = Swedish News Agency

c. 10000 B.C.–A.D. 1523
Sweden Emerges

VILHELM MOBERG SAYS that 'Sweden's greatest national archive is the Swedish soil' and it is true that owing to the paucity of written documents dating from Sweden's early history it is the archaeologist who has contributed most to our knowledge of Sweden until the Middle Ages.

The first inhabitants were small groups of nomadic hunters and fishermen who moved northwards as the ice receded between 10000 and 8000 B.C. Then there are signs that by about 3000 B.C. people were settling in the south of the country and were cultivating the soil and raising domestic animals. There are also traces of the Boat-Axe people, so-called because of the boat-shaped stone axes peculiar to them. These latter people appear to have been warriors who moved into Sweden from the Baltic. Their culture spread rapidly in the southern and central areas and a widely accepted theory held by Swedish archaeologists is that they formed an élite. Certainly the wealth of decorative objects found in the richer graves of this period suggests that there was a nobility in the country. It is not certain whether we are dealing with three successive migrations into Sweden or whether (less likely) one culture developed out of another, but in any case, by the end of the Stone Age the three had fused together.

During the Bronze Age (*c.* 1500–500 B.C.) the Boat-Axe people traded extensively with countries in the South, importing bronze (which they learnt to work with great skill) and exporting furs and amber. The large finds of bronze ornaments from this period show that the period was a comparatively rich one, but it was followed by a difficult 500 years from about 500 B.C., when the deterioration of the climate in Sweden coincided with the rise to prominence in Europe of the Celtic tribes who severed the Scandinavians' trade routes.

As the Romans penetrated into Gaul, however, they came into contact with, and influenced, the Germanic tribes, including the Scandinavians. This influence spread further to the Germanic world when Germanic tribes penetrated into lands bordering the Rhine and the Danube. Tangible evidence of this influence is found in the use of runes, Germanic adaptations of Greek and Roman letters. Trade routes were now open from Scandinavia to the Mediterranean and a great many Roman coins dating from the era of the Roman Caesars have been found in Scandinavia.

The Scandinavian Germanic tribes are specifically mentioned in classical literature for the first time during this period. Pliny the Elder (A.D. 23–79) mentions, in his *Historia naturalis*, an island far to the north called *Scandinavia*, but it is in Tacitus' *Germania* (A.D. 98) that reference is made by name to a Swedish tribe, the *Suiones*, i.e. the Svear, who, Tacitus relates, had their strength in men, weapons, and ships.

By the mid-sixth century Jordanes, the Gothic historian, mentions over twenty tribes in the Scandinavian peninsula, including the Götar, Svear, the Finni (Finns), and Scridfinni (Lapps). Little is known of the feuds during the first centuries of the Christian era, but at some stage the Svear must have gained supremacy over the powerful Götar. In Beowulf it is related that early in the sixth century the Svear kings subjected a people called *Geatas*, and there is much speculation as to whether these *Geatas* are the Götar. The first Svear king known definitely to have been king of the Götar too was Olof Skötkonung, but that was in A.D. 1000. Whatever the details, it was the Svear who emerged as the rulers of the whole of Sweden except the south, and they have given the country its name, *Sverige* in Swedish, i.e. *Svea rike*, the Kingdom of the Svear. The district which they settled, the rich pasture land round Lake Mälaren with its many easily-defended islands and a rich forest hinterland in the north well stocked with fine animal furs, established itself as the centre of Swedish culture, a position it has held ever since.

The history of the Svear kings, the Yngling dynasty, belongs more properly to mythology than to history. Odin himself is said to have come to the Mälar district accompanied by Frej, the god of plenty and fertility, also called Yngve, from whom the Ynglings are said to stem. They had their seat in Uppsala where in their role of priests as well as kings they sacrificed to the Nordic gods. Every nine years there was a particularly bloody ceremony when human sacrifices were offered to Odin, Frej, and Thor. The Icelandic *Ynglingatal* gives a list of the kings as handed down by tradition. Doubtless some of these were genuine monarchs but little is known about them. King Erik the Victorious is known to have ruled until A.D. *c.* 994. His son Olof Skötkonung who ruled from *c.* 994 to 1022 was said to be Sweden's first Christian king, which perhaps angered

his divine forebears, for his two sons were the last of the line and the
Yngling dynasty died with them in 1060.

The Viking Era

'From the fury of the Norsemen, O Lord, deliver us'. This
anguished prayer offered up in Christian churches and monasteries
in northern France in the tenth century is a stark indication that the
Scandinavians were occupying a central position in European
history. Several reasons have been given for the sudden emergence
of the Vikings as a dominant force from about 800 to 1060: a rise in
population in Scandinavia; the Vikings were both polygamous and
proud of their virility, and since they also had adopted a system of
primogeniture, many younger sons went abroad to seek their
fortune; the changing political situation in Europe (after the Arab
invasion had disrupted trade routes in the western Mediterranean
area, trade increased in northern Europe, with the Rhine developing
into a major trade route. Charlemagne was strong enough to defend
his lands, but after his death in 814 the Frankish Empire began to
disintegrate, exposing to the Vikings rich, ill-defended coastal
regions); also important is the Vikings' great skill both as ship-
builders and as sailors; and not least their bold spirit of adventure
and bravery in battle. The *Hávamál* (The Sayings of Odin), which
reflects in essence many of the Norse attitudes, contains the lines
'Cattle die, kinsmen die, I myself shall die, but there is one thing
which I know never dies: the reputation we leave behind at our
death'. To achieve honour in battle was one of the Vikings' aspira-
tions, and they were willing to sacrifice their lives to this end. It
was this, together with their prowess as both warriors and seamen,
that made them such formidable enemies.

Since many of the contemporary accounts of the Vikings were
written by ecclesiastics, it is hardly surprising that the Norsemen
have gone down in history as fierce, murderous pirates who specialized in pillaging monasteries and other holy places. While this
aspect cannot be ignored, they were also brave explorers and
intrepid merchants who pushed back the limits of the known world
and were instrumental in bringing south-east European and Asian
culture to the North. In truth, the distinction between merchant
and pirate is occasionally very fine indeed, for they plundered for
provisions *en route* and their merchandise usually consisted not only
of furs, wax, and honey but also of slaves they had seized during
their journey.

For the Vikings land divided and water united, and although
Vikings from all three Scandinavian countries took part in expeditions irrespective of nationality, it was natural that they tended to

set out on the sea that washed the coasts of their own country. Thus it was largely the Norwegians and Danes who settled, raided, or conquered Iceland, the Faroes, Orkney and Shetland, the Isle of Man, parts of Ireland and the Scottish mainland, England, northern France, and even Greenland and America, while the Swedes, broadly speaking, turned their attention eastwards. Archaeologists have found near Libau in Latvia evidence of a Swedish colony in the seventh and eighth centuries, proving that the Swedes were already in contact with countries on the other side of the Baltic. In the ninth century these contacts developed into a large Swedish expansion eastwards. Vikings followed a route from Aldeigjuborg (Old Ladoga) along the Volkhov to Novgorod across Lake Ilmen, along the Lovat, and then down the Dnieper to Kiev and the Black Sea; or alternatively, from the Gulf of Riga they sailed up the Dvina, then went overland to the Dnieper and on to the Black Sea. They also travelled from Aldeigjuborg to the Volga or up the Svir to Lakes Ladoga and Onega, on to Bjelozersk, south along the Syeksna and on to the Volga and down to the Caspian Sea. Thus they established contact with the Byzantine Empire, centred on Constantinople, and the Arab Caliphate with its capital in Baghdad.

As it became increasingly important to protect their valuable trade routes, the Swedes became colonizers as well as traders. *Nestor's Chronicle* (allegedly compiled *c.* 1100 by a Kiev monk) relates that in 862 several peoples in Russia, weary of political anarchy, asked the Rus (the Swedes) to send a powerful prince to rule over them. Three brothers answered their call and settled Aldeigjuborg, Bjelozersk, and Isborsk. When the younger brothers died, Rurik the eldest claimed all three settlements and then proceeded south to build Novgorod. His successor Helgi (Oleg) conquered Kiev, taking *en route* the settlement where modern Smolensk now lies. This is a naïve account of how the Swedes founded communities at key points along their essential routes from the Baltic down to South Europe into Asia. Vast numbers of Arabic coins found buried in Swedish soil, especially on Gotland and Birka in Mälaren, show that this period was one of great wealth for the Swedes.

Gradually the Swedish settlers in Russia were assimilated with the Slav population and by the end of the Viking period ties with their homeland had been severed. It is a quirk of history that the name *Russia* is derived from *Rus*, the name the Slavs gave the Viking traders and settlers (the word presumably comes from the coastal district of Roslagen, north of Stockholm), and that those most Russian of names Oleg, Igor, and Vladimir are derived from the Swedish Helgi, Ingvar, and Valdemar.

Viking activities gradually ceased during the eleventh century. Well-organized states were emerging in Central and western Europe, the Normans (of Viking stock themselves) had settled in England, and it was becoming difficult to penetrate these countries' defences. The Vikings had played an important part in the economic and political life of Europe for over two centuries, but by the end of the eleventh century Scandinavia returned, to a certain extent, to its former isolation. However, their travels had brought them well within the bounds of Christendom and in contact with a different way of life; and as Christianity spread, they were increasingly influenced by the Roman Catholic Church and were slowly drawn into the orbit of a general European culture.

Nineteenth-century nationalistic Romantic writers loved the story of a messenger in France who asked approaching Vikings 'What is the name of your master?' and received the answer 'None, we are all equals'. It contains an element of truth, of course. On Viking expeditions there was joint responsibility for the provision of men and ships, and although one man may be the instigator and leader of the expedition, he was considered the *primus inter pares* whose companions retained their independence.

The backbone of Viking society was the peasant, who owned perhaps only a small plot of land but was a free man. Viking law was based on the *Thing*, the Assembly of free men. The king himself had to be elected by the chieftains and his power was subject to the consent of the Assembly. Communities had their own assemblies where the peasants would discuss matters of common interest. There they elected their leaders and their lawman—a man with authority and a good memory, since he had to recite the unwritten laws where appropriate at the Assembly. Each province developed its own laws and was self-governing, although Uppland's importance grew with the power of the Svear.

The basis of democracy thus goes a long way back in Swedish history. The peasant has retained his freedom throughout the centuries, although it was a close-run thing in the seventeenth century, and has played a major part in the building-up of a modern democratic state. Sweden at this period was not, however, a bastion of individual freedom. Much of the menial work in society was performed by thralls, slaves captured in war, victims of Viking raids, born or sold into slavery. They were the property of their owners with no more rights than other domestic animals; the provincial laws offered them no protection and demanded no redress if they were slain. Vilhelm Moberg calculates that some 20 per cent of the Swedish population in the eleventh century were thralls. The figure is open to question, but the indisputable fact remains that there were many thralls in Sweden until Christianity became an active force there, and that serfdom persisted until the fourteenth century.

The Coming of Christianity

Sweden was one of the last countries in Europe to accept Christianity and perhaps it isn't surprising that a proud and sensuous people who admired physical strength, loved battle, and considered vengeance as a duty, had difficulty in accepting Christ's teachings. Louis I the Pious, whose Frankish kingdom was subjected to Viking attacks and who would therefore have a material as well as a spiritual interest in Christianizing the Norsemen, sent Ansgar, a Benedictine monk, to Sweden in 829 to spread the gospel. He was well received by a king Björn at Birka and was allowed to build a church there. Björn's sentiments were evidently not shared by the populace, for when Ansgar left Birka after a few years, they turned on the other missionaries, expelling some and slaying others. Twenty years later Ansgar, by then archbishop of Hamburg-Bremen, returned to Birka and once more organized his congregation, but its influence was negligible. In the 930s a further mission set off from Hamburg, but again with no lasting effects.

The erection at the beginning of the eleventh century of runic stones bearing Christian symbols shows that some Swedes were Christian at that time. By then Norway and Denmark had accepted Christianity and were soon sending to Sweden missionaries who understood the Swedes and their language. They were joined by missionaries sent by the archbishops of Hamburg-Bremen, by Christians from England, France, and even from the Eastern Orthodox Church in Russia. The magnet was the heathen temple at Old Uppsala, the stronghold of the old pagan religion. Several Swedish kings allowed themselves to be baptized–Olof Skötkonung is thought to have been baptized by Sigfrid, an Englishman, in 1008 and during his rule a bishopric was established at Skara in Västergötland. His successors–his son Anund, Anund's half-brother Emund, and Stenkil–were all Christians, and during Stenkil's rule a bishopric was founded at Sigtuna.

Sigtuna, which lies near Old Uppsala, became the centre of the Christian faith in the Mälar district and there are ruins there today of churches built by English missionaries. The old religion was remarkably tenacious in the heart of the Svear country, however, and as late as 1066 heathens drove out the bishop of Sigtuna. Nor was the struggle over when heathens were converted. Adam of Bremen, the German ecclesiastical historian, wrote about 1075 that both Skara and Sigtuna were without a bishop. Aelnoth, an Anglo-Danish monk from Canterbury, noted early in the twelfth century that the Svear and Götar would acknowledge Christ if things went well, 'but enemy attacks or outbreaks of fire–then they persecute the religion they seem to honour . . . they revenge themselves on the Christians and seek to banish them completely out of their country'.

At the end of the eleventh century the Svear banished their Christian king Inge for refusing to perform pagan rites, regarded by them as part of his duty, and they installed Blót (i.e., Sacrifice)-Swein. (One of the victims of this rising was said to be the English bishop Eskil who was buried at Tuna, now known as Eskilstuna.) It was the last large-scale act of defiance. Inge regained control and the temple at Uppsala was subsequently demolished, and a Christian church was built on the same site. In the 1130s Uppsala replaced Sigtuna as the episcopal seat, thus symbolizing Christ's victory over Odin, Thor, and Frej.

There had been an element of competition between Hamburg-Bremen and Canterbury during the eleventh century, as both sent missionaries into Scandinavia, and German influence was particularly strong in Denmark throughout the century. By 1103, however, the Danes freed the Scandinavian Church from Hamburg-Bremen. The following year Archbishop Asser was appointed archbishop of Lund and primate of Scandinavia, and the Swedish Church too passed from the control of Hamburg-Bremen to Lund, at that time part of Denmark.

The Middle Ages

At the end of the Viking era the Swedish provinces were virtually independent, having their own law Codes and their own Assembly, or *Thing*. The only visible link between them was the king, who on election had to ambulate from *Thing* to *Thing*, taking the royal oath and in return receiving the oath of allegiance. During the Middle Ages the provinces were gradually formed into a more unified kingdom, comprising the territory now embracing modern Sweden with the exception of Skåne, Halland, and Blekinge, which were Danish, and Bohuslän, Jämtland, and Härjedalen, which formed part of Norway, while Gotland changed hands but managed to remain relatively independent of the mainland. The king's authority increased, and by the late thirteenth century laws concerning the keeping of the 'king's peace' had been accepted by the whole country, and offenders could be outlawed not just from the province where the offence had occurred but from the whole realm. In 1296 the king himself played a part in codifying the Uppland laws and by the middle of the fourteenth century King Magnus Eriksson was able to draw up a code of laws for the whole country.

The king's source of income was originally derived from the crown lands in Uppland and a share of fines imposed by the provincial assemblies. His subjects were also obliged to house him and his retinue as they progressed, and to supply armed, provisioned warships in time of war. Gradually these obligations were replaced by regular taxes which enabled the king to administer the whole country in times of peace as well as war.

The period was one of great turmoil in Sweden as ambitious leaders, deriving support from different provinces, struggled for the crown, and meanwhile groups of nobles strove to prevent the centralization and strengthening of royal authority.

The Yngling kings were superseded in 1060 by the Stenkils, and when they died out, two families, the Sverkers and the Eriks, strove for over a century for supremacy. The first King Sverker (*c.* 1130–56), a religious man, donated land to allow the founding of Cistercian monasteries in Sweden. The first of these were built at Varnhem in Västergötland and Alvastra in Östergötland, where the ruins of the chapel and Sverker's castle are still standing. Sverker was murdered, and he was succeeded by Erik, who became the patron saint of Sweden. According to the *Legend of St Erik* (dating from *c.* 1270) King Erik went on a crusade to Finland (still a heathen country then) accompanied by Bishop Henry, an English-born bishop. He was later killed at Uppsala in 1160 and by the end of that century the date of his death, 18 May, was being celebrated as a church festival. The significance is more nationalistic and ecclesiastical than dynastic: a Swedish archbishop had been installed at Old Uppsala in 1164, and by the end of the century Sweden had her own patron saint (not to be outdone by Norway which now had St Olav); by 1220 at the latest the remains of St Erik were laid in Uppsala Cathedral which soon became the object of pilgrimages.

King Erik was succeeded in 1161 by Sverker's son Karl who in turn was slain and succeeded by Erik's son Knut, a forceful ruler who subdued other claimants to the throne and created a period of stability in the country. It was during his reign that a stronghold was erected on the site of modern Stockholm to protect Lake Mälaren from marauding pirates. Under the protection of this fortress the future capital grew up. Knut also helped the Church to organize more effectively. The boundaries of the dioceses were established – apart from the archbishopric at Uppsala there were now five sees in Sweden proper: Skara, Linköping, Strängnäs, Västerås, and Växjö; and one in Åbo (Turku) in Finland.

After Knut Eriksson's death in 1196 civil war broke out again as the Sverkers and Eriks strove to establish dynasties. One result of this continual feuding was a weakening of the king's power and the rise of the so-called *jarl* or earl, an administrator for the whole country, chosen from the ranks of the leading nobles and second only to the king. When Erik Eriksson, the last of his line, died in 1250 the power passed to his *jarl*, Birger, who became king in all but name and saw to it that his son Valdemar was elected king. The Folkungs, a powerful family bitterly opposed to increasing royal power and the consequent weakening of the authority of the provincial assemblies, had helped to bring about the fall of the Eriks. Now they turned on Birger Jarl, but he crushed the revolt. Their name has been transferred inaccurately to Birger Jarl, who has gone down in history as the founder of the Folkung dynasty.

Birger was virtual ruler of Sweden until his death in 1266, and Sweden prospered during that time. His son Valdemar took over the reins of government in 1266, but in 1275 he was deposed by his brothers Duke Magnus[1] and Erik, and Magnus was elected king. Magnus had inherited his father's administrative ability and quickly set about consolidating his position. Previous kings had arranged occasional meetings of spiritual and temporal leaders, but Magnus gave these meetings a more regularized form, setting up a Council of the Realm comprising certain powerful nobles, bishops, lawmen from different provinces, and three officials who helped in the administration of the country, the Lord High Steward, Chancellor, and Marshal. To prevent the Council from becoming too powerful, however, Magnus also forbade the members to meet without his approval. He also decreed that nobles were no longer to claim accommodation for themselves and their followers when they journeyed about the country, a decree which is said to explain his sobriquet Ladulås (i.e., Barn-lock).

The Age of Chivalry came to Sweden in Magnus's reign. The art of warfare was changing and mounted warriors in full armour were supplanting the untrained freemen who had answered the king's call to arms in emergencies. Magnus and the Council decided at a meeting on Alsnö in 1279 that those who served the king fully armed, trained, and mounted would be exempted from taxes. This freedom from taxes was not hereditary, but since the same rich families for several generations provided armed knights, an aristocracy was established.

The Church and the king gave each other mutual support. Magnus was crowned at Uppsala and was declared king 'by grace of God'. This enabled him to introduce a new concept in Sweden,

---

[1] After quelling risings against himself and his son Valdemar, Birger Jarl strengthened his family's position by granting his son Magnus the title Duke of the Svear. The title reflects the influence of continental feudal ideas on Sweden.

lèse-majesté, a formidable weapon against nobles seeking to curb his authority. In return he extended the privileges of the Church, granting in 1281 tax exemption on all church lands.

The growth of the Church's power is best illustrated by the large number of cathedrals built in this period, the famous Gothic cathedral at Uppsala being the best example. During the thirteenth century both the Franciscan and the Dominican Orders were founded in Sweden and played an important role in the cultural life of the people. As distinct from the Cistercian monks, the Franciscans and Dominicans brought their teaching to the people, building their monasteries in towns and serving as cultural centres for the poorer members of the community. Education was in the hands of the Church, the only schools being cathedral schools.

To safeguard his crown Magnus had his eldest son Birger elected king when only four years old in 1284, but he also granted virtually independent duchies to his younger sons Erik and Valdemar, which proved fatal. Magnus Ladulås had been strong and astute enough to hold his nobles in check, but when he died in 1290 his son, King Birger Magnusson, was only ten and the government was taken over by the Council, led by the powerful magnate Marshal Torgils Knutsson. Although he aroused the envy of the king's brothers, he had the support of the Council and seemed secure. However, he overreached himself when he attacked the privileges of the Church, and Dukes Erik and Valdemar exploited the opposition that was aroused. They persuaded King Birger that Torgils was threatening his crown, and Birger had him executed in 1306. This was a prelude to a decade of civil strife involving all Scandinavia, for Birger had married a Danish princess, while his brothers Erik and Valdemar had both married Norwegian princesses. Erik and Valdemar captured Birger on his estate at Håtuna and forced him to agree to a division of the kingdom. Birger accepted the situation only until he had the opportunity to avenge himself. He invited his brothers to a peace banquet at Nyköping in 1317, had them put into the dungeons, and according to popular tradition threw away the keys so that they starved to death.

Ultimately it was the Council who gained most. Appalled by Birger's treachery, they drove him into exile and in 1319 elected as their king Duke Erik's three-year-old son Magnus who, on the death of his maternal grandfather, had already inherited the Norwegian crown. Thus the Council established Sweden again as an elective kingdom and moreover set up a regency government during the new king's minority, which offered the nobles an opportunity for aggrandizement.

Magnus Eriksson, the last of the Folkung monarchs, was a hapless king. Strindberg's historical play *Folkungasagan* (The Saga of the Folkungs) depicts him as the innocent king visited by the sins of his fathers, which is one way of explaining why such a well-meaning monarch had such a troubled reign. During the regency the leading member of the Council, Mats Kettelmundsson, had negotiated successfully with the Russians the Peace of Nöteborg (1323) which established the frontiers between the two countries. Denmark was disunited during this period and the people of Skåne (still a Danish province) appealed to Magnus for help against the Holstein counts, then in possession of the province. In 1332, on payment of 34,000 silver marks, Magnus was accepted as ruler of Skåne, Blekinge, and part of Halland. He was already ruler of Swedish Finland and king of Norway–all in all one of the largest kingdoms in fourteenth-century Europe.

Magnus appears to have had the interests of his people at heart. He abolished thralldom finally in Sweden and it was also during his reign that the *Landslag* (the national law) was introduced, replacing the old provincial laws and laying the foundation for Sweden's first constitution. He was a religious man and bestowed on his kinswoman Birgitta (St Bridget; *c.* 1302–73) the royal estate of Vadstena, where her famous convent was built.

However, his seemingly strong position was largely illusory, for he was persistently dogged by crippling debts, by a powerful Council determined to lose none of the privileges acquired during the regency, and, it seemed, by fate.

The Russians violated the Peace of Nöteborg in the 1340s, and Magnus went on a crusade to Finland, where he was defeated. The debts incurred in these wars, plus the ransom of 34,000 marks paid for the southern provinces, led to a critical situation, exacerbated when the Black Death, the dreaded plague, reached Sweden in 1349 and, on the rough estimate it is possible to make, carried off about one-third of her population in the 1350s. As whole families succumbed, farmsteads were abandoned, and no taxes could be paid to the crown, Magnus borrowed from abroad, his brother-in-law Albrekt of Mecklenburg standing surety, and then tried to alleviate his financial difficulties at the expense of the nobles. He had already angered the Council in 1344 when he had had his younger son Håkon declared king of Norway and his elder son Erik designated successor to the Swedish throne; for this was interpreted as a renewed threat to an elective crown. Now the nobles rose against him, joined by Erik, who had viewed with envy his brother Håkon enjoying authority in Norway while he had had nothing but promises for the future. After a series of abortive agreements the breach between Magnus and the magnates became irreparable and the

Council offered the crown to Albrekt's son, also called Albrekt of Mecklenburg, and imprisoned Magnus. (During this period of unrest, in 1359, Magnus summoned a *Riksdag* at which all four Estates of the realm were to be represented–the Nobles, Clergy, Burghers, and tax-paying Peasants. It was presumably the first Swedish *Riksdag*.)

The nobles soon found Albrekt a greater threat to their privileges than Magnus, for he continued the policy started by the Folkungs of building fortified castles, but he placed them and the land supporting them in the care of Mecklenburgers on whom he also bestowed high office. When Magnus's son, Håkon of Norway, raised a revolt and marched on Stockholm, Albrekt hastily promised to favour only Swedes and to consult the Council on all important issues. Magnus was released and given the provinces of Västergötland, Värmland, and Dalarna, but he never regained power. He went to join Håkon and was drowned in a shipwreck off Norway in 1374.

The Kalmar Union

In its attempt to hold King Albrekt in check the Council was led by the Lord High Steward, Bo Jonsson Grip, a powerful magnate who amassed vast estates in Sweden and Finland, not just from personal ambition but to prevent land from falling into German hands. The most famous of his private castles is Gripsholm on Lake Mälaren which still bears his name. When Grip died in 1386 the executors of his will, a group of magnates, acted on his instructions and prevented his German widow from inheriting his wealth. Albrekt tried to turn the situation to his advantage, supporting the widow's claim and appropriating much of the property himself. This time he had gone too far and the nobles turned on him. He sought military aid in Germany while the Council turned to Norway for support. Håkon had died in 1380 and his widow, the extremely able Queen Margareta, was the effective ruler not only of Norway where her son Olav was still an infant but also of Denmark on the death of her father, King Valdemar, in 1375. Her son Olav died just when the executors of Grip's will sought her aid and when she had been declared ruler of Denmark and Norway. In 1388 she added Sweden to her realm and for the first time the three Scandinavian crowns were united under one ruler. Her first task was to expel the Mecklenburg army. Albrekt was captured at Falköping in 1389 and although his supporters held Stockholm for a further nine years with help from Mecklenburg, the rest of Sweden accepted Margareta. To ensure the continuation of the Union she put forward as her successor her great-nephew, Erik of Pomerania, who in 1397 at the age of fifteen, was crowned in Kalmar king of Norway, Denmark, and Sweden.

A union of these three Northern countries made sense in many ways. The people shared common origins, customs, and outlook on life, and spoke mutually comprehensible variations on a common Norse language. By influential marriages across the respective borders or by direct purchase several nobles also owned property in more than one of the Scandinavian countries. And yet ultimately it proved as impossible in the fifteenth century as in the nineteenth, and indeed in this century, for the Scandinavian countries to accept political unity.

The period of the Kalmar Union is characterized by the continued struggle between the crown and the nobles; but now an important new element can be discerned: the rise of the common people and a spirit of nationalism.

Desiring to create efficient government in Sweden Queen Margareta appointed bailiffs who were directly responsible to the crown. In order to improve the royal finances she also restored to the crown sections of land previously acquired by the Church and certain nobles. Her foreign policy was geared to the resistance to German influence and the expansion of Denmark's frontier southwards. It says much for her statesmanlike qualities and her remarkable personality that she increased the crown's effective power at the expense of the nobles and especially the Church, and financed a war against the Order of the Teutonic Knights without arousing too much animosity among either the members of the Council or the Swedish peasants. She was careful not to bestow too many favours on Danes in Sweden; she spent a large proportion of her time in Sweden; she supported St Bridget's religious foundation and visited Vadstena frequently. As long as she was alive criticism of the crown was without venom. During a visit to Flensburg in 1412 to further her Danish policy she succumbed to the plague and died, whereupon Erik became king in deed as well as name.

Erik possessed more ambition that Margareta and viewed his three kingdoms as a potential Baltic empire. By marrying Henry V's sister Philippa and bestowing favours on English merchants he hoped to establish an ally in his struggle for Schleswig-Holstein. Throughout almost his entire reign Erik was caught up in this struggle, which brought him into conflict with the Hanseatic League. He exacerbated the situation by his introduction in 1429 of a toll on ships passing Elsinore and by his support of Danish merchants at the expense of Hanseatic merchants.

He showed less tact in Sweden than Queen Margareta and alienated most sections of society by appointing Danish and German royal bailiffs and depriving Swedish nobles of political influence; by interfering in clerical appointments, taxing the peasants heavily to pay for his Danish wars, and residing so rarely in Sweden that he lost touch with affairs there. His downfall came, however, as a result of a blockade imposed by the Hanseatic League from 1426.

The Swedish economy throughout the Middle Ages, and indeed until the late nineteenth century, was essentially agricultural. It was also a 'storage economy',[2] with almost all food being salted and preserved. Although largely self-supporting, the one commodity such an economy had to import was salt. Among the few Swedish exports of the period were iron and copper which from the beginning of the Middle Ages were mined in the Bergslagen district. Cutting off this vital trade could therefore quickly undermine the foundations of Sweden's primitive economy. It was the miners in Bergslagen, led by Engelbrekt Engelbrektsson, a mineowner, who started the rising against Erik. It took on the character of a freedom movement and was joined by many other miners and peasants throughout the country. In three months Engelbrekt and his supporters were in control of the whole of Sweden except Stockholm and a few fortifications. Several spiritual and temporal leaders also joined the opposition to Erik and when Engelbrekt called a national assembly at Arboga in 1435, he was elected regent. The Swedish magnates had considered him a tool against Erik and now felt it necessary to curb his power. They appointed Karl Knutsson Bonde as regent and intrigued against Engelbrekt, who was murdered on a journey to Stockholm in 1436. Whether dead or alive, however, Engelbrekt had touched a patriotic chord. Shortly after his death Bishop Tomas of Strängnäs wrote a stirring poem about his struggle for freedom, while the *Karlskrönikan*, a contemporary verse chronicle, reveals a certain patriotic fervour when dealing with Engelbrekt. The nobles had been against Erik's ambitions rather than against the Union, but they had helped to foster a nationalistic sentiment that ultimately made the Union untenable.

There were now in Sweden both pro- and anti-unionists. After risings in Norway and Denmark Erik had been deposed there and succeeded by his nephew, Kristoffer of Bavaria. The Swedish pro-unionists accepted him (and on his death in 1448 his successor, Christian I of Oldenburg) as king of Sweden, but the anti-unionists rallied round Karl Knutsson. Three times Karl Knutsson was king, but never with security of tenure. On his death in 1470 Sten Sture was elected regent, but Christian I sailed to Stockholm with an army to re-establish the Kalmar Union. The Swedes under Sten Sture defeated him decisively at Brunkeberg in Stockholm in 1471

[2] E. Heckscher, *An Economic History of Sweden* (Cambridge, Mass., 1954), pp. 20–22.

and hailed the event as a national victory. There followed a series of nationalistic measures, including the founding of a Swedish university. At the request of Archbishop Jakob Ulfsson Pope Sixtus IV founded in 1477 the University of Uppsala, the first in Scandinavia, and Ericus Olai, often called the 'father of Swedish history', was appointed as one of its first professors. Bernt Notke gave artistic expression to the surge of nationalism in his wood and elk's horn statue of St George and the Dragon, commissioned by Sten Sture and still in Stockholm Cathedral in *Gamla Stan* (the Old Town).

There was more emotion than logic in the situation, for the struggle had been as much a civil war as a war of liberation. Several Swedish magnates had supported Christian, and one of Karl Knutsson's most dangerous enemies had been the Swedish Archbishop Jöns Bengtsson Oxenstierna. By 1483 the Council had accepted Christian's son Hans as king of Sweden, although the wily Sten Sture succeeded in delaying the enforcement of this decision for fourteen years and in remaining regent until his death in 1503, when the struggle against the Danes was continued by his successor, Svante Nilsson Sture, and on his death in 1512 by Sten Sture the Younger. The latter was only twenty when he became regent, but he was able and ambitious and planned to assert Swedish independence and his own claim to the Swedish throne. In this he was opposed by the Council, led by the forceful Archbishop Gustav Trolle. Sten, whose support came largely from the commoners, persuaded the *Riksdag* to have Gustav Trolle removed from office, and crowds subsequently razed the archbishop's castle, Stäket, to the ground.

The king of Denmark, now the ambitious Christian II, countered this by persuading Pope Leo X to excommunicate Sten Sture and his supporters and attacking Sweden in the name of the Church as well as the Kalmar Union. Sten Sture held him in check in 1518 at the battle of Brännkyrka, when Christian contented himself with establishing a cease-fire and sailing back to Denmark with six Swedish nobles as hostages. In 1520, however, he returned with a large force, battle was joined on the frozen Lake Åsunden (near present-day Ulricehamn), Sten Sture was mortally wounded, and his supporters defeated.

Christian penetrated as far as Stockholm, which opened its gates on his promise of an amnesty. Once inside the capital, however, Christian, urged on by Gustav Trolle, began reprisals. Sten's widow, Kristina Gyllenstierna, was imprisoned in Denmark, while many of the Stures and their supporters were convicted by Trolle of heresy and handed over to the king for execution. Almost one hundred high-ranking Swedes, including two bishops and several Council members, met their death in what became known as the Stockholm Massacre. Sten's body was disinterred and publicly burnt. On his return to Denmark through the southern provinces Christian continued his ruthless policy, determined to stamp out opposition. It earned him the name of Christian the Tyrant, but did not further his cause—indeed it had the reverse effect.

One of the hostages seized by Christian was the young Gustav Eriksson Vasa, nephew of Sten Sture's widow and also related to the Stures. He had escaped to Lübeck and slipped back into Sweden by the time of the Stockholm Massacre, which claimed his own father. Gustav Vasa made for Dalarna, the province that had supported Engelbrekt and the Stures, and tried to raise a rebellion. Legends not unlike those connected with Alfred the Great colour this period of Gustav's life. According to the version he dictated to his own chronicler, Peder Svart, he was at first unsuccessful and was making for the Norwegian border pursued by the king's agents when news of Christian's atrocities reached the Dalarna peasants. These proud men of Dalarna hurried after Gustav and joined him in a bid to liberate their country. The rising quickly spread until by 1521 Gustav's army was in control of the whole country except the stronghold of Kalmar and Stockholm itself. Gustav Vasa was declared regent and persuaded Lübeck to supply money, ships, and men in order to oust the remaining Danes. By 1523 Christian had to withdraw and Gustav entered Stockholm in triumph. At a *Riksdag* in Strängnäs in June 1523 he was elected king of Sweden, bringing to an end any hope of a revival of the Kalmar Union and ushering in a new era in Swedish history, a period when the foundations of modern Sweden were laid.

Chapter 2

1523–1718
The Rise and Fall of the Swedish Empire

GUSTAV VASA WAS faced with a formidable task at the outset of his reign. His own claim to the throne was suspect; the crown was heavily in debt; Sweden's trade was dominated by Lübeck and her economy was primitive; the government machinery was in a state of decay; and after many decades of near civil war the country as a political unit seemed in danger of disintegrating.

It soon became obvious that Gustav had expelled the Danes not to reinstate the Stures but to found the Vasa dynasty, and in 1524 Sture supporters, incited by Sten's widow, Kristina Gyllenstierna, who had been released from her Danish prison, rose against him. Gustav quelled the riot, but by 1527 was faced with a similar rebellion, this time led by a man who claimed to be Sten Sture's son Nils, and who has gone down in Swedish annals as *Daljunkern*.

The Reformation

By the time of this second revolt Gustav had started on his reorganization of the country, but, although supported by large sections of both the nobles and the burghers, he was constantly restricted by his menacing Lübeck creditors, who had largely financed his campaign against Christian II, and desperately needed the room to manoeuvre that only solvency could bring. The richest institution within his realm was undoubtedly the Catholic Church, which owned over 21 per cent of the land, free of tax, as opposed to the crown's 5·6 per cent. By 1526, however, Olaus Petri (*c.* 1497–1552), who had studied in Wittemberg, was preaching the Lutheran doctrine in Stockholm, and many people who viewed with dismay the decadence of certain prelates and lesser clergy and with disapproval the selling of indulgences, were attracted to the idea of a reformed Church. Gustav Vasa was quick to see the potentialities of the situation. He directed at the churches and richly-endowed monasteries increasing demands for financial support, and when they were reluctant to respond, he called a *Riksdag* at Västerås in 1527. In a skilful address he stated that he had done his duty by his people but had been poorly served by them. He then played off the Estates of the Nobles, Burghers, and Peasants against the Clergy, emphasizing where the real wealth of the country now lay. Finally he threatened to abdicate and leave the Estates to sort out the present crisis as best they could. It was a masterful speech and led to the resolutions Gustav had hoped for: the *Riksdag* offered to assist in punishing those causing unrest in the kingdom; the king was to claim the surplus revenues of the bishops, cathedrals, and canons and to take over the bishops' castles; the nobles could under certain conditions reclaim estates given to the Church by their ancestors since the mid-fifteenth century and moreover the monasteries were to be handed over to them as fiefs.

The immediate result of the Västerås Assembly was that the rising under *Daljunkern* was quickly suppressed with the extra support Gustav Vasa had obtained. Much more lasting and far-reaching, however, was the fact that the king became head of the Church, and appointed the bishops. Implicitly Sweden had broken with Rome. Gustav quickly used, and indeed abused, the powers afforded him. He permitted the clergy to retain only enough land to support their immediate needs, the rest becoming crown lands, and he replaced the existing loose ecclesiastical organization by a centralized administration that was in turn part of the overall national organization he was setting up. Many treasures belonging to churches and monasteries found their way to the royal coffers and their precious parchment manuscripts were used by the king's bailiffs to keep their accounts.

Gustav Vasa had little interest in the doctrinal aspects of the Reformation and remained uncommitted towards Lutheranism for some time. The Västerås Assembly had decreed that 'the word of God should be preached in the realm purely and plainly' and Olaus Petri worked zealously to spread Luther's teaching in Swedish. In 1526 he published the first hymnbook in Swedish and for the next decade produced a steady flow of religious tracts in his native tongue, including the first Swedish translation of the New Testament, which appeared in 1526, and parts of the Old Testament, which appeared in the Gustav Vasa Bible of 1541. When in 1531 Gustav made Olaus secretary of Stockholm (a post which he combined with thunderous, audacious sermons in Lutheran vein from the pulpit of Stockholm Cathedral) and in that same year appointed Olaus's brother, Laurentius Petri (1499–1572), archbishop of Uppsala, Lutheranism seemed to have been given official approval. Swedish Lutherans were subsequently appointed to vacant sees and by the late 1530s the Mass was heard in Swedish throughout the country.

The king had made Olaus his Chancellor, but soon tired of his sermons and replaced him in 1538 with the more malleable German Konrad von Pyhy. Olaus considered the Church and the crown as two independent powers, but Gustav would tolerate no suggestion that the Church should be a state within a state. The inevitable clash between these two dominant personalities came in 1539 when Olaus and his brother Laurentius were convicted of high treason. Gustav acted with the ruthlessness that made him greatly respected rather than loved. They were tortured and then condemned to death, although the sentence was later commuted to excessively heavy fines. Olaus continued to defy the king until his death in 1552, but Gustav had demonstrated that the Church fitted into the broader state organization and that he was the overlord.

Gustav Reorganizes his Kingdom

Gustav took over what was a medieval country and reorganized it. By the 1530s the administrative districts were no longer ruled by magnates obliged to supply the king with defence forces, but otherwise virtually independent viceroys. Bailiffs answerable directly to the king were appointed instead to collect taxes and effect the king's commands. The nobles who would naturally have been opposed to this new order had been notably weakened by the recurring civil wars and were unable to resist. In any case Gustav had cleverly compensated them at the Church's expense. An Exchequer was established to keep a check on the bailiffs, who soon learnt the wisdom of giving the king his full dues, for Gustav was an astute manager and examined the accounts himself. His well-organized tax system afforded the means of retaining troops and building a fleet, a much more effective method than relying on the nobles' contribution to a defence force. Other government business was channelled through the *Kansli*, a central office organized with the help of German jurists, to deal with all the king's correspondence.

Gustav had need of his loyal professional soldiers at home, for his position was seriously threatened twice more, in 1531 by rebels in Dalarna and as late as 1542 by the southern provinces under Nils Dacke, a Småland farmer. In each case he acted promptly and firmly, quelling the riots and dealing severely with the instigators. However, the Dacke rising subsequently led to Gustav's treating his commoners with more circumspection. It also convinced him that he must secure the succession once and for all. At a *Riksdag* at Västerås in 1544 the four Estates accepted his proposal that the crown should pass to the monarch's male heir in direct succession – for the first time the Swedish crown was hereditary, not elective.

A feature of the Vasa period was the series of castles, often founded by Gustav and then completed by his sons, erected at strategic points to protect ports, boundaries, important waterways, and highways. Many of them were built on the old site of a former castle or fortification owned by a magnate, bishop, or religious Order. Several of them still stand today (at Uppsala, Vadstena, Gripsholm, Kalmar, for instance), solid, imposing edifices like medieval strongholds with large reinforced towers to withstand the increased strength of artillery in the sixteenth century. They served as centres of government, or garrisons for Gustav's troops and storehouses for his supplies (taxes still being paid largely in kind at that time). But they were also royal palaces, a characteristic blend of stark utilitarianism and luxury, with the walls adorned by gobelins and portraits by German and Dutch masters of the king, princes, and nobles.

Gustav Vasa's reign was from a material point of view a happy one, with satisfactory harvests; exports of butter, hides, iron, copper, and silver; unimpeded imports of necessities, especially salt and spices; and a stability guaranteed by a powerful, active monarch. In intellectual matters, however, it was a retrograde period. Uppsala University had ceased to function before 1521 and Gustav did nothing to remedy this. Swedes wanting to study attended a Lutheran university, usually Wittemberg (as did Olaus Petri) or Rostock. The good schools run by monks naturally closed after the Reformation. Chapter and municipal schools had been geared to boys wanting to take the cloth, but after 1527 the clergy was reduced to such straitened circumstances that the career no longer attracted able youths and the schools fell into decay. The visual arts too suffered, for their focal points had been the Catholic churches, a role the more austere Lutheran churches did not fulfil to the same extent.

In his foreign policy Gustav's ambitions were limited to securing his country's existing boundaries. Apart from a border war in Finland against Russia (1555–57) he was involved in only one foreign war during his reign, and that could be construed as a war of defence. His arch-enemy, Christian II (the Tyrant), had been deposed and succeeded in Denmark by Frederik I. On Frederik's death in 1533 Christian II, supported by Lübeck, attempted to regain the Danish throne. Gustav had every reason to foul such an attempt by a man who had once been crowned king of Sweden and good cause too for wishing the defeat of Lübeck. He therefore sent his new fleet to support Frederik's son, Christian III, and his soldiers to subdue Skåne (then part of Denmark). The combined Danish and Swedish fleets defeated the Lübeck ships in 1535, the Swedish privileges enjoyed by Lübeck merchants were suspended, and the remaining Swedish debt to Lübeck was settled in Sweden's favour. The Hansa towns retained their power in the Baltic until it was usurped by Holland at the end of the century, but Gustav had at least won immediate relief from Lübeck dominance.

Gustav Vasa's demise in 1560 brought to an end the settled period in home and foreign affairs. Ironically, the terms of his will were partly to blame for unrest at home, for although his eldest son automatically succeeded him as Erik XIV, his younger sons received large independent duchies and Erik found that a substantial part of his kingdom was outside his control. The nobles whom Gustav Vasa had firmly contained during his rule now saw an opportunity of regaining influence and Erik became involved in two different struggles, the monarchy versus the nobility and Vasa versus Vasas. Gustav Vasa had married three times, first to Katarina of Saxony-Lauenburg, who had died when Erik was very young; then to two Swedish noblewomen: Margareta Leijonhufvud, the mother of the princes Johan, Magnus, and Karl; and finally to the young and beautiful Katarina Stenbock who survived him. Erik, who had inherited in full measure the Vasa's suspicious temperament, considered as potential enemies not only his father's old rivals, the Sture family, but also his half-brothers and their powerful relations the Leijonhufvuds and the Stenbocks, a fear that became an obsession during the eight years of his reign. One of his first acts as king was to call a *Riksdag* at Arboga in 1561 when he reduced his half-brothers from virtually independent princes to subjects of the crown, and although he created a number of peers, he was careful to give the most important offices of state to commoners. In a very short time he caused dissatisfaction among his relatives and his nobles, and his use of an efficient spy system to keep himself informed of the comings and goings of the aristocracy and the setting-up of a supreme court to deal with them did nothing to increase his popularity.

The Vasas' Expansionist Policy

Gustav Vasa had built up his armed forces to protect his kingdom's existing boundaries. Erik XIV increased them but with a view to expansion. Gustav had been something of a homespun farmer, but he had given his sons an education in true Renaissance style so that they were versed not only in the arts but also in Machiavellian views on the art of government, and they were all willing to exploit a confused situation in order to gain territory or prestige. Such a situation had arisen in the Baltic towards the end of Gustav Vasa's reign. The Teutonic Order of Knights was disintegrating and the Baltic countries were all looking for pickings. The Tsar of Muscovy, Ivan the Terrible, was also beginning to look westwards and wanted ice-free harbours to allow trade with western Europe. When still crown prince, Erik had seen the weakness of Sweden's position. Her only outlet to the west was at Älvsborg near the present-day Gothenburg, the territory to the north and south belonging to Denmark-Norway, while the Danish southern states of Skåne, Blekinge, and the island of Gotland cut her off from north Germany. His remedy then was to seek an alliance through marriage and he sought the hand of Elizabeth of England, whose evasive answer was a masterpiece of diplomacy, and then of Christine, daughter of the Landgrave of Hesse, but in both cases his suit was finally rejected. Nevertheless, Erik decided that the Baltic situation demanded action. The Russians had taken Narva and were trying to subject Estonia, which Sigismund II of Poland also coveted. Finland was becoming too vulnerable. In 1561 Reval and parts of Estonia agreed to acknowledge Swedish rule in return for Swedish protection. Erik's brother Johan, duke of Finland, chose this moment to act independently of his brother. He had married Sigismund's sister, Catherine Jagellonica, hoping to secure himself an ally in the southern Baltic, and now he turned his attention to securing bases on the southern side of the Gulf of Finland. Erik would not countenance such a dangerous alliance and had Johan imprisoned in Gripsholm Castle and his duchy confiscated.

Frederik II of Denmark seized the opportunity offered by civil strife in Sweden, formed an alliance with Poland and Lübeck, and in 1563 launched the Northern Seven Years' War, a brutal, bloody affair with both sides using propaganda methods to fan the flame of hatred. (The Swedish fleet, incidentally, for the first time sailed under a new ensign–'Golden cross on blue ground'–which is still the national flag of Sweden today.)

Sweden seemed about to gain the upper hand when civil war broke out again. Erik was convinced that the Stures were plotting against him and had their leaders arrested; but before their trial was concluded, he had an attack of madness and had them murdered while he himself looked on. Although, when his sanity had been restored, he tried to make amends, it was too late. Discontent among the nobles increased when Erik, tired of trying to arrange an acceptable marriage, legitimized his relationship with the low-born Karin Månsdotter, and reached boiling-point when he re-instated as his secretary his favourite, the commoner Jöran Persson, who had been removed from office during the king's madness. Duke Johan, his brother Karl, the nobles, commoners, and troops all rose against Erik, who was arrested in 1568 and placed in Gripsholm Castle while Johan succeeded him as Johan III. Erik was held prisoner until his death in 1577, and it was rumoured that he died from poison administered on Johan's orders, one of the many 'not proven' cases in history. The Seven Years' War ended in 1570 with the Peace of Stettin. No territory changed hands, but Sweden had to pay a heavy ransom to retrieve Älvsborg. Since Johan, Sigismund's brother-in-law, had become king the war with Poland ended too.

Johan, who admired the aesthetic aspects of the Catholic religion, attempted during his reign to bring the Lutheran and Catholic religions closer together and produced a liturgy, his notorious 'Red Book', to that purpose. Despite the recent origins of the Swedish Lutheran Church Johan's efforts were flatly rejected and many clergymen chose exile rather than use his liturgy. They found asylum with Duke Karl who had Calvinistic leanings and refused to have the Red Book in his duchy, which comprised the provinces of Värmland, Närke, and Södermanland.

The religious question gained importance again on the death of Johan III in 1592. He was succeeded by his son Sigismund, who had been king of Poland (as Sigismund III) since 1587 and who had also accepted his mother's Catholic faith. Duke Karl played on the Swedish fears that Sigismund would try to impose Catholicism on his Swedish subjects. Before Sigismund arrived from Poland, Karl called a meeting in Uppsala in 1593 when the Augsburg Confession was formally accepted, Johan III's liturgy rejected, and no other religion but Lutheranism allowed to be practised publicly in Sweden. When Sigismund reached Sweden later that year, he refused to acknowledge the decisions of the Uppsala meeting, Catholic services were held in several Stockholm churches, and there were bloody encounters between Swedes and Poles. Duke Karl, strongly anti-Catholic, hectored his nephew, who soon returned temporarily to Poland, leaving the government in the hands of Karl and several provincial governors who were to be directly responsible to the king. Karl appealed to a *Riksdag* called at Söderköping in 1595, was declared regent as long as Sigismund was in Poland, and was to rule together with the Council. Several members of the Council found co-operation with Karl impossible and fled to Sigismund.

In 1598 Sigismund returned to Sweden to suppress the rebels. After sporadic fighting Sigismund suddenly abandoned his attempts to subdue his unruly Swedish subjects and returned to Poland, leaving to the mercy of Duke Karl those Swedish nobles who had remained loyal to the king. Mercy was not one of Karl's attributes and he exacted bloody vengeance on them at Linköping in 1600, the so-called Linköping Massacre. A *Riksdag* in 1599 had declared Sigismund formally deposed and Karl the hereditary ruler. After a few years he took the title of King Karl IX and his eldest son was recognized as the heir apparent.

The last years of Karl IX's reign coincided with the time of troubles in Russia and Karl endeavoured to exploit the situation himself and to prevent Poland, now his natural enemy, from doing likewise. His war with Poland which he waged in Livonia was unsuccessful. So too was the Swedish force sent under Jacob Pontusson De la Gardie, a Swedish general and aristocrat of French descent, to Russia to support a pretender to the Russian throne and his plan to have his younger son, Karl Filip, elected to the Russian throne. Indeed, the only successes Sweden enjoyed were the capture by De la Gardie of Keksholm, the Russian stronghold on Lake Ladoga, and of Narva.

Meanwhile, seeing that Sweden was engaged in the East, Christian IV of Denmark attacked, quickly capturing Kalmar and pressing hard a Sweden bereft of allies. At this time, in 1611, Karl IX had a stroke and died, leaving his country threatened on all sides. He was succeeded by his eldest son, Gustavus II Adolphus (Gustav II Adolf), an untried seventeen-year-old, but destined to become the great Lion of the North.

His immediate task was to save the country. The Danes had taken Älvsborg and their fleet was in Stockholm archipelago. They could not press home their victory, however, and by 1613 the Peace of Knäred was signed, a significant feature of which was that Älvsborg was ransomed for the enormous sum of one million *riksdaler*. The money had to be borrowed through Dutch creditors and by 1619 the Danes withdrew. Russia was so torn by internal strife until Michael Romanoff came to the throne that she was prepared to cede to Sweden considerable territories. By the terms of the Peace of Stolbova in 1617, Russia evacuated Ingria and south-west Karelia. Thus Sweden established overland communications between Finland and Estonia, Russia had in effect withdrawn from the Baltic, and the pressure was off Sweden.

Gustavus Adolphus had inherited the best qualities of the Vasas—intelligence, energy, great ability—but brought to them qualities that previous Vasas had lacked—great military acumen, an inner harmony, and generosity of spirit. He had the happy knack of gaining confidence and affection and inspiring people to give of their best. The conflict between monarch and nobles which had become extremely bitter in his father's time was resolved during his reign. He granted to the nobles important privileges, which were formalized in the Act of 1617, but in return he expected them to serve the crown as officers and administrators, and in this he was not disappointed. It was important now to establish who had the right to these privileges, and from 1626 families with a claim to the Estate of the Nobility registered their names at the House of

Nobility (*Riddarhuset*). A large building to house the Estate was finally completed in Stockholm in the 1670s and can still be admired today.

Sweden as a European Power

Sweden was on the threshold of what is called the Age of Greatness, during which for the first time since the Viking period large sections of her population either served abroad or knew personally someone who had done so, and the insignificant Northern kingdom suddenly became part of the mainstream of Europe again. With the co-operation of its able nobles, headed by the gifted Axel Oxenstierna (1583–1654), whose statue appropriately stands outside *Riddarhuset* in Stockholm, Gustavus Adolphus set about reorganizing the administration and initiated a system of central government based on principles still valid today. The Council appointed by the king was the centre of government. Five leading members headed 'Colleges' equivalent to modern government departments: the Chancellor, Marshal, Admiral, Treasurer, and Steward in charge of foreign affairs, the army, navy, economy, and justice respectively. A *Riksdag* was called almost annually, at which the four Estates (Nobles, Clergy, Burghers, and Peasants, i.e., free peasant proprietors) met and deliberated separately.

An educated class was obviously needed to cope with this more sophisticated form of government and to that end Gustavus Adolphus donated a large sum to the hitherto neglected University of Uppsala. The success of the new administrative system and the spirit of co-operation between king, Council, and Estates was shown in the smooth way affairs of state were managed, even though the king was on campaign for so much of his reign.

Gustavus Adolphus also realized that to be a European power his country must alter the basis of its economic life, which was still overwhelmingly orientated towards agriculture with most taxes rendered in kind. Towns were founded, the most notable being Gothenburg, which Gustavus Adolphus had rebuilt after its almost total destruction in the Danish war of 1611–13, and to which he extended full privileges in 1621. Foreign merchants were invited to invest in them, while craftsmen from more advanced countries were encouraged to come and populate them. Several Dutch and German names date their arrival in Sweden to this period–the Dutch entrepreneur Louis De Geer (1587–1652) became one of the most influential and died one of the richest men in Sweden. More important still was the rich supply of ore which has played such an enormous part in Swedish history. The king encouraged the development of iron-mining in the Bergslagen district and the exploitation of a rich vein of copper found in the Falun copper-mines. Production reached its peak there in the first half of the seventeenth century and since copper was in great demand in Europe at the time and Sweden could command a good price for her exports, the metal played a large part in financing Sweden's wars.

A system of recruitment was established whereby one peasant in ten could be called to his provincial regiment while full-time cavalry soldiers were granted land from the crown. These would form the core of the Swedish army, but mercenaries, Swedish and foreign, could be taken on as necessary.

Perhaps subconsciously Gustavus Adolphus had thus been preparing his country for war. He was a convinced Protestant and married Maria Eleonora, daughter of Johan Sigismund, elector of Brandenburg, thus identifying himself with the Protestant camp. In 1621 he decided to wage war against Poland, a traditional Swedish enemy ever since Karl IX had usurped the throne from his nephew Sigismund and a Catholic state which, according to rumour, was contemplating an attempt to place Sigismund III on the Swedish throne and to bring Sweden back to the Catholic faith. He quickly took Riga, and large parts of Livonia. Then in 1626 he attacked Prussia, thus cutting off Polish access to the Baltic.

Denmark, also a Protestant state, had entered the Thirty Years War but had suffered defeat by the imperial forces at the Battle of Lutter in 1626. Large parts of northern Germany were then occupied and it seemed to be the intention of the imperial forces to establish a fleet in the Baltic with Stralsund as its base. To prevent this, both Danish and Swedish troops went to the defence of Stralsund, but Jutland was occupied and Denmark placed in a perilous position. When at this juncture the imperial forces offered King Christian IV of Denmark an advantageous settlement provided he withdrew from the war, he accepted the offer.

It seemed that Sweden would now be drawn into the war and Gustavus Adolphus, his Council, and the Estates decided that it was better in that case to fight on foreign soil than on their own. There is much speculation as to whether Gustavus Adolphus was motivated by a desire to defend his faith or to make political gains. The answer is probably both. At the outset he wanted to defend Protestantism while fulfilling Swedish ambitions in the Baltic dating from the time of Erik XIV and Johan III. By 1630, however, his defence of Protestantism was linked with his plan for a far-reaching confederation of German states with a Swedish Protestant king at its head.

Through the mediation of Richelieu a treaty between Poland and Sweden was arranged in 1629 which gave Sweden Livonia and several Prussian harbours from which port duties would help to finance a war. With his rear firmly covered and with control of the most important grain-exporting areas in Europe, Gustavus Adolphus felt free to embark on a German campaign, and landed in Pomerania shortly after midsummer 1630. It was a fortunate moment to enter the arena, for Wallenstein, the brilliant commander of the imperial forces, had through his driving ambition threatened many German princes, who succeeded in arousing the suspicions of the Emperor Ferdinand II against him. Ferdinand relieved Wallenstein of his post, but there was no general of equal calibre to lead the Catholic forces. The German Protestant princes were reluctant to join Gustavus Adolphus, but he took matters into his own hands, forcing Brandenburg to form an alliance and then going to the aid of Saxony when it was attacked by Tilly. He defeated the army of Tilly, the Catholic general of the imperial forces, decisively at Breitenfeld in 1631 and was hailed as the saviour of the Protestant cause. He turned now to the Rhineland and set up camp at Mainz and Frankfurt, and experienced soldiers flocked to join his army. His headquarters became the centre of European diplomacy. In 1632 he moved into Bavaria, crossed the Lech despite opposition from Tilly, who was killed in the encounter, and made for Munich. Wallenstein was now recalled by the desperate emperor and he and Gustavus Adolphus fought an indecisive battle at Nuremberg in September. Wallenstein withdrew to winter quarters in Saxony, but Gustavus Adolphus followed and on 16 November attacked at Lützen. The victory went to Sweden, but the price was enormous, for Gustavus Adolphus was mortally wounded in the battle.

Without his magic touch the Swedish achievements were greatly reduced. The two Protestant commanders, Gustav Horn and Bernhard of Weimar, quarrelled and were well beaten at Nördlingen in 1634 by the Catholic forces under Archduke Ferdinand, king of Hungary and Bohemia, and son of Ferdinand II. Fortunately for Swedish troops in Germany two young military disciples of Gustavus Adolphus, first Johan Banér and then Lennart Torstensson, took over the command and saved the Swedish position. A familiar hazard arose nearer home, however, for Christian IV, afraid of Sweden's increasing power, threatened to attack while her forces were deployed in Germany. Torstensson had to hurry north to counteract Danish moves. Gustav Horn invaded Skåne while Torstensson moved into Holstein and then Jutland, and Dutch ships joined the Swedish fleet under Karl Gustav Wrangel. Despite a gallant defence the Danes were overwhelmed and had to accept the Peace of Brömsebro in 1645, an extremely important one for Sweden, since among her gains were Jämtland, Härjedalen, Halland (for a period of thirty years), Gotland, and Ösel, and exemption from the sound dues. For the first time Sweden had a proper outlet to the North Sea.

The Swedish army meanwhile returned to Germany. Sweden was in a good strategic position during the negotiations leading to the Peace of Westphalia which was concluded in 1648 and did well out of the final settlement, her gains including western Pomerania, which gave her control of the mouth of the Oder; the bishoprics of Bremen and Verden, and thus control of the Elbe and the Weser; and 5 million *riksdaler* to pay off her armies.

Gustavus Adolphus's only child, Kristina, was only six years old in 1632 and a regency of five high officials was appointed, dominated by Axel Oxenstierna, who was virtually regent until Kristina came of age in 1644. The pressing need was to find the means to finance the German war and this was often done by the alienation of crown land either in lieu of payment to an officer or as a means of raising money, which increased even further the power of the nobles. In the struggle between king and nobles the latter had gained the ascendancy. Not only did they constitute a threat to royal power but also to the very roots of the peasant's traditional freedom in Sweden, for when a crown estate was donated the peasants on that estate found themselves paying taxes to the new owner instead of to the crown and being treated much more like serfs than freemen. Many of the nobles had had experience in Germany and the Baltic states, where feudal customs still existed, and brought back concepts foreign to Sweden. Per Brahe, who held the office of High Steward, was quoted as saying, 'We are all subjects of the crown, the peasants indirectly and we [i.e., the nobles] directly'. The peasants were fully aware of the danger and used the channels open to them, mainly the Peasant Estate in the *Riksdag*, to draw attention to their grievances.

In accordance with her father's wishes Kristina had been afforded the education a male heir would have received. She had inherited the Vasas' intellectual gifts, was a brilliant scholar, attracted famous men to her court, including Descartes, and was interested in government, but appears to have had one serious shortcoming, a lack of interest in finance. She was disinclined to allow Oxenstierna to retain his great influence and skilfully used the dissatisfaction in the *Riksdag* to her advantage. She had no desire to marry, but could not persuade the nobles to accept her cousin Karl Gustav as heir to the throne – it was never in their interests to have an able-bodied, strong-willed crown prince ready to seize the reins of government. By playing off the lower Estates against the nobles, however,

Kristina succeeded against Oxenstierna's wishes in having Karl Gustav appointed commander-in-chief of the Swedish troops in Germany and then in 1650 formally accepted as heir to the throne.

There is something larger than life about Swedish monarchs in the Period of Greatness and Kristina, with her eager but restless intelligence, is no exception. In the early 1650s she faced a crisis when her sense of duty as sovereign of a Protestant state collided with a strong and, as it proved, irresistible urge to embrace the Catholic faith, a strange situation for the only child of the great defender of Protestantism. As a Catholic she could not wear the Swedish crown, and in a moving scene at a *Riksdag* at Uppsala in 1654 she took a ceremonious farewell of her people. She went first to Belgium and on to Innsbruck where she was formally converted to the Catholic faith. Then in 1656 she journeyed to France where she was involved with Cardinal Mazarin in a secret plot to capture Naples, whereupon she would bear the Neapolitan crown for life, after which it would revert to France. The plot was betrayed by Kristina's own Chamberlain, Monaldeschi, and Kristina moved on to Rome where she was drawn into papal politics and where, too, she founded a learned society and surrounded herself with precious works of art. In 1660–61 and in 1667 she revisited her native country, essentially in order to guard her economic interests there, but Rome had become her temporal and spiritual home and she died there in 1689.

During her reign, Kristina preserved peace, realizing perhaps that the country desperately needed time to recover from its military enterprises. Unfortunately she never allied this with that other necessity, a determined effort to put to rights the country's finances. It was left to her cousin, who succeeded her in 1654 as Karl X Gustav, to implement the policy of reclaiming crown lands. The process was started, but then the king, not an adherent of his predecessor's peace policy, went off to war and plans were delayed. The Russians had emerged from their time of troubles and by the 1650s were occupying large parts of Poland. Karl Gustav decided to join in the war while Poland was under stress, partly to force the Polish king, Jan Casimir, to abandon all claim to the Swedish throne and partly to seize the Polish littoral. He had initial successes, but then the Catholic Poles rose against the Swedish infidels and while King Karl Gustav was fighting desperately in northern Poland, the Russians in 1656 concluded a truce and invaded Ingria and Livonia. Brandenburg had turned on Karl Gustav, and Denmark seized the opportunity and declared war on Sweden.

Karl Gustav attacked the Danes first as being geographically closest to home and therefore the most dangerous. He pushed northwards and occupied the whole of Jutland in 1657, leaving himself in a vulnerable position, for the Poles were in Pomerania, Austrians were in Prussia, Brandenburg was numbered among his enemies, and the freezing sea was threatening to keep him locked in Jutland. Karl Gustav, who was renowned for his audacity and surprise tactics, and who on one occasion was quoted as saying that he 'did not mean to commit a madness by halves', now excelled himself. Trusting to his luck and to the thickness of the ice, he marched his army across the frozen Little and Great Belts by way of the small islands and soon threatened Copenhagen itself. The Danes, unable to procure aid, quickly had to submit to the Peace of Roskilde in 1658, one of the most significant in inter-Scandinavian relations, for Skåne, Halland, Blekinge, and Bohuslän were ceded to Sweden, giving her a long, unimpeded outlet to the North Sea, an equal share with Denmark to the entry of the Sound, and rounding off her territory in the Baltic.

All this proved insufficient to still Karl Gustav's ambition, and in 1658 he broke the peace and landed in Zealand with the intention apparently of making Norway and Denmark Swedish provinces. Inspired perhaps by his famous uncle, the Lion of the North, he saw himself as the head of a united Scandinavia. Copenhagen would be destroyed and Malmö, Swedish since the Peace of Roskilde, would become a base, while Norway would have a Swedish governor. But by this time Karl Gustav had exhausted his great fund of good fortune. He roused the Danes to a heroic, desperate defence of their capital and also brought upon himself other Baltic powers which were becoming alarmed at his increasing power. King Frederik III of Denmark gallantly defended Copenhagen until the Dutch arrived, while forces from Poland, Austria, and Brandenburg entered Holstein and forced the Swedes to withdraw.

Karl Gustav called a *Riksdag* at Gothenburg in 1660 while planning an attack on Norway but, unpredictable as ever, he suddenly collapsed and died shortly afterwards, only thirty-eight years of age. All plans for continued hostilities died with him and Sweden entered peace negotiations instead. She was fortunate in being able to retain most of the territories she had won at the Peace of Roskilde. In a limited way Karl Gustav's gamble had paid off and Sweden retained her position as the strongest of the Scandinavian countries.

Karl Gustav's only child, Karl, was only four when his father died, and so the country once more faced the prospect of a long regency period. Once more the nobles emerged as the virtual rulers of the country, though in this case it almost amounted to the regents (presided over officially by Karl Gustav's widow, the inoffensive Queen Hedvig Eleonora, but in effect dominated by the Chancellor,

Magnus De la Gardie) being given enough rope to hang themselves.

Sweden was faced with the problem of peace. For many years war had been her normal state and peace the exception. What was now needed was some kind of order in the state finances and a means of safeguarding peace, preferably by gaining the support of a powerful ally. The regents proved unsuccessful on both counts. A further reclaiming of land by the crown from the nobles was necessary, but it was perhaps expecting too much of the regents to denude their own Estate of wealth and power, and the necessary measures were not implemented. In foreign affairs the Chancellor, Magnus De la Gardie (1622–86), wanted Sweden to ally herself with Louis XIV of France, whose ambitions in the 1660s were threatening to alter the map of Europe. De la Gardie's opponents at first pushed through in 1668 the Triple Alliance between Britain, Holland, and Sweden, but when Louis XIV began preparing for war against Holland in 1672 De la Gardie succeeded in changing Swedish policy and forming an alliance with France. It soon became evident that he had backed the wrong horse. Louis forced Sweden, as his ally, into war with his enemy Brandenburg and the Swedish army was defeated at Fehrbellin in 1675 (the setting, incidentally, of Kleist's play *Der Prinz von Homburg*). Sweden's other enemies, Holland, Austria, Denmark-Norway, countries that had watched her expansion in the Baltic area with much apprehension, took the opportunity to declare war. Danish troops landed in Skåne in 1676 and Norwegian forces were ready along the western borders. The situation showed up clearly Sweden's weaknesses.

Karl XI, who at the age of sixteen took over the government of Sweden in 1672, deprived the regents at this moment of imminent danger of all their powers, and took over the defence of the country himself. After a desperate bloody battle at Lund in 1676 he finally expelled the Danes from the southern provinces. By 1679 peace was restored, no territory was lost to Denmark, and through the mediation of Louis XIV Sweden regained most of the territory that she had lost to Brandenburg. Dano-Swedish relations were improved when Karl XI shortly afterwards married the sister of Christian V of Denmark, Ulrika Eleonora.

Although he acquitted himself well at the Battle of Lund, Karl XI has gone down in history as a man of peace who restored the economic affairs of the crown. The *Riksdag* in 1680 and 1682 gave him the opportunity he needed to deal ruthlessly with the nobles, whose property, it is estimated, was reduced by some 50 per cent. The lower Estates gave him their wholehearted support, especially the peasants who now saw the awful threat of serfdom effectively removed. It is estimated that by the turn of the century as much as one-third of all land in Sweden was again owned by the crown. The king's authority increased until by 1693 when Karl put a direct question concerning his sovereignty to the *Riksdag*, he received the remarkable reply that he was 'an absolute all-powerful sovereign King who is responsible to no one on earth for his actions but has power and might at his own pleasure and as a Christian King to govern and rule his Kingdom'. The Council became a Supreme Court, but otherwise was retained in an advisory capacity only and referred to at the king's pleasure.

Having solved the internal problem of state finances Karl then concentrated on building up an efficient defence force. A system of earmarking revenue from certain estates for government expenditure was extended to the army. Crown land in certain districts was given in return for the provision of cavalry and foot soldiers. These districts were divided into small units, each of which had to provide one soldier and find him a cottage and plot of land to support himself and his family.

The functions of the Swedish navy were carefully examined too. Stockholm obviously was not the ideal location for the main base since it was too far from the obvious enemies, Denmark and Holland, and in any case the waters tended to freeze in winter. Karl had a new naval base built at Karlskrona in Blekinge under the supervision of Hans Wachtmeister. It soon became one of the largest towns in Sweden, while the well-known Wachtmeister family still has close ties with Blekinge.

If Karl XI lacked the intellectual gifts and the panache of his predecessors, he nevertheless gave the country the peace and stability it needed and left it in a much healthier state than he had found it.

The Wars of Karl XII

The reverse is true of his son and heir, that most enigmatic king, Karl XII, who had the most adventurous reign of all but left his country exhausted, disorganized, and bereft of all her Baltic possessions. Although only fifteen when his father died in 1697, Karl was immediately declared of age and thus absolute monarch. The Swedish Baltic empire had been built up at the expense of other countries caught in weak situations. Several of these–Russia, Saxony, Poland, Denmark-Norway–joined in an alliance against Sweden in 1699, judging that with many nobles smarting under the effect of Karl XI's reclamation policy and the government under an untried young king Sweden herself would be vulnerable. In 1689 Karl XI had championed Albert, duke of Holstein-Gottorp, father of his future son-in-law Frederick IV, against Denmark. In 1700 Danish troops attacked strongholds in Holstein, planning to remove this Swedish ally that they had at their rear, while Augustus II, the Strong, king of Poland and elector of Saxony, invaded Livonia. Karl XII decided to take the initiative. In 1700 he left his capital, never to see it again, and turned on Denmark. Frederik IV quickly made peace with the duke of Holstein and left the alliance against Sweden. Karl then moved his main army to Livonia, from which the Saxons soon withdrew; but then he heard that Tsar Peter was threatening Narva. With a force of only 10,000, Karl relieved Narva and won a decisive victory over the Russians who outnumbered the Swedes by three to one. He then turned his attention to Augustus; won a series of battles, taking Warsaw and Cracow; then decided to take the war into Saxony; and forced Augustus to make peace at Altranstäd in 1706. Augustus was forced to renounce his claim to the Polish throne, to accept Karl's candidate, Stanisław Leszczyński, as king of Poland, and to leave the alliance against Sweden.

Karl was now at the height of his fame and he was visited by many European diplomats, including Marlborough (soliciting support in the War of the Spanish Succession), at his winter quarters at Altranstädt. His attention, however, was fixed firmly on Russia. Tsar Peter had penetrated into Ingria, Estonia, and Livonia, and had laid the foundations of his new capital, St Petersburg, in 1703. With characteristic boldness (or foolhardiness?) Karl decided to go to the heart of the Russian force and with 40,000 men he marched on Moscow. He was to be joined by a Polish army sent by Stanisław and a Swedish force under Adam Ludvig Lewenhaupt coming from Livonia, but neither reached him. The Russians meanwhile adopted a scorched-earth policy, and like Napoleon and Hitler after him Karl experienced the vastness of Russia. Since it proved impossible to reach Moscow, he decided to move instead to the Ukraine, hoping to be joined by the rebel Cossack leader Mazeppa. That winter (1708–09) was one of the severest on record and took a heavy toll of the Swedish soldiers. Karl's hopes lay in a pitched battle against Tsar Peter and presumably with this aim in view he besieged Poltava in 1709. Peter rose to the bait, arriving with an army 45,000-strong as opposed to the Swedish 18,000. It was a hard-fought battle and Karl might yet have achieved the impossible, but he had sustained a foot injury in a skirmish before the battle which precluded his usual mobility. He was defeated and with a thousand men went south to Bender in Bessarabia where he remained for no less than five years trying to raise Turkish help. Tsar Peter skilfully removed the causes of enmity between Russia and Turkey, and Karl

D

found himself being treated by the Sultan Ahmed III not as an ally but as an embarrassing guest. He was finally forced to leave Bender and at the beginning of October 1714 set off for Sweden, riding through Hungary and then via Vienna, Regensburg, Nuremberg, Bamberg, Würzburg, and on to Kassel and then Stralsund. It was not the most direct route, but he had to avoid the territory of his enemies, Poland and Saxony. It has been calculated that he covered 1,430 miles in under sixteen days on horseback, and it is said that when he dismounted in Stralsund in November, he was limping badly, for he had not had his riding boots off for eight days and his feet were swollen.

Meanwhile after Poltava Augustus, who had succeeded in regaining his Polish kingdom once his adversary had lost his Swedish backing, and Frederik of Denmark had formed an alliance with Tsar Peter. A Swedish defence force beat off an attempted Danish invasion of Skåne in 1710, but when the Swedish commander, Magnus Stenbock, tried to take the initiative in 1713 and attacked Denmark, he was defeated in Holstein. The Russians occupied Estonia and Livonia, and moved on into Finland. George, elector of Hanover (and king of Great Britain since 1714), and Frederick I of Prussia also joined the allies, eager to seize Swedish possessions in Germany.

Karl eschewed any suggestion of suing for a peace that would result in loss of territory, even though all Swedish territory outside Sweden was occupied by enemy forces. When he reached Lund in 1715, he set about the task of breaking the ring of enemies surrounding his country. As absolute monarch he ignored his Council and imposed on his subjects, already suffering from the effects of protracted wars, plague, and famine, a series of desperate measures including a drastic form of conscription, a compulsory loan scheme, and a debasing of the currency.

By 1718 he had an army of 40,000 at his disposal and was ready to attack. Denmark-Norway was to be the first target and he sent General Armfelt with a small force to cross the mountains into the Trondheim district while he himself advanced with 30,000 men into southern Norway. While besieging the fortress of Frederiksten near Frederikshald Karl was shot dead on 30 November 1718 and historians ever since have been trying to decide the truth of the rumour that the king was murdered. It seems appropriate that this most controversial warrior-king remained an enigma to the end. Was he an outdated warrior who thought that a bared sword at the head of an army could solve the balance of power in the whole of Europe or a brilliant leader who staved off the inevitable fall of the Swedish empire for a decade? Voltaire saw him as a myth in his own lifetime, a larger-than-life character whose very prowess in battle prevented him from being a successful king; the Swedish writer Olof von Dalin in his allegorical *Story of a Horse* of 1740 called him a Hercules whose renown was immortal. Samuel Johnson in 1749 saw him as a hero:

> He left a Name at which the World grew pale,
> To point a Moral or adorn a Tale.
>
> *(The Vanity of Human Wishes)*

Many other Swedish writers, notably Esaias Tegnér in the early nineteenth century, idealized him as a great fearless warrior-king; but towards the end of the nineteenth century he emerged as the villain of Swedish history, who brought about the downfall of the Swedish empire and caused great privation among his people. Visitors to Stockholm are reminded of him as he stands in Karl XII:s Torg (Charles XII Square) dressed in his characteristically austere military overcoat, riding boots, and long sword and pointing towards Russia.

On his death the Swedish armies returned to Sweden and the new Swedish government sued for peace. Bremen and Verden were lost to Hanover in 1719; Swedish Pomerania south of the Peene and the islands of Usedom and Wollin went to Prussia in 1720; Sweden lost exemption from sound dues; and at the Peace of Nystad in 1721, Ingria, Estonia, Livonia, and the large part of Karelia including Viborg went to Russia.

Seventeenth-century Enterprise and Culture

The Swedish empire had gone and the Period of Greatness was over. It had left its mark, however, on the development of Sweden. It was a period of expansion and as such attracted to Sweden people of spirit and enterprise. Not only was foreign capital invested in the expanding mining industries and new towns, but skilled German, Dutch, and Walloon craftsmen arrived too. Able army officers joined Gustavus Adolphus during the Thirty Years War and many of them, often ennobled for their services to the king, settled in Sweden after the war. Aristocratic Swedish families with Scottish names can be traced back to this period: Duvall (McDougall), Hamilton, Sinclair, Ramsay, etc.

The spirit of enterprise was manifest in 1638 when Sweden founded the North American colony of 'Nya Sverige' (i.e., New Sweden), comprising parts of the territory now known as Delaware, plus parts of Pennsylvania and of New Jersey. The Swedes bought the land from the Indians and established several settlements such as Fort Christina and Vasa. New Sweden was taken over by the Dutch in 1655 and absorbed by the neighbouring New Amsterdam which in turn became New York only ten years later. Some 500 to 600 Swedes remained there and the Swedish language was extant in the area until the end of the eighteenth century.

Louis De Geer founded an African trading company and in the 1650s had a fort built on the Gold Coast, at what is now Cape Coast Castle. It was a financial failure and was taken over by the Dutch in 1663; but it is yet another indication of Swedish enterprise and self-confidence in the seventeenth century.

There was a cultural expansion in Sweden during this period. A new form of school, the *gymnasium*, was established in 1623 (the first was in Västerås) where the classics, Hebrew, theology, history, and mathematics were taught up to university level by graduate teachers. Not only was Uppsala University given royal patronage, but new universities were founded in Swedish overseas territories— Dorpat, Åbo, and Greifswald. After the Treaty of Roskilde a Swedish university was established at Lund, the *Academia Carolina Conciliatrix*, founded in 1668. The rapid success of the gesture may be illustrated by the fact that Dalin, acknowledged as the best exponent of modern Swedish in the first half of the eighteenth century, studied at Lund in 1721.

As the wealth of the nobles increased, they began to build mansions, and palaces more splendid than anything built before–or indeed since–by private Swedish citizens. The old city wall of Stockholm was pulled down and in 1640 Stockholm was replanned. With a centralized government administered by the nobles and situated in Stockholm, leading members of the Estate of Nobles commissioned town houses as well as country seats. Wrangel's residences, for instance, can still be seen today; his town palace, which now houses the Supreme Court, is on Riddarholmen, while Skokloster is on Lake Mälaren. (One of his prize possessions here was the *Codex Argenteus*, taken from Prague in the Thirty Years War, and now lodged in the Uppsala University Library.) Renowned architects were also attracted to Sweden. The Frenchman Jean de la Vallée completed the *Riddarhus* (begun 1642, completed 1674), while the German Nicodemus Tessin designed the charming palace of Drottningholm on Lake Mälaren. When the old castle Tre Kronor was burned down in 1697 Tessin's son, also called Nicodemus, designed the new palace, although it was not completed until 1757.

Painters were also drawn to the centre of the Northern empire. The French artist Sébastien Bourdon painted portraits of many royal and noble Swedes, including both Kristina and her cousin Karl Gustav; the German David Klöker (later ennobled as baron

von Ehrenstrahl) depicted Karl XI and his family; and the artist
David von Krafft became famous towards the end of the period for
his portraits of Karl XII.

The Swedish court, especially in the reign of Kristina, became
known for its extravagance. Kristina patronized the arts and many
Swedish writers came to prominence. It is characteristic of the
period that they all spent much time abroad. The most important
was Georg Stiernhielm (1598–1672) who studied at Greifswald,
Strassburg, and Leiden, and served in Livonia and Ingria. This
brilliant poet, philologist, mathematician, and lawyer (and from
1669 member of the Royal Society in London) epitomizes the spirit
of Sweden and the Age of Greatness. Lars Wivallius (1605–69), one
of Sweden's first lyric poets, enjoyed the distinction of having been
captured by both Wallenstein and Tilly in the Thirty Years War
and escaping from both. Lucidor (the pseudonym of Lars Johans-
sson; 1638–74) spent part of his childhood in Pomerania and studied
at Greifswald. He too reflects the spirit of his times; he was proud,
independent, expressed a *carpe diem* sentiment, and ended his life
in a tavern brawl. Samuel Columbus (1642–79) travelled widely
in Europe; Urban Hiärne (1641–1724) was born in Ingria; Gunno
Dahlstierna (1669–1709) was a surveyor in Livonia and Pomerania.
Johan Runius (1679–1713) journeyed to Reval, and Haquin
Spegel (1645–1714) studied at universities in Germany, England,
Holland, and Denmark.

These poets reflected in their work the patriotic zeal of the period.
The Swedes had acquitted themselves well in war and saw themselves
worthy descendants of the old Goths. Interest in old Scandinavian
literature was kindled and in 1667 a College of Antiquity was formed
in Stockholm.

The Swedish empire had lasted less than a century, and on the
death of Karl XII in 1718 there was little on the map beyond the
bounds of Scandinavia to show for it. But within Sweden itself the
cultural developments of the period remained and many of the fine
palaces and their paintings can still be admired today.

Chapter 3

1718–1866

The Road to Parliamentary Democracy

The Age of Liberty

'The history of Sweden is the history of her Kings', wrote Geijer in the nineteenth century, but an exception must be made for the period known as the Age of Liberty (1718–72). Swedes of all classes were weary of war and alert to the evils of an absolute monarchy, and since there was no direct heir to the Swedish throne on the death of Karl XII, they had an excellent opportunity of electing a monarch on their own terms. Karl XII's sister Ulrika Eleonora was offered the crown in 1719, only on condition that she accepted a new constitution. The following year her consort Fredrik became king, again on condition that the new constitution first be accepted.

The royal couple were little more than figureheads and real power was held by the Council responsible to the four Estates who could dismiss Council members for misconduct. The twenty-four members of the Council were officially appointed by the king, but a *Riksdag* committee shortlisted eligible candidates. The king himself had only two votes and a casting vote on the Council, a measure of his authority in this period. The leading Council member was the Chancellor, the most powerful man in government. It was not a truly democratic system, for the influence of the Estate of Nobles was much greater than that of the other three Estates, while the landless peasants, a large section of the farming community, were not represented at all.

The office of Chancellor was held from 1720 to 1738 by Count Arvid Horn, who had distinguished himself both as a soldier and a diplomat during the wars of Karl XII but had become a convinced pacifist and an opponent of absolute monarchy. His task as he saw it was to build up the country's economy again and to avoid wars. For nearly twenty years he succeeded in doing both and during his term of office economic conditions improved, and there was a steady rise in population. Sweden was still overwhelmingly an agricultural country and since only the more extreme parts of Sweden proper had been invaded during the wars (the Danes were in Skåne in 1710 and the Russians ravaged the east coast in 1719–21), there was no large-scale damage to repair. There was also a steady demand for iron in Europe and Swedish iron commanded a good price in European markets. The state regulated production and prevented the export of poor-quality iron. (Thus even in the eighteenth century the Swedes established a reputation for reliable-quality goods.) The general peace in Europe helped shipping and by the 1730s Swedish merchant-ships dominated the Baltic. Trading companies were set up, the most notable being the East India Company (established in 1731 in Gothenburg by a number of merchants including Colin Campbell, a Scotsman). Horn's home policy was mildly protectionist, enough to help Swedish industry to thrive but not to encourage foolhardiness.

Horn established friendly relations with both France and Britain (Sweden's best customer for iron)–straightforward when the two leading statesmen, Sir Robert Walpole and Cardinal Fleury, were anxious to avoid war and while the Treaty of Hanover (1725) was valid. It became more complicated after 1731 when the Anglo-French alliance foundered and Britain seemed to be veering towards Russia.

Opposition to Horn grew up among a young generation who remembered nothing of the privations of the Great Northern War, but were conscious of having lost a Baltic empire. To them Karl XII was a hero, Russia was their natural enemy, and Horn's caution bordered on cowardice. They clamoured for renewed hostilities against the Russians in an attempt to regain lost territory. Many burghers joined this opposition, hoping for greater tariff protection and more state subsidies for industry. Since a Swedish war against Russia would serve France's purposes, the French minister in Stockholm encouraged and subsidized the opposition who organized themselves into a political party. They called Horn's supporters (who included the older generation of nobles) *Natt-mössor*, abbreviated to *Mössor* (i.e., 'nightcaps' or 'caps'), and they themselves became known as the *Hattar* (i.e., 'hats') because of the tricorn worn by army officers.

When war broke out between Russia and Turkey in 1738, the Hats considered it a heaven-sent opportunity and were determined to oust Horn. They gained a majority in the *Riksdag* of 1738 and sent Major Malcolm Sinclair on a mission to contact and co-operate with the Turks against Russia, and to arrange for subsidies from France. The Russians had Sinclair killed on his way home, and Hat propaganda whipped up public opinion against Russia and demanded a war of revenge. The inflammatory *Sinclairsvisan* or

Sinclair song, still found in Swedish song-books, dates from this time. Horn resigned, his closest followers were dismissed from the Council by the *Riksdag*, and a Hat, Carl Gyllenborg, became Chancellor–an exercise in parliamentary government, if not exactly true democracy, since the Estates were not sufficiently representative of the whole nation.

When Princess Elizabeth, daughter of Tsar Peter, solicited Swedish aid to secure the Russian throne, the Hats seized the opportunity and at the 1740–41 *Riksdag* pushed through a declaration of war on Russia. The Swedish army organization, however, was hopelessly run down. A Swedish force set off for Finland, but before they had fired a shot their commander, Charles Emile Lewenhaupt, learned that Elizabeth was already the Tsarina. Irresolute, he quartered his men in Finland where the Finnish winter, disease, and desertions took their toll. When Elizabeth now turned on the Swedes in Finland as enemy invaders, Lewenhaupt's force was unable to defend itself. By 1742 the Swedish army had capitulated in Helsinki and the Russians occupied the whole of Finland.

The Hats saved face partly by using Lewenhaupt and his deputy, Henrik Magnus von Buddenbrock, as scapegoats and having them executed, and partly by obtaining lenient peace terms from Tsarina Elizabeth by accepting her candidate for the Swedish throne. Queen Ulrika Eleonora had died in 1741 and the Hats agreed to elect Adolf Fredrik of Holstein-Gottorp, Elizabeth's cousin, as Fredrik I's successor. In return Sweden had to cede to Russia only the southeastern part of Finland.

It was in France's interests to keep the Hats in office, while the Russians hoped to see the Caps regain control. Both countries bribed freely, but the Russian minister in Stockholm, Baron J. A. von Korff, was so blatant that public opinion, always ready to see the Russians as the enemy, was outraged at this interference in internal affairs and favoured the Hats, the anti-Russian party, as a consequence.

When, on the death of Fredrik I, Adolf Fredrik came to the throne, he and his ambitious wife, Lovisa Ulrika, sister of Frederick II (the Great) of Prussia, expected the Hats to revise the constitution in their favour, in acknowledgement of their role in Sweden's negotiations with Russia; but they were disappointed. A court party was formed and when relations between the royal couple and the Hats deteriorated even further, Lovisa Ulrika planned a *coup d'état*. It was an unrealistic scheme, but was in any case never put to the test, for it was betrayed. Several members of the court party were arrested. Eight were executed, and the royal couple suffered the embarrassment of public rebuke by their own subjects.

Partly to humiliate the queen even further and partly to satisfy the French, the Hats joined a coalition against Frederick the Great. Swedish troops were sent to Pomerania during the Seven Years War (1756–63), but they were no match for the well-trained Prussian troops and the queen enjoyed a moral victory when the Hats were obliged to solicit her aid in negotiating a lenient peace settlement with her brother.

Throughout their period of office the Hats devoted much attention to the economy; seeing how countries like Holland and England had prospered by exploiting their resources, they wanted Sweden to do likewise. They intensified Horn's protectionist policy and subsidized manufacturers. The National Bank was equally eager to put capital at the disposal of manufacturers without collateral. A number of manufactories were started, especially in the Stockholm area, while Jonas Alströmer set up textile factories at Alingsås.

Agricultural reform was also initiated in this period. The old system of dividing strips of arable land among members of village communities had reached the point where a peasant could well own up to fifty small plots in as many different places. It militated against change, but thanks initially to Jacob Faggot, a surveyor, in 1757 the Estates accepted in principle the need for consolidation. The difficulties of reapportioning the land so that everyone was treated fairly and of persuading peasants to change a way of life that had been handed down for generations were enormous. By 1783 Rutger MacLean, a wealthy landowner of Scottish descent, began experimenting with the enclosure system on his estate in Skåne, setting up his tenants on compact plots. The improvement in production persuaded others to follow suit and gradually reforms were effected.

The Hats had a practical approach to life. They founded the Academy of Sciences in 1739, a founding member of which was the renowned botanist Carl von Linné (Linnaeus; 1707–78). The Estates at this time financed Linnaeus's journeys to various Swedish provinces to assess the land and its potential. In 1749 Per Wargentin (1718–83) started compiling reliable statistics on population and in 1776 he was appointed a member of a committee on statistics, the first in Europe. Other Swedish names of this period won universal acclaim, such as Emanuel Swedenborg (1688–1772), anatomist, astronomer, mineralogist, and philosopher, and Anders Celsius (1701–44), professor of anatomy, founder of Sweden's first observatory, and the innovator of the centigrade thermometer.

The realistic attitude is reflected too in a new approach to history. Professor Sven Lagerbring (1707–87) laid the foundations for a critical study of the subject. When Olof von Dalin (1708–63), the best-known writer of the period, was commissioned by the Estates to write a history of Sweden, he followed Lagerbring's guidelines and criticized the bombastic xenophobic historians of the seventeenth century. Dalin himself is remembered particularly for his periodical *Then Swänska Argus* (The Swedish Argus; 1732–34), based on (indeed on occasion plagarizing) Addison's and Steele's *Tatler* and *Spectator* – a realistic, commonsense, moralizing periodical which set the standards of modern Swedish prose for many years to come.

Opinions on this period differ. In Tegnér's assessment, written in the nineteenth century, it was a period when 'everything was attempted, nothing was completed, a time without King or honour'. Professor Eli Heckscher, on the other hand, the famous economic historian, saw the period, with its interest in science, industry, economics, statistics, etc., as the time when the foundations of modern Sweden were laid. There is fairly general agreement, however, that the period ended in confusion, mismanagement, and corruption. Many factories hiding behind protective import barriers tried to force poor-quality goods on the public, but this led to smuggling on a large scale, which in turn led to manufacturers leaning even more heavily on state subsidies. The Bank's policy of printing more banknotes than it could cover led to a highly inflationary situation. This was exacerbated by the Seven Years War, and by the 1760s prices were three times the 1740 level–the newly-instituted Statistics Bureau must have found their material far from encouraging. Dissatisfaction over the mismanagement of the war and the economic situation generally led to the Caps' return to office in 1765. In their determination to rectify previous mistakes they removed subsidies, restricted the Bank's credit, demanded repayment of outstanding loans, and brought prices down so drastically that many manufacturers went to the wall and there was widespread unemployment. The poet Carl Michael Bellman (1740–95) was one of many who went bankrupt in the 1760s and the many dissolute characters he portrays, Stockholmers who haunted the numerous gin-shops in the capital, illustrate one hectic reaction to the dire economic situation at that time.

The Hats exploited the general discontent and asked the *Riksdag* to be reassembled. The Council, with its majority of Caps, tried to reject their demands and the king, who had agreed to help the Hats in return for increased power, threatened to abdicate in protest. The Caps retaliated by issuing a rubber stamp with the king's name on it; but the civil servants, the majority of whom were Hats, refused to accept this. The *Riksdag* was then assembled in 1769, in the face of a campaign characterized by blatant use of bribes and external interference, especially by Russia. The Hats won a majority and a predominantly Hat Council was constituted, but when this Council tried to honour its promises to the king, the Hats in the Estates threw out its proposals. At this point of impasse, in 1771, Adolf Fredrik died and his eldest son, Gustav, who was in Paris, hurried home, although not without first assuring himself of French aid should it be necessary in re-establishing effective government in his country.

The Gustavian Era

Evidence shows that Gustav III made a genuine attempt to make the parties work together, but when they proved irreconcilable, he staged a *coup d'état*. The army was loyal to him and it soon transpired that he also had the enthusiastic backing of most of his subjects. No blood was spilt–no one apparently thought the Age of Liberty was worth that much–the Council was arrested, and forced to resign. Two days after the *coup* the Estates were assembled and presented with a new constitution which Gustav III had already drawn up. It was immediately accepted and the Age of Liberty had given way to the Gustavian Era.

The constitution was based on the principle of a balance of power between the king, Council, and Estates, but many issues were phrased in vague terms and the trend was now obviously away from parliamentary power towards a greatly increased royal authority. The success of the new constitution would depend on the strength and the personality of Gustav III. He was a complex character, reared in the spirit of the Enlightenment and a great admirer of Voltaire–humane, tolerant, artistic, histrionic, and with a talent for charming people in his presence. Combined with these qualities was a love of pomp and circumstance. He loved the brilliance of the French court and hoped to create during his reign a Swedish Versailles–and indeed court life played a larger part in Swedish history during the first part of his reign than ever before or since.

Gustav had sufficient scope for improvement when he came to power, for the confusion of the final years of the Age of Freedom had precluded effective government. His immediate task was to supervise the distribution of imported grain in 1772, for the crops had failed and there was starvation and ensuing disease.

On the advice of the gifted Johan Liljencrantz (1730–1815) he then set about restoring the Swedish currency to some form of stability. By 1776 Liljencrantz had borrowed sufficient silver from abroad to enable the National Bank to redeem its notes up to half their face value. The *riksdaler* was introduced and for a time at least the economy was calculated on a stable currency.

The civil service was also improved on the king's initiative and matters were dealt with that had been waiting for attention for up to ten years. The worst examples of excessive sentences such as the death penalty for witchcraft, theft, rape, and bigamy, were removed from the penal code. Foreign residents in Sweden were allowed religious freedom and this tolerance was extended in 1781 to Jews, who were permitted to reside and trade in Stockholm, Gothenburg, and Norrköping and to have their synagogues there–although admittedly this tolerance had a more cynical edge to it since it was expected that the Jews would thereby bring considerable capital with them and help the Swedish economy. In the spirit of Adam Smith, various trade restrictions were lifted, including those governing imports. Many craftsmen and tradesmen were also allowed to start their own concerns.

Necessary though these reforms were, they nevertheless collided with the interests of many sections of the community and the wave of popularity that Gustav enjoyed in 1772 soon receded. The nobles, although treated with deference because of their birth and breeding, felt they were gradually being denuded of real authority and were becoming nothing but adornments at court. The clergy, often rigidly formalistic Lutherans, objected to the new religious tolerance and deplored the open selling of ecclesiastical appointments in the king's gift. The burghers objected to the removal of trade restrictions which threatened their profits, while peasants bemoaned their unalleviated economic plight. The population was rising sharply during this period, moving from approximately 1,781,000 in 1750 to almost 2,218,000 in 1780, and this increase had led to farms being divided into increasingly uneconomic units, and many peasants were permanently underemployed and wholly unemployed if there was a bad harvest. They were furious, too, at the setting-up of a crown monopoly of distilleries and a law forbidding home distilling of grain.

Opposition was at first neither co-ordinated nor vocal, but at the *Riksdag* of 1786 Gustav was for the first time made fully aware of the extent of the discontent. He removed some of the causes immediately, but never regained his former popularity.

At this point war broke out against Russia. Gustav had been fortunate in foreign affairs up to now, in that the traditional enemies of Sweden were engaged elsewhere or were not inclined to be belligerent. He had used the respite to complete Sveaborg, sometimes called the Gibraltar of the North, a great naval defence on the islands off Helsinki which had been started in the late 1740s, and to build up a strong fleet in the Stockholm archipelago. (The work was partly directed by F. H. af Chapman, a shipbuilder of

English descent whose name is now borne by the Stockholm Youth Hostel, a renovated sailing-ship moored at Skeppsholmen.) However, the Russian threat was growing; the Russian minister in Stockholm had been given instructions in 1784 to resuscitate the 'Russian Party' with the aim of undermining the Swedish constitution, while in Finland an independent movement had started up among young army officers with hopes of freeing Finland from Sweden and placing her under Russian protection. When war between Russia and Turkey broke out in the spring of 1788, Gustav decided to attack.

The great advance that he had hoped for eluded him and when the army officers refused to take part in a war which they said was a breach of the 1772 Constitution, his position became dangerous. A group of about a hundred Finnish officers, known as the Anjala League, wrote to the Tsarina Catherine II asking for peace negotiations. This was open treason and helped the king, as, ironically, did the Danes at this point by attacking Sweden. Gustav made a tour of his peoples, appealing for their help to beat back the invaders of their beloved country. He met with an enthusiastic response. The immediate threat of invasion was averted and Gustav called a *Riksdag*. The mutineers in Finland had been members of the Estate of Nobles and Gustav used this fact to increase the existing animosity that the other three Estates felt towards the nobles. He pushed through his 'Act of Union and Security' which made him virtually an absolute monarch.

With the means to continue the war granted, he returned to the attack against Russia. In 1790, after several defeats, the Swedish fleet enjoyed a victory decisive enough to allow Gustav to arrange a treaty with Russia without losing face. At Värälä the *status quo* was restored and Russia promised not to interfere again in Swedish internal affairs.

The nobles realized now that they had lost most of their privileges and their hatred of Gustav was intense. Under the leadership of old General Carl Fredrik Pechlin (1720–96) a number of aristocrats plotted to assassinate the king. The taciturn Jacob Johan Anckarström, a former Captain of the Guard with a personal grudge against the king, was assigned the role of regicide and at a masked ball at the Opera-House in Stockholm on 16 March 1792 he shot and fatally wounded Gustav, who died two weeks later.[1] It is a mark of Gustav's personal courage (and of his streak of panache, perhaps) that although he had received an anonymous warning beforehand, he refused to cancel his engagement.

---

[1] Verdi's opera *Un ballo in maschera* (A Masked Ball) is based on this incident, although to comply with censorship, the action was placed in Boston. The Swedish poet Erik Lindegren translated the libretto in 1958 and, like E. J. Dent, restored the action to Sweden.

The conspirators had expected the assassination to trigger off a military *coup*, to be followed by a new constitution restoring the nobles' superiority. Instead, as Gustav lay dying, a wave of affection for him and of hatred for the perpetrators swept the country. The nobles were fearful for their lives and Gustav's son, Gustav IV Adolf, succeeded to the throne with no curtailment of the monarch's power.

The Gustavian period is characterized by a flowering of the arts. The Age of Liberty, admittedly, had not been wholly lacking in cultural pursuits. Dalin's contemporary Hedvig Charlotta Nordenflycht (1718–63; whom Kellgren called ironically a Swedish Sappho), Gustaf Philip Creutz (1731–85), and Gustaf Fredrik Gyllenborg (1731–1808) formed the nucleus of a literary society, *Tankebyggarorden*, founded in 1753, and although none of them aspired to literary greatness, they all produced elegant, pleasing verse.

The musical societies and *collegia musica* found in Europe generally during this period had a counterpart in the amateur musical groups found in Sweden and in *Utile Dulce*, founded in 1766, a society for the promotion of both literature and music. Johan Helmich Roman (1694–1758), the composer who has often been called the 'Father of Swedish music', fits squarely into the Age of Liberty. A gifted instrumentalist, he studied in England for over four years from 1715, sponsored by the Swedish king, and on his return to Stockholm he directed his energies to the improvement of the court orchestra. He helped to bring about co-operation between his professional court musicians and proficient amateurs, and by 1731 was able to embark on public concerts. In 1753 he was able to say with obvious satisfaction that when in 1720 he had performed with the court musicians they were only twenty in all, 'but now we number well over one hundred, and all within Stockholm'. The music they performed included works by Handel and by Roman himself. He was a prolific and versatile composer, producing overtures, symphonies, *concerti grossi*, concerti for violin and for oboe, suites, chamber and choral music. Seen in perspective his music seems to bridge the late Baroque and Viennese Classicism. Despite his talent Roman was unable to create a lasting Swedish school of music, however, and there was no one of similar calibre to take over his work when he withdrew from the musical life of the capital.

Nor did Lovisa Ulrika's efforts to establish opera in Stockholm show lasting results. The sister of Frederick the Great, she had been reared in a court which showed great respect for music as an art form and one of her cherished desires as queen of Sweden was to have regular performances of opera in Stockholm. To this end she hired foreign companies, one of the more renowned being an Italian company under the management of Francesco Antonio Uttini who performed at Drottningholm in the 1750s. The royal purse during the Age of Liberty was not able to cope with the expenses involved in this kind of patronage, however, and it fell to her son, Gustav III, to ensure a rich cultural life in his capital and its surrounds.

Assured of the king's patronage, first-rate poets, painters, sculptors, and architects became respected members of the community. Earlier in the century the Rococo style in art had replaced the heavy Baroque. Like his mother, Queen Lovisa Ulrika, Gustav was drawn to this graceful form and to the neo-classical art that he had seen in France and Italy. One began to speak of the 'Gustavian style', a Swedish variation of Louis XVI, revealing a strong French influence.

In 1782 Gustav established a Royal Opera-House, in 1786 he founded the Swedish Academy to guard the Swedish language and encourage national literature, and in 1788 he set up the Royal Dramatic Theatre. He also had a court orchestra of some fifty players. His love of the theatre was such that even when on campaign in Finland during the Russian War, he arranged to be kept up to date with theatre productions in Stockholm. Both the king and Swedish aristocrats commissioned works by Swedish architects, sculptors, and painters. Carl Fredrik Adelcrantz (1716–96) designed the China castle at Drottningholm, the Adolf Fredrik Church in Stockholm, and the Royal Opera-House (which was destroyed and replaced in the 1890s by the present building in Stockholm); Johan Tobias Sergel (1740–1814) the sculptor, a pupil of Pierre-Hubert L'Archevêque, who had also been active in Sweden where he resided from 1755 to 1776, came into prominence in this period. His statue of Gustav III is to be seen at Skeppsbron in Stockholm and several of his works can be admired in the National Museum in Stockholm, another of Gustav's projects. There too can be seen many charming portraits by Alexander Roslin (1718–93). Two other painters who catch the spirit of the period are Pehr Hilleström (1733–1816), whose subjects included Bellman, and the landscape painter Elias Martin, famous for his views of Stockholm and its environs in the late eighteenth century.[2]

Gustav had often performed in amateur theatricals when crown prince. Decorum made it more difficult for him to do so as king, but he found an outlet by writing plays, notably his historical drama *Gustaf Wasa*, attending productions by others, and supporting other

---

[2] There is in the National Museum a fine painting by E. Martin of Alexander Pope's house in Twickenham.

authors. Bellman, the popular poet, musician, and entertainer, was given a sinecure; Johan Henrik Kellgren (1751–95) and Carl Gustaf Leopold (1756–1829) were welcome at court, as were many actors and musicians, including the composer Uttini.

Visitors to Sweden today can still see something of Gustav's charming world. He had the forbidding castle of Gripsholm, prison of Erik XIV and others, renovated and provided with a small court theatre. Drottningholm too was improved and the formal French park was laid out. Operas known in the Gustavian period are again being performed at the small, perfectly equipped theatre at Drottningholm.

Gustav IV Adolf came of age in 1796 when he took over the government from his uncle Duke Karl, who had acted as regent for four years. He is surely one of the most pathetic of the Swedish kings. He grew from a lonely inhibited child to an industrious, frugal formalistic king, religious, steadfast (or stubborn), possessing a strong sense of duty and of justice but little of his father's intellect or charm.

K. Hagberg,[3] writes that Gustav Adolf was an able enough leader in peacetime when there were norms to follow, but that when war started and traditional concepts were in the melting-pot, he could not cope. It was Gustav Adolf's foreign policy that brought about his downfall. His aim at first was to preserve Swedish neutrality and in 1800 he joined Denmark, Russia, and Prussia in an alliance of armed neutrality as a protection against cavalier treatment by British vessels of neutral shipping. Gradually his policy shifted its emphasis and when war broke out between Britain and France in 1803, he joined a coalition with Britain, Russia, and Austria against Napoleon. It was a reasonable enough policy since Britain was both a leading naval power and Sweden's best customer for iron, but it was not popular with many Swedes, who followed Napoleon's exploits with admiration; it also had a more fantastic cause, for Gustav Adolf had become convinced that Napoleon was the beast in the Apocalypse and that he had been sent to do battle with him. The first time he actually engaged Napoleon's forces was in Pomerania, where his troops capitulated and were lucky to be allowed to withdraw in good order.

Even so, Gustav Adolf's policy made sense until 1807 when at Tilsit Napoleon and Tsar Alexander I formed an alliance against Britain. Denmark had hoped to remain neutral, but Britain seized the Danish fleet to prevent it from falling into French hands. In their indignation at this action the Danes joined France and Russia. Thus they too were aligned against Sweden; but Gustav Adolf

[3] K. Hagberg, *Av Vasarnas ätt* (Stockholm, 1929), p. 247.

remained steadfastly opposed to Napoleon and his allies. Danish troops, augmented by a French contingent under Marshal Berna-dotte, prepared to invade Skåne while the Norwegian army stood by, ready to move over the border. Swedes seemed so convinced of Napoleon's invincibility that their defence forces were dispirited. Fortunately the British fleet prevented the invasion from ever taking place.

Meanwhile Alexander tried to force Gustav to join the Continental Blockade and when he refused in 1808 Russian troops moved into Finland. They were not unduly efficient or numerous, but the Swedes were defeatist from the outset and put up little resistance. Their humiliation culminated in the surrender of Sveaborg, the Gibraltar of the North, almost without a struggle. By the end of 1808 all Swedish troops had evacuated from Finland and Sweden herself was threatened.

In this crisis Gustav Adolf proved incapable of getting to grips with the situation and opposition leaders among the Swedish nobles seized the initiative. In 1809 Lt-Col. Georg Adlersparre, who was with the western army in Värmland, the province bordering on Norway, marched on Stockholm. Gustav Adolf prepared to join his forces in Skåne, convinced that they would remain loyal to him. General Carl Johan Adlercreutz, who was in Stockholm, feared a civil war at this juncture and, acting quickly, he arrested the king. The accounts of the terrified Gustav Adolf, always mindful of his father's assassination, being dragged screeching and vomiting down the palace stairs make ugly reading. The Estates were assembled and Gustav IV Adolf was formally deposed.[4] His uncle Duke Karl became King Karl XIII, but not until he had accepted a new constitution, drawn up within a month, limiting the king's powers and giving more authority to the *Riksdag*.

In this Constitution of 1809 the balance of power was again to be maintained between king and *Riksdag*. The king was given executive powers, but he was to consult the *Riksdag*. Both the *Riksdag* and the king had the power to legislate, while taxation was in the hands of the *Riksdag* alone. Suggestions that the four Estates should be replaced by a more democratic *Riksdag* consisting of only one chamber were rejected. Å. Holmberg maintains that

> it was in the interests of those civil and military officials, over-whelmingly aristocrats, who had carried out the revolution and took the lead in Sweden's fortunes to have a reform that ulti-mately favoured the bureaucracy and privileged Estate. The

---

[4] He went into exile and after travelling in Europe finally settled in Switzerland as the poor obscure Colonel Gustafsson and he died in St Gallen in 1837.

1809 revolution was the final phase in the old struggle between the power of the king and the nobles.[5]

During the *coup* Sweden's enemies were poised all round her borders, and indeed Russian troops were by this time within her borders. Since the new king was both childless and senile, the election of an heir was important, and the choice was affected by differing views on Sweden's future foreign policy and the best means of ending the war. One faction, led by Adlersparre, believed that Sweden could persuade the Norwegians to reject Denmark and align themselves with Sweden, and to this end they succeeded in pushing through the election of Prince Kristian August of Augustenborg, a member of a branch of the Danish royal family and Danish commander-in-chief in Norway. He accepted, but only on condition that peace was arranged between Denmark and Sweden, and the *status quo* restored.

Meanwhile, with Gustav Adolf gone, Sweden was able to begin friendly overtures with Napoleon and sought his assistance in helping to restore Finland to Sweden. Napoleon ironically referred them to the generosity of Tsar Alexander. This was far from boundless and the Swedes had in 1809 to accept the Peace of Fredrikshamn which deprived them of all of Finland, the Åland Islands, and a section of Västerbotten as far west as the Torne and Muonio rivers—in all, more than one-third of the territory which had been considered Swedish for hundreds of years was now in Russian hands.

The Founding of the Bernadotte Dynasty

The new crown prince, Kristian August, reached Sweden early in 1810 and then died suddenly of a heart attack while watching military manoeuvres in May the same year. Adlersparre's faction was not to be deterred. Kristian August had a brother and they would have him as crown prince instead; the Council gave its consent, and sent a delegation to Napoleon to secure his approval.

The French Revolution had influenced Swedish thinking and there was an implicit desire among many people for a strong radical man of action to run the country. Lt Carl Otto Mörner, one of the delegates sent to Napoleon in Paris by the Council, obviously adhered to this view, for when in Paris he first visited Jean-Baptiste Bernadotte (the son of a French lawyer, who had advanced rapidly from the ranks of the revolutionary army serving under Napoleon and received from him the Marshal's baton) and asked him if he would allow his name to go forward as crown prince of Sweden. When Bernadotte agreed, Mörner, having made sure that Napoleon

<hr>

[5] Å. Holmberg, *Sverige efter 1809* (Stockholm, 1969), p. 6.

approved of his Marshal, then returned to Stockholm to urge his candidacy. Bernadotte's record suggested a first-rate soldier, a radical, and a friend of Napoleon–here surely, it was reasoned, was the man to restore Swedish confidence and regain Finland. The *Riksdag* adopted him unanimously.

From his arrival in Stockholm in October 1810 with his wife Desirée, Bernadotte, who assumed the name Karl Johan, was virtually in charge, for Karl XIII was too old to rule and moreover had a touching faith in his adopted son. Karl Johan at first simply kept channels open without committing Sweden to any country or course of action. Napoleon insisted on Sweden joining the Continental Blockade and declaring war on Britain, and Karl Johan accepted this; but hostilities were avoided and smuggling increased. He established friendly but unprejudiced relations with Tsar Alexander, but also proposed to Napoleon a military alliance if France would help Sweden to regain Finland and to wrest Norway from Denmark.

The 1812 Policy

It was Napoleon who forced Karl Johan's hand in January 1811 by moving into Swedish Pomerania which he knew was being used as a centre for smuggling British goods into Germany. It was a blatant act of aggression and Karl Johan allied himself with Napoleon's enemies, and turned to Russia. There was a personal meeting in Åbo between him and Alexander in 1812 when an alliance between their countries was confirmed and it was agreed that with Russian support Swedish troops would move into Denmark and force Denmark to abandon Norway, after which Swedish troops would join Russia and engage Napoleon in north Germany. This, Karl Johan's so-called 1812 policy, marked a change in the traditional Swedish attitude. For every Swede Finland was emotionally part of Sweden and Russia the enemy. Bernadotte had none of this inbuilt Swedish emotion, but simply looked at the map, decided that Norway and Sweden formed a geographical entity and that it was logical to replace an eastern province with the western one. He was hardly to know that he was sparking off a conflict that was to last just under a century.

Karl Johan was forced to play a more active part than he wished in the campaign against Napoleon in Europe in 1813 and it was only after Napoleon's defeat at Leipzig that he could leave the main arena of war and move his troops into Denmark. With no allies to come to her aid, Denmark quickly capitulated and at the Peace of Kiel in 1814 ceded Norway to Sweden.

Karl Johan soon discovered that the matter wouldn't end there.

A strong feeling of nationalism was growing in Norway and the Norwegians refused to accept the terms of the Peace of Kiel. On 17 May 1814 (a date still celebrated fervently in Norway every year) at Eidsvold they declared Norwegian independence and accepted a new constitution, after which Prince Kristian Frederik, the Danish viceroy and cousin of Frederik VI of Denmark, was elected king of Norway. Karl Johan moved his troops into Norway and forced on the Norwegian people the Convention of Moss, by the terms of which the Eidsvold Constitution had to be modified so that the king of Sweden would also be king of Norway; foreign policy of the two countries would be decided in Stockholm; and the king would appoint both a governor to represent him in Norway and members of the Norwegian Council in the Norwegian capital. The Act of Union was formally accepted and in 1815 Karl XIII was crowned king of Norway. The Act of Union was not what most Swedes had hoped for, since it left Norway autonomous with her own parliament (the *Storting*) and with a wholly Norwegian civil service; the king commanded the armed forces but all the officers had to be Norwegian; there was no royal court in Norway and no legislative or other body was superior to the *Storting* in Norway. However, the Act of Union was at the time considered a victory for Karl Johan. Karl Johan soon destroyed most of the preconceived Swedish notions about him when he came to Sweden. It was soon evident that he was not such a close friend of Napoleon after all and although obviously a gifted military commander he did not intend to make—and certainly couldn't have made—Sweden a military power. It is another irony of Swedish history that this former marshal at the outset of his Swedish career concluded Sweden's last war and became the first Swedish monarch to avoid war throughout his entire reign. (Karl XIII died and his adopted son became Karl XIV Johan in 1818.) Nor did he attempt to regain Finland, but continued to stand by the implications of his 1812 policy, despite the lack of Norwegian co-operation in making the Union work.

The Eidsvold Constitution gave the king a veto, but if a motion were passed by three successive *Storting*, then it was carried despite the king's opposition. Thus the *Storting* in 1821 abolished in Norway the privileges of the aristocracy even though Karl Johan protested. The Norwegians caused him even more discomfort when they refused to sanction the payment of their share of the Danish-Norwegian debt incurred before the Peace of Kiel. Karl Johan had negotiated skilfully with Denmark to Norway's advantage, but then encountered the intransigence of the *Storting*.

A similar embarrassment occurred in 1821 when the Norwegians

arrested an English merchant for smuggling goods into the newly-
founded town of Bodø. He claimed compensation for wrongful arrest
and the British government backed up his claim. To prevent the
situation from growing out of all proportion Karl Johan as king of
Norway offered to meet the claim in part, which the merchant
accepted, but the Norwegians were incensed by the settlement.

By the 1830s the Norwegians were demanding greater independence of Sweden in matters concerning foreign trade. As a sea-
faring nation they found dependence on the Swedish flag and on
Stockholm in consular and diplomatic affairs both galling and in-
efficient. By 1839 a Union Committee was set up to examine a
series of political issues. It worked well at the outset and the Union
problems did not take up much of Karl Johan's last years, although
they caused his successors all the more trouble.

Conservatism and Liberalism

In the reactionary post-Napoleonic Europe Russia had assumed
the role of defender of the old order and supporter of legitimate
monarchs of Europe. It was perhaps this that persuaded Karl
Johan to draw closer to Russia after the revolutions in 1830 when
the Poles rose against Russia, the Belgians against Holland, and
crowned heads, even perhaps his own, seemed less secure than
immediately after the Congress of Vienna. Despite the Russophobia
of the majority of his people, Karl Johan maintained his own
foreign policy, and even the increasing opposition in Sweden could
not dispute his words, included in his address to the *Riksdag* in 1840,
that 'our geographical position decides our policy. All foreign
powers continue to give us proof of their confidence and friendly
relations'.

The notion that Karl Johan would be a radical ruler thus proved
to be unfounded and the reign of this former leader of the revolutionary army was characterized by an increasing struggle between
conservatism and liberalism, with Karl Johan firmly on the side of
conservatism. One of his first acts was to revive the press ordinance
of 1810 so that the government could impound periodicals, ostensibly to prevent the spread of seditious literature, but in fact to
prevent opposition to the king's views. (One of Karl Johan's better-
known exclamations was 'Opposition, c'est conspiration'.)

There was very little opposition to worry about in the first years
of his reign. The king was the effective ruler; he had a Council of
nine including Ministers of Foreign Affairs and Justice, who were
served by state secretaries. Although the *Riksdag* could hold these
councillors responsible, it was the king who actually appointed
and dismissed them and they thought of themselves not so much as

politicians as civil servants administering the king's decisions, which were usually directed towards maintaining the *status quo*.

This conservative spirit pervaded much of the intellectual life of the country. Writers of the Gustavian era had been associated with France and the Enlightenment, but by the time of Karl Johan's accession to the throne the influence was predominantly German. Poets of genius emerged in this period: Per Daniel Amadeus Atterbom (1790–1855), Erik Johan Stagnelius (1793–1823), Esaias Tegnér (1782–1846), Erik Gustav Geijer (1783–1847), Johan Olaf Wallin (1779–1839), all influenced to some extent by the Romantic movement. For most of them the 'real' material world we inhabit was merely a shadow of an ideal perfect world of the spirit which they longed to reach. Such a longing was conducive to beautiful lyric verse but not to an interest in improving man's immediate mundane needs. Several of these writers expressed strong nationalistic sentiments, but again in the Romantic mode. They countered the bitter defeats, the loss of Finland, and Swedish humiliations with stirring reminders that Swedes had after all inherited a great tradition. *Götiska Förbundet* (The Gothic Society) was formed in Stockholm in 1811 and its organ, *Iduna*, published poems (including Geijer's 'Vikingen' ('The Viking') and 'Odalbonden' ('The Yeoman Farmer') extolling the sterling qualities of the Swedes in the past. Tegnér published his *Fritiofs Saga*, a romanticized version of the exploits of the Viking Fritiof the Bold. Per Henrik Ling (1776–1839), also a member of the Gothic Society, evolved his system of gymnastics–Ling's modern contemporaries were to be as physically fit as his forbears.

The same spirit of conservatism was found in politics and was developing into a philosophy. Led by Hans Järta (1774–1847; a former revolutionary who played a large part in the drafting of the 1809 Constitution) and Geijer, the conservative element centred round the so-called 'historical school' which embraced the theory that every institution is an organism with its own inherent laws which regulate its development. With such a belief in historical continuity a case could be made for preserving, for example, the Estates system which had grown up organically to meet a need in society.

An opposition evolved, led by Johan Gabriel Richert and Carl Henrik Anckarsvärd, embracing more liberal views and believing in the freedom of the individual and his right to be represented. It was an irritant rather than an effective opposition until 1830 when, stimulated by the July revolutions of that year, L. J. Hierta brought out the first number of *Aftonbladet*, Sweden's first modern newspaper. Although himself an aristocrat, Hierta allied himself with the growing industrial bourgeoisie and his paper followed a liberal but not dogmatic line. The government realized how important *Aftonbladet* was for the liberal cause and frequently impounded it; but Hierta was well prepared. *Aftonbladet* was followed by *Nya Aftonbladet* (The New *Aftonbladet*) and when the twenty-first *Aftonbladet* appeared, the Chancellor knew it was time to throw in the sponge.

The struggle grew fiercer and the opposition learned how to harass and embarrass the government in the 1830s. When in 1832 Anders Lindeberg forgot himself sufficiently to criticize not only the government but the king personally, he was convicted of *lèse-majesté*, the punishment for which was death. Karl Johan commuted this to three years imprisonment, but Lindeberg knew his rights, would be a martyr, and insisted on the full sentence. To prevent further embarrassment an amnesty was granted to all political prisoners and it says much for Sweden that Lindeberg was the only one in the country at that time. A similar case in 1838 involved M. J. Crusenstolpe, a liberal journalist whose sentence of three years imprisonment led to rioting in Stockholm. The government was now on the defensive and suffered another blow in 1838 when Geijer, hitherto a bulwark of the 'historical school', made public the fact that under the influence of the workers' movements in England (a country he knew well) and the writings of Saint-Simon, he had become a liberal. He expresses poignantly his isolation after this 'apostasy' in a number of short poems dating from 1838.

The struggle came to a head in the 1840–41 *Riksdag* when liberals were determined to concentrate all their energies on the one central issue: a change in the system of government. They kept up pressure against the Council members by censuring and indicting them, and threatened to refuse to vote taxes to run the government if need be. The Council members lost their nerve and proffered their resignations, but Karl Johan steadfastly refused any new form of representation. However, honours were divided equally, since he did accept the resignation of the oldest members of the Council and a measure of reform in the Council itself. There would be ten members, seven of whom would be Heads of Departments, thus being directly in charge instead of working through state secretaries. They could acquire expert knowledge in their own field and so be better placed in dealing with the king. The changes were a far cry from the sweeping reforms that many liberals had wanted, but they increased the power of the *Riksdag* and drew some of the sting out of the political controversy.

It would give a false impression to think of the government and opposition as firm political parties or of the conservatives as wholly opposed to any change and the period a wholly stagnant one. The agricultural reforms of the eighteenth century were accelerated with a new ordinance in 1827; grain imports were insignificant by the 1820s and had ceased altogether by the mid-nineteenth century. There was a marked increase in the Swedish population at the time. At the end of the eighteenth century approximately 2·3 million people were living in Sweden proper; by 1835 the figure had reached the 3 million-mark and was approaching 4 million by the 1860s–a hundred per cent increase in little over half a century. Tegnér, in one of his famous remarks from the 1830s, said the increase had come about 'with the assistance of peace, vaccination, and potatoes'. Jonas Alströmer had begun cultivating potatoes on his estate, Nolhaga, on his return from England as early as 1724, but for decades even peasants starving to death were too suspicious of this novelty to plant it. By the 1830s, however, it had become accepted, not least (alas) because it was found to make a potent alcoholic drink when distilled. Vaccination against smallpox had become widespread by the 1820s.

Unfortunately the increase in population coincided with great difficulties for Swedish industry. New English methods of processing iron, using coke instead of charcoal, made Swedish iron difficult to sell, while European countries were also beginning to turn to other sources of supply for timber. In this period before emigration, agriculture had to absorb the increased population and the result was an increasing agricultural proletariat: cotters, farmhands, people without property or prospects.

Investigations into several social and industrial fields were instigated during the reign of Karl Johan, although in some cases the benefits were not realized until after his death. In 1826 a school commission, whose members included both Tegnér and Geijer, was set up. It recommended that every parish should have its elementary school, with parents responsible for seeing that their children attended, and that training colleges should be set up to guarantee adequate trained staff. These recommendations were incorporated in the Education Bill of 1842. Compulsory schooling thus came to Sweden more than thirty years before a corresponding law was passed in Great Britain.

A move was also initiated in the 1820s to remove restrictions on both import and export duties and on crafts and trade regulated by the guild system, but it was only in 1846 that real progress was made.

The government realized the necessity of improving communications and earmarked large sums to this end. Most spectacular was the building of the Göta Canal, completed in 1832 after twenty years, linking Gothenburg with Stockholm. It never fully realized its economic potential because it was so quickly superseded by the railways; but it was a remarkable feat and tourists today can enjoy a lazy three days traversing some beautiful stretches of the Swedish countryside.

Karl Johan died in 1844, over eighty years of age, and although his passing was tinged with national regret and gratitude to the man who had saved Sweden, it was also the signal for liberal reforms under his son, Oscar I.

Oscar had been only eleven when he was brought to Sweden, young enough to assume both the language and customs of Sweden. When crown prince, he often expressed very different views from those of his father and it was confidently expected that he would be a liberal monarch. Both his home and foreign policies certainly mark a change from the previous reign and a move away from Karl Johan's 1812 policy. Although not prepared to risk a break with Russia, Oscar's general inclination was towards a united Scandinavia allied with the West against possible attack from Russia. There was a growing feeling of kinship in Scandinavia at this time, especially in Scandinavian university liberal circles, which developed into a pan-Scandinavian movement aimed at drawing together people with a common heritage.

Oscar's first opportunity of demonstrating his Scandinavian sentiments without alienating Russia came in 1848 when risings encouraged by Prussia and the German Confederation broke out in Schleswig and Holstein against Frederik VII of Denmark. With the *Riksdag*'s approval Oscar sent Swedish troops to Denmark and informed Prussia of his intentions. Russia added her support, Prussia gave way, evacuated the occupied areas of Jutland, and in Malmö in 1848 agreed to an armistice. About 4,000 Swedish troops occupied northern Schleswig until 1850, when a definitive treaty was signed between Denmark and Prussia.

The outbreak of the Crimean War enticed Oscar on to a more daring course. In 1853 Russia was at war with Turkey and by the following year France and Britain had joined in the war. By allying himself with the Western powers against Russia, Oscar could conceivably regain Finland and the Åland Islands. His concept was perhaps too ambitious, but in any case he overplayed his hand. Bypassing the official channels, he secretly contacted Napoleon III and the British government led by Palmerston, and signed the November Treaty, a defensive treaty guaranteeing British and French aid against Russian attack on any part of Oscar's realm. When Russia accepted the allies' peace terms in Paris early in 1856 and the Crimean War unexpectedly came to an end, Oscar's plans were stranded. His only gain was a ban on Russian fortifications on the Åland Islands, which was more than offset by strained relations between Russia and Sweden, his ministers' disapproval of his highhanded handling of the whole affair, and Danish suspicions of his real motives. When in 1857 Oscar offered Denmark a defence alliance, his offer was rejected because it did not include Holstein.

In that same year Oscar was seriously ill with a brain tumour and he died in 1859. His son Karl acted as regent and then succeeded him as Karl XV. He was a popular monarch of regal appearance, artistic, less formal than previous monarchs but also lacking in their authority. Not only Scandinavianism but the personal power of the monarchy itself suffered a fatal blow during his reign.

The Norwegians had been watching Oscar's tactics with apprehension, which was not diminished when the recommendations of the Union Committee set up in Karl XIV Johan's reign were turned down. At the outset of his reign Karl XV wanted to improve relations between his two countries and as a gesture of goodwill promised the Norwegians that he would abolish the office of Governor, his official representative in Norway. It had always been an unpopular office and the *Storting* quickly acted on Karl's promise. In December 1859 it decided to abolish the Governorship. The *Riksdag*, however, insisted that it must have a say in the matter and the king's ministers threatened to resign if he approved the *Storting*'s decision. Karl had to give way and in April 1860 had to break his promise to the Norwegians and veto the *Storting*.

When the Dano-Prussian War broke out in 1864, Scandinavianism was put to a crucial practical test. Karl was prepared to help Denmark defend the line of the Eider, the river dividing Schleswig and Holstein, but his ministers would not agree unless France and Britain also came in. This they refused to do and once more Karl's impotence was revealed. German troops quickly invaded and although some Swedish volunteers went to Denmark, no official aid was forthcoming. Nineteenth-century pan-Scandinavianism ended in bitterness and recriminations. Ibsen, the Norwegian dramatist, was furious at what he considered his country's betrayal of Denmark and in his play *Brand*, written in 1866, he poured scorn over Norwegian hypocrisy and cowardice.

In internal affairs the reigns of Oscar I and Karl XV mark the breakthrough of liberalism in Sweden. The literature of the period clearly reflects the change as realistic descriptions of life in different sections of the community supersede romantic, often transcendental, lyric verse. C. J. L. Almqvist (1793–1866), a prolific writer, part visionary, part social commentator, and often *enfant terrible*, awakened his readers to many of the social problems of the day: poverty, religion, the institution of marriage, women's dependent position in society, etc. Fredrika Bremer (1801–65), in such novels as *Familjen H——* (The H—— Family; 1830–31) and *Grannarne* (The Neighbours; 1837), describes everyday life in middle-class homes and also focuses attention on the plight of the unemancipated woman wholly dependent on male guardians, and with no outlet for her intellectual energies. A more aristocratic milieu, in Stockholm and in the country, is depicted in the novels of Sophie Knorring (1797–1848), while Emilie Flygare-Carlén (1807–92) captures the much more rugged life on the west coast. August Blanche (1811–68) in, for example, his *Hyrkuskens berättelser* (Tales of a Livery Man; 1863) depicts a variety of Stockholm characters from all walks of life. The works of these novelists, together with the liberal press that became important under the guidance of men like L. J. Hierta and Magnus Jakob Crusenstolpe, served to make the middle classes more aware of themselves and of the society in which they lived.

When Oscar I became king in 1844, he appointed ministers much more liberal than those who had served under his father, and a series of social and commercial reforms date from this time. The liberals supported Jeremy Bentham's view that the state should afford the greatest happiness to as many of its members as possible and they set about achieving this aim in a practical way. In 1847 a Poor Law was passed obliging every parish to take care of its poor, sick, and unemployed. Women were allowed their equal share of an inheritance from 1845 and were in 1858 declared legally of age at twenty-five. The penal code was reformed, flogging was abolished, the death penalty, although retained, was rarely enforced. The real mark of progress in criminology was that Richert won over many to his belief that punishment should be corrective as well as punitive. Prisons were improved and prisoners were given some form of training. All these improvements were consolidated in the Penal Code of 1864.

In 1860 Jews were given the same rights as other citizens to own property and in 1861 Swedes of a different persuasion from Lutheranism could hold public services.

A social evil which has never been wholly eradicated was drunkenness. Consumption of alcohol in the 1830s was alarmingly high and having grave effects on the population. Peter Wieselgren, a clergyman, saw some of the effects at first hand. He was preaching at Östraby one Sunday in 1833 when

> during the sermon two women began to fight in church, drowning the voice of the preacher. The more intoxicated of the two had to be led out, but when she was standing immediately in front of the pulpit, she raised a clenched fist at the preacher and

screamed, 'listen parson, don't stand there chastising the Väster-stad men 'cos they're wiser and better than you even if you stood for three hours preaching. We don't understand much of what you say and don't want to either!' When Wieselgren descended from the pulpit a drunken man on one of the benches below began to be sick, at which point his neighbour hurried to hold his hat in front of the man's mouth.[6]

Wieselgren founded the Swedish Temperance Society, the 1853–54 *Riksdag* imposed a heavy tax on distilleries, and in 1860 the distilling of spirits at home was forbidden. Consumption fell, but drunkenness remained a problem.

The liberals in Sweden, influenced by Adam Smith, wanted freedom in the world of trade and industry. In 1846 restrictions imposed by the guild system were removed and import and export duties were relaxed. The great step forward was taken in the *Riksdag* of 1853–54 when the state decided to build certain main-line railways, leaving the laying of branch lines to the private sector, and raising a loan abroad for the purpose. The easing of restrictions and the great improvement in communications paved the way for the vast industrial expansion that was about to begin.

The Reform of the Riksdag

The great political issue of the time, however, was the reform of the *Riksdag*, and here Oscar proved anything but radical. The February Revolutions in Europe in 1848 had had only slight repercussions in Sweden with some stone-throwing and window-breaking and minor civil disorders, but they alarmed the king who became increasingly conservative in his views. A proposal was put before the four Estates in 1850–51 for the abolition of the Estates system and the adoption of a bicameral form of *Riksdag*, but it was hedged in by too many restrictions and won little approval, and there the matter rested for some time. Under Karl XV, however, who was a more pliable man than his father, liberals went into action again determined to force through a new reform bill.

Karl had appointed extremely able, forceful ministers, the most able of all being Louis De Geer (1818–96), who was Minister of Justice and who became Sweden's first Prime Minister in the modern sense of the word. He drafted a bill proposing an Upper and a Lower House, the former to be elected indirectly by local councils, the latter directly by a general election. If the king would not help its passage through the *Riksdag*, then De Geer was prepared to resign. Karl complied and in 1865 the proposal was laid before the *Riksdag*.

---

[6] S. Wieselgren, *Peter Wieselgren. En lefnadsteckning 1900.*

The tension grew in December 1865 as it transpired that the Burghers and Peasants had accepted the proposal, the Clergy were prepared to follow the lead of the Nobles, and that all therefore depended on the great four-day debate in the *Riddarhus*, the House of the Nobles. Louis De Geer's own memoirs capture some of the excitement of those four days when many brilliant speeches were made and the final voting cut across family relationships.

> Count Liljencrantz was one of the leaders for the opposition but his son Baron Johan L. Liljencrantz made a talented speech for the proposal. The Cederström brothers, Karl and Rudolf, spoke immediately after each other and the former supported the motion as warmly as the latter rejected it eloquently, [etc.]

The voting was 361 for the proposal and 294 against; the Clergy then accepted it too and in June 1866 the four Estates officially voted themselves out of existence. It was a victory for parliamentary rule and at least a step in the direction of fair political representation.

Chapter 4

1866–1914
The Industrial State Emerges

THE PERIOD FROM the middle of the nineteenth century until the outbreak of World War I saw the 'great transformation',[1] the time when Sweden was transformed from a backward agricultural country to a modernized industrial state and the economic foundations were laid that made the Welfare State possible. Most of the changes were triggered off by international conditions outside Swedish control and depended basically on the natural resources that Sweden suddenly discovered were a blessing (and on a series of coincidences). It must be added, however, that the way these conditions were exploited demonstrates the Swedes' great technical inventiveness and industriousness.

There had been little demand for Swedish timber until the middle of the nineteenth century. Great Britain had looked to Norway and Canada, even protecting the latter with tariffs. In the 1840s, however, when these tariffs were removed, there was an increased demand for timber which Norway could not meet. Steam-driven sawmills were being introduced into Sweden just when her timber was being offered an opening. Sawmills were located at the mouths of rivers instead of on sites suitable for water-wheels, rivers were cleared for floatage, and vast areas of forest land in central and northern Sweden were bought up by entrepreneurs. Many a Norrland small farmer was duped, accepting a mere pittance for acres of virgin forest land which was then ruthlessly exploited. There were two booms, in the 1850s and the 1870s; companies were formed, capital borrowed, workers rushed to where employment was offered, and Norrland, the neglected province, became a speculator's paradise. There was a fourfold increase in the output of sawn timber between the years 1856 and 1896, and the timber industry from 1870 to the end of the century accounted for 40 to 50 per cent of total Swedish exports.

By the turn of the century the ruthless exploitation had exhausted the supply of virgin forests, but the Goddess of Fortune had obviously

[1] So called by E. Heckscher, op. cit., pp. 209 ff.

decided to smile on Sweden, for just at this time, when a shortage of timber threatened, the pulp industry opened up on a large scale. Until the middle of the nineteenth century, paper had been made with expensive linen rags, but the rise in literacy and in the production of newspapers and books on both sides of the Atlantic created a demand that this method of production could not meet. Chemical wood pulp had been invented, but the earliest method resulted in a poor-quality paper. Significant progress was made in the 1870s, however, when Carl Daniel Ekman evolved a method of dissolving lignum from wood by the use of sulphides and leaving pure cellulose, from which good-quality paper could be made. Alvar Müntzing meanwhile invented the 'sulphate' method of making brown Kraft paper. The first chemical pulp factory in the world was set up at Bergvik in northern Sweden in 1872, but it was in the 1890s that the industry developed on a large scale. It was not spectacular like the timber industry, it needed no pioneers to open up new territory, it gave off offensive smells, and consequently it didn't catch the imagination of the public and the novelist as the timber industry had done. What is spectacular, however, is the rise in pulp production: a tenfold increase is recorded between 1894 and 1914. It became Sweden's largest single export, and by 1914 Sweden had become the leading pulp exporter in the world. Its development dovetailed with that of the timber industry, for it absorbed workers in Norrland threatened by the exhaustion of the timber supply there and it could use spruce and even wood waste not suitable for the sawmills.

The iron industry recovered from the difficult period early in the nineteenth century and began to use the new techniques being evolved. The Lancashire process had already been introduced into Sweden in the 1830s. Then Sir Henry Bessemer carried out his early experiments in Sweden, assisted by the Swede G. F. Göransson, who later founded the Sandviken Ironworks where the Bessemer process was introduced in 1858. This process used little fuel and produced steel in quantity at the required quality. Close on its heels came the Thomas Gilchrist method, which used more fuel but had the great advantage in Sweden of utilizing iron-ore of high phosphoric content, thus opening up the mining of ore around Kiruna beyond the Arctic Circle and Grängesberg in the Bergslagen area. The new operations were on too large a scale for the traditional iron-masters and gradually the small iron foundries ('bruk') amalgamated or closed down. The Domnarvet Ironworks, founded in the 1870s, for instance, replaced some nineteen *bruk*, spread over the whole province of Dalarna. Other large ironworks established included Uddeholm and Fagersta.

European demand for steel was so great and the price it commanded so high that it proved financially worthwhile for iron-works in Central Europe to import iron-ore from central and northern Sweden. Ore was first exported from Grängesberg in 1887, from Gällivare in 1892, and from Kiruna in 1902. Thus a new Swedish export reached impressive proportions by the turn of the century. All this occurred at a time when railways were being built; which speeded up the transport of ore. This was particularly true of the line completed in 1902 from Kiruna to the Norwegian ice-free harbour at Narvik, which simplified the export of northern Swedish ore all the year round.

With a good supply of indigenous iron and steel and a much improved transport system Swedish engineering developed at a great pace and offered scope to the Swedish national gift for invent-ing machines. Railways themselves needed locomotives and thous-ands of miles of track. Farming methods were improving and from the 1870s onwards there was an increasing demand for farm imple-ments. Gustaf de Laval invented the mechanical cream-separator in 1878. (He was the Swede who also greatly improved Charles A. Parsons's steam turbine.) By the turn of the century standardized goods, such as the bicycle and the sewing machine, were coming on to the market. At this time too, many Swedish concerns which have since become international household names were set up. Sven Wingqvist invented the ball-bearing and in 1907 SKF (Svenska kullagerfabriken, i.e. Swedish Ball Bearing Company) was founded. F. W. Lindqvist's Primus cooker, G. Dalén's acetylene gas units, C. E. Johansson's precision instruments were all developed about this time.

By the 1890s electro-technology had become an important branch of the Swedish engineering industry. The telecommunications firm L. M. Ericsson started making telephones in 1876 and by 1883 a public service company, Stockholms Allmänna Telefon AB, was set up to make and operate telephone lines. Also in 1883 Elektriska AB, the firm subsequently called ASEA, began making electrical machinery at Arboga. It was then moved to Västerås where it still remains today: Sweden's electrical centre and a firm of international repute.

All branches of the economy seemed to be affected by change. Farmers had begun to invest in better equipment and machines, to use fertilizers, to import good stock for breeding purposes, and agri-cultural yield rose out of all proportion to the number of people employed on the land.

There was a great move of population in this period. In 1870 more than 70 per cent of the population still earned their living from agriculture and its subsidiaries, but by the turn of the century this figure had fallen to 50 per cent. Conversely, the urban population in 1870 was less than 13 per cent of Sweden's total, but by 1910 was over 25 per cent. All this altered the pattern of life and needs of the public. Farmers got better returns for their products from the larger urban population and devoted more time to agriculture and less to the traditional handicrafts–spinning, weaving, carpentry, etc. Factories sprang up to produce consumer goods on a large scale: textiles, cotton, ready-made clothing and shoes; then beer, spirits, tobacco, sugar, and even bread and confectionery. The process started in the 1870s, gathered momentum in the 1890s, and then expanded rapidly until World War I.

In other fields too, Swedish inventive genius revealed itself. Gustav Pasch invented the safety match in 1844 and laid the foundation of an industry based on Jönköping. That strange genius Alfred Nobel (1833–96) patented his invention, dynamite, in 1867, a product that played a great part in blasting paths through mountains in Sweden and elsewhere so that roads and railway tracks could be laid. He also improved firearms and in 1894 bought the Swedish firm of Bofors-Gullspång where he produced munitions. He became a multi-millionaire and in an effort to alleviate some of the destructive effects of his inventions he asked in his will that some 33 million *kronor* should be invested and the interest 'annually distributed in the form of prizes to those who during the preceding year shall have conferred the greatest benefit on mankind'. There were to be five prizes, in Physics, Chemistry, Physiology or Medicine, Literature, and in the Promotion of Peace. Nobel died in 1896, the first prizes were awarded in 1901, and apart from the war years have been awarded annually ever since.

A necessary adjunct to the growth of industrialization was an efficient and reliable banking system, and in the second half of the nineteenth century the important Swedish banks were formed: Stockholms Enskilda Bank, founded in 1856 by André Oscar Wallenberg, still one of the most powerful names in Sweden today; Skandinaviska Banken[2] in 1863; Stockholms Handelsbank (now Svenska Handelsbanken) in 1871. *Riksbank*, the National Bank, was given the exclusive right to issue paper money in 1877, at which time it ceased commercial business and assumed the role of a central clearing bank. The extent of the development of the banking world is shown in K. Samuelsson's figures:

In 1860 there had existed 12 banks housed in 27 offices. By 1880 the number had risen to 44 banks with 205 offices and in 1913 to

[2] Stockholms Enskilda Bank and Skandinaviska Banken merged in 1971.

F

75 banks with 630 offices. Between 1877 and 1896 outstanding claims of commercial banks rose from 450 to 900 million kronor averaging out an increase of 20 million kronor per year. Advances then rose at an annual rate of 100 million kronor up to 1913, when they began to approach the 3,000 million mark.

Large sums of capital were also accumulated in savings banks and, as the century neared its end, in insurance companies. At the close of 1913 there were 440 savings banks with total deposits of 953 million kronor, mostly invested in building credits and bonds.[3]

Emigration

With the aid of statistics and production charts it is easy to give too glowing a picture of this period. The general trend upwards is unmistakable, but many an individual concern overstretched itself, went bankrupt, and left a trail of suicides in its wake. Nor was there any attempt at an even distribution of the newly accumulated wealth and, paradoxical though it may seem, this period of expansion coincides with large-scale emigration, mostly to the United States. A stream of Swedish emigrants to North America started in the 1840s and by the 1850s there were some 15,000 Swedes in the United States, many of them in Minnesota. The landscape there, with its forests and lakes, reminded these Swedes of home and it became the largest centre for Swedish immigrants. As a result of the run of disastrous harvests in Sweden from 1867 to 1869 some 80,000 Swedes went to America between 1868 and 1870. The culminating point in emigration was in the 1880s. The Swedish population had continued to rise, the agricultural industry with its use of improved methods could not offer employment to new generations of landless farmhands, and the developing industries could not yet absorb them all. When cheap cereals from Russia and America flooded the markets, the position of the agricultural proletariat became desperate and emigration reached record figures. There were regular sailings across the Atlantic and German and British shipping firms worked through advertisements and agents in Sweden. A shipping firm in Liverpool, for instance, had a general agent in Gothenburg who in turn had some two hundred agents spread over Sweden at this period. It is estimated that 325,000 Swedes went to the United States in the 1880s.

In the 1890s the economic situation in Sweden was favourable and emigration slackened off, although the number involved was still substantial. The Swedes concerned were mostly impecunious agricultural workers and kept to their trade in the New World, but

[3] K. Samuelsson, *From Great Power to Welfare State* (London, 1968), p. 198.

towards the turn of the century increasing numbers went to the large
cities. In 1900 Chicago, for instance, had some 49,000 Swedish
inhabitants. The Swedish population in the United States reached
its peak in 1910 when there were some 665,000 Swedish immigrants
and 700,000 second-generation Swedes there. Since the population
in Sweden was about 5½ million at the time, one Swede in five was
thus on the other side of the Atlantic. In the holiday season one can
hear in Sweden today American visitors who still speak Swedish or
in many cases a singular blend of nasal American and a southern
Swedish dialect.

Gradually the Swedish authorities became alarmed at the proportions of this strange phenomenon and began to offer counter-
attractions, setting up a committee in 1907 to examine the causes
of emigration and introducing such measures as arranging home
ownership. Nowadays emigration is not viewed as having been a disadvantage. At worst it acted as a safety valve, helping Sweden with
her problem of poverty and unemployment; and one of the more
tangible results was that some 200,000 Swedish Americans returned
to their homeland, often with capital and new technical expertise
which benefited Sweden. The Swedish novelist Vilhelm Moberg
has given a moving fictionalized account of the hardships endured
by Swedish pioneers both before and after they sailed for America
in his tetralogy, *Utvandrarna* (The Emigrants; 1951), *Invandrarna*
(translation title Unto a Good Land; 1954), *Nybyggarna* (The Settlers; 1956), and *Sista brevet till Sverige* (The Last Letter to Sweden;
1959). The work has been filmed and it has already become an
accepted part of Swedish social history.

The Bicameral Riksdag

Compared with changes on the economic front, the Swedish
political scene after the 1866 Reform Bill seems strangely stagnant.
In order to get the bill accepted at all De Geer had had to include
a great many safeguards, and the first bicameral *Riksdag* which
assembled for the first time in January 1867 was hardly what the
reformers had hoped for. Only some 6,000 people in the whole
country were eligible for the Upper House and of the 125 members
elected over half were aristocrats; about half the members were high-
ranking civil servants or officers, and well over half owned estates.
They were, moreover, elected for a nine-year period and returned
successively, only a small proportion of the chamber being elected
annually, so no violent changes could be envisaged. The Lower
House was dominated by well-to-do farmers who held about three-
quarters of the 190 seats, formed themselves into the Farmers'
Party (*Lantmannapartiet*), and could outvote representatives of the

rising industrialists and the civil servants. They were not interested in the altruistic reforms urged by the old liberals in the four-Estates *Riksdag*, but frankly aimed at improving the farmers' lot. They wanted the abolition of land tax and of the old defence system which they considered a burden specifically on farmers (it was the old *indelning* system introduced by Karl XI) and the avoidance of any heavy government expenditure.

A New Liberal Party (*Nyliberalerna*) did emerge in 1868, led by Sven Adolf Hedin, advocating an enlargement of the franchise and an increase in the *Riksdag*'s influence on the government, and it was supported by the liberal press that had helped bring about the Reform Bill; but it effected very little at this stage. The electorate refused to be roused and if those with the franchise registered their votes at all (and polls were singularly low for the first two decades of the bicameral system), they tended to do so on personal and local rather than political issues.

This remained true in the 1870s when the question of defence was the dominant issue. Sweden had enjoyed many years of peace and had allowed her defences to run down. Her fleet had only wooden vessels and her soldiers had only thirty days' training. The Dano-Prussian, Austro-Prussian, and Franco-Prussian Wars were a reminder of potential danger, and if the occasion should arise, it was obvious that Swedish forces would be no match at all for the well-trained Prussian army, equipped with the latest weapons. The government, led by De Geer until 1870, put forward a proposal for the reorganization of Sweden's defence system; but the Farmers' Party rejected it, reasoning that it was unnecessary and would inevitably mean an increase in taxes. De Geer resigned and successive ministries led by Axel Gustaf Adlercreutz in 1870, Edvard Carleson in 1874, De Geer again in 1875, Count Arvid Posse in 1880, juggled with compromises linking defence with the farmers' desire for the abolition of land taxes in stick-and-carrot schemes. A settlement was finally reached in 1885 under Oscar Robert Themptander: military service was to be increased to forty-two days; the government was to take over 30 per cent of the cost involved; and land tax was to be reduced by 30 per cent. External events helped persuade the *Riksdag* to accept later measures; with Russia's threat to Finland in 1895, increased tension in relations with Norway, and the outbreak of the Boer War playing their part in the final abolition in 1901 of the old *indelning* system and its replacement by a general conscription with an eight-month training period. The land tax was phased out completely. What caused the political pulse to quicken was not defence or land tax, but the free trade versus protectionism issue which had a direct bearing on almost everyone in the country. Free trade had been an article of faith for the liberals, but by the 1880s it met with increasing opposition. A cheap plentiful supply of cereals was coming on to the Swedish market from America and Russia and was forcing down the price of home-produced grain. Swedish industrialists were also beginning to smart under the competition from highly developed industrial countries such as Britain. Opinion cut right across party allegiances, some farmers being joined by industrialists and adopting the slogan 'Sweden for the Swedes'; others, including dairy farmers and town-dwellers, favouring the retention of a free-trade system and taking up the cry 'No starvation tariffs'. Exercising his royal prerogative for the first time, Oscar II dissolved the Lower House and called a special election in 1887. Prime Minister Themptander, who favoured free trade, won a majority and by way of confirmation the ordinary elections held in the autumn of that same year produced approximately the same results. It was not allowed to be as simple as that, however, for one of the candidates on the Stockholm voting list had not paid his taxes, which according to the law at that time meant that not only his but the other twenty-one names on the same list were invalid. This gave the majority to the protectionists and Themptander resigned. The immediate outcome of the issue was a split in the Farmers' Party (which divided into the Old Farmers' Party, a free-trade party led by Carl Ifvarsson, and the New Farmers' Party which was protectionist) and the imposition of moderate tariffs on grain and protective tariffs to help industries producing goods for the home market. The longer-term results were more vital, however. Public interest had been roused in politics and organizations had been set up to inform the electorate. This interest remained and, as we shall see presently, was channelled into (among other things) a campaign for enlarging the franchise and improving representation in the *Riksdag*.

Popular Movements. The Founding of the Social Democratic Party

One of the remarkable features of nineteenth-century Swedish social history is the forming of idealistic movements, associations, and societies which brought about changes in society. The most important towards the end of the century were instrumental in improving conditions for the working classes.

Industrialization had come relatively late to Sweden and many of the extremes of poverty and deprivation experienced in some European countries had been avoided; but the working conditions of the new proletariat were often both wretched and dangerous, with a high accident-rate. Living conditions were often deplorable. Large numbers of people had moved into towns ill equipped to receive them; there was a shortage of adequate accommodation, serious overcrowding, and poor hygiene. Few towns in the nineteenth century could boast of a satisfactory water and drainage system, infectious diseases were rife, tuberculosis a dreaded word. By the time these serious problems arose in Sweden, however, they had long been discussed in leading industrial countries and Swedish workers in some respects benefited from earlier mistakes. Swedish employers had themselves observed the English situation and many of them were prepared to accept measures already introduced there. It was on their initiative that a law restricting child labour was introduced as early as the 1850s. In the 1880s working conditions and occupational hazards were investigated, and in 1889 certain minimum safety requirements were stipulated by law and factory inspectors were appointed to guarantee their enforcement.

And happily the new Swedish proletariat had a comparatively short period to wait before the rise of international socialism which helped to improve their conditions. Ingvar Andersson[4] mentions that De Geer was taking the waters in Karlsbad in 1874 and there saw Karl Marx. De Geer records that 'they glared at one another between glasses without getting acquainted'. Before many years Swedish Prime Ministers could no longer ignore Marx and his doctrine.

With many workers gathered in one spot in factories or large sawmills, often owned by a number of faceless shareholders, Swedish industrial workers had the opportunity to form associations which the isolated agricultural workers, operating under a personal, if paternalistic, system, had lacked. A number of trade unions were formed in the 1860s and 1870s, aimed primarily at protecting the financial interests of their members (with their own insurance schemes, sickness benefits, etc.) rather than at changing the structure of society. The situation became more pointed after the Sundsvall strike in 1879. It was no coincidence that the first major labour dispute in Sweden broke out in Norrland where the timber industry had grown so rapidly, where both men and forests had been exploited and the guiding line had been simply quick profits. Five thousand workers went on strike, but were dealt with summarily and ruthlessly by troops. In strikes elsewhere many were driven from their homes and replaced by strike-breakers from other districts. It became obvious to the unions that they needed more than insurance schemes to protect their members.

At about this time, in 1881, August Palm, a tailor who had lived

4 I. Andersson, *A History of Sweden* (London, 1965), p. 368.

in Denmark and there been in contact with Marxists, came to Malmö and began to agitate for trade unions affiliated to the Social Democratic movement. His campaign gained little ground at first, and although trade unions were being formed (by 1885 there were over one hundred of them), they were not inclined to identify their organizations with Palm and socialism; but gradually the situation changed. By a narrow majority a Scandinavian trade union congress in Gothenburg declared that private systems run by the trade unions prevented 'the spread of happiness and contentment' in society. These private schemes were in other words obstructing the mounting of a more effective system and were to be superseded by an integrated, potentially much stronger, national trade union organization.

Meanwhile Palm had set up his political headquarters in Stockholm and in 1885 founded a socialist paper, *Social-Demokraten*, with Axel Danielsson as co-editor. The next year they were joined by Hjalmar Branting (1860–1925), only twenty-six at the time but destined to become the Grand Old Man of Social Democracy in Sweden, the first Social Democrat to sit in the *Riksdag*, the first Social Democrat to become a member of the Cabinet, and eventually the first Socialist Prime Minister. The son of a professor, and a graduate of Uppsala University, Branting knew many of the dominant people in Swedish political life at the time. From 1883 he had been on the staff of *Tiden*, a democratic daily paper whose contributors included Adolf Hedin and August Strindberg, with whom Branting became well acquainted. His intellect and personality were of a different calibre from Palm's, who was soon pushed into the background. This had important consequences for the development of Social Democracy in Sweden generally, for Branting was a very moderate Marxist, a revisionist who believed admittedly in the class struggle but who was undogmatic, and preferred to avoid excesses and to co-operate with bourgeois democracy in order to further the aims of the working classes. It is typical of the man that although he was an atheist himself, he opposed Viktor Lennstrand's attempt to make the struggle against Christianity one of the points in the Social Democrats' programme. He also fought those who advocated the use of extensive extra-parliamentary means to bring about reform. Thus his superseding Palm as the leading figure in the movement meant that the moderates, ready to work side by side with liberalism, had taken over from the radical advocates of class warfare.

In April 1889 trade union representatives met in Stockholm and formed the Social Democratic Labour Party, but of some two hundred and fifty trade unions in the country only about fifty joined the

Labour Party at this stage. When in 1898 *Landsorganisationen* (Confederation of Trade Unions) was formed, however, it was decided that within a period of three years all unions within the confederation would be affiliated to the Social Democratic Party. The party had thus become a force to be reckoned with, but so few of its members had a vote that for some few years to come it was not able to effect much directly, but acted rather as the Liberals' junior partner.

A feature of the Swedish Labour movement was its emphasis on educating and informing its followers. Some of the first trade unions had evolved out of workers' study groups, while from 1880 onwards workers' institutes were founded in different parts of the country.

Outside the unions adults could broaden their education at one of the Folk High Schools, a movement started in Denmark by the Romantic theologian and educationalist N. F. S. Grundtvig. Unhampered by formal curricula and examinations, adults with a desire to improve their minds could attend short courses in the liberal arts at these residential schools.

Another of the many edifying movements of this period was the Temperance Movement. Despite Wieselgren's improvements, drunkenness had remained a problem, but in the 1870s a new wave of interest in temperance emanated from America, aiming this time not just at moderation but total abstinence. The founding of a Swedish lodge of the Order of Good Templars in 1879 was an important cultural advance, for the movement deployed large sums of money not just to deter the consumption of alcohol but also to stimulate interest in education and culture. The movement's influence was increased by its close links with the socialist movement.

Even more important were the various Free Church societies that figured so prominently in the latter part of the nineteenth century. George Scott had introduced Methodism into Stockholm in 1830 and was active until 1842 when pressure from the Lutheran State Church persuaded him to return to Scotland. His disciples carried on his work, however, and when the Conventicle Act was repealed in 1860, Swedish Methodism was officially recognized.

Scott's most important successor was Carl Olof Rosenius, who helped to bring about the National Evangelical Foundation, which dates from 1856 and forms part of the State Church. Rosenius had a big following in the province of Norrland. In 1878 the Swedish Mission Society was formed under the guidance of Peter Paul Waldenström, who drew a lot of his support from central Sweden and Småland. 1866 saw the founding of the Swedish Baptist

Free Church, based on the American Baptist movement and under the influence of American Swedes. It became a powerful movement, but lost many of its members to the Pentecostals who began holding their meetings in Stockholm in 1907 and under the present-day leadership of Lewi Pethrus have become one of the largest of the Free Church movements in Sweden.

In 1882 the Salvation Army was introduced into Sweden, a branch of the international organization centred in London with its emphasis on practical social work.

The vast majority of Swedes have remained Lutheran, for even those who joined a Free Church seldom left the Church of Sweden; but these Free Church movements showed clearly that the authority of the State Church, which had grown dogmatic and intolerant of innovation, was being eroded by the changes in society now gathering momentum.

Another movement intent on changing society was the movement for women's rights. Fredrika Bremer had gained a hearing for women's independence in her novel *Hertha* (1856), and her most important disciple was Sophie Adlersparre, a Swedish aristocrat who devoted her energies to improving educational openings for women. She also formed the Fredrika Bremer Society in 1864, 'an association of men and women active and interested in the elevation of women morally, intellectually, socially, and economically'.

The Co-operative movement was also launched in this period, at first on a modest scale to help protect the consumer. The first co-operative society was set up in 1850 at Örsundsbro; others quickly followed; by 1899 they were consolidated into the nationwide *Kooperativa Förbundet* (KF), which by 1908 had over 68,000 members.

All these popular movements helped to inform the public and arouse interest in various aspects of the community. The Swedish press, too, began to play an increasingly important part in politics and social affairs towards the end of the nineteenth century. On 23 December 1864 Rudolf Wall produced the first issue of *Dagens Nyheter* at the sensationally low price of 5 öre a copy. It became, and still is, the most important liberal newspaper in Sweden. *Dagens Nyheter* had a formidable rival in *Stockholms-Tidningen*, which first appeared on 2 December 1889 at 2 öre a copy, and aimed at capturing the lower orders of society looking for a cheap means of satisfying their newly-acquired literacy. In 1884 the conservative daily newspaper *Svenska Dagbladet* was founded, but it got off to a shaky start and was in danger of folding up altogether. However, by 1897 it was reorganized and under the leadership of the famous Swedish author Verner von Heidenstam emerged, as he himself expressed it, as a quality newspaper 'which would above all be an organ for the educated classes and for science and art'. It is still the leading moderate conservative paper on the Swedish market. Outside Stockholm other newspapers emerged, notably the Gothenburg daily *Göteborgs Handels- och Sjöfartstidning*, which under the leadership of S. A. Hedlund became a highly respected organ for the modern Liberals, a reputation it still enjoys; and the *Sydsvenska Dagbladet Snällposten*, based on Malmö. Its editor-in-chief, Carl Herslow, like S. A. Hedlund, was a member of the Lower House of the *Riksdag*, a moderate Liberal who wanted to inform rather than to indoctrinate.

Particularly significant at a time when the Social Democratic Party was still unrepresented in the *Riksdag* was the appearance of several socialist newspapers: *Social-Demokraten*, *Ny Tid*, and *Arbetet* were all founded in the 1880s and '90s. *Social-Demokraten*, which first appeared in 1885 and lasted until 1958 (by that time called *Morgon-Tidningen*), numbered among its editors such outstanding Social Democratic leaders as Hjalmar Branting, Per Albin Hansson, and Z. Höglund.

At this time of far-reaching social and economic changes, when the broad public was better informed than ever before, energies were turned towards the all-important question of reforming the franchise.

The years 1891–1905 form a transitional period in Swedish politics and, apart from a two-year break, the Prime Minister throughout that time was Erik Gustav Boström. He was a moderate Conservative (adhering to the majority *Riksdag* group that called itself *Högern* (i.e., the Right), as opposed to the *Vänster* (i.e., the Left), those wanting far-reaching reforms). Boström was a protectionist, and a believer in a sound defence force and a lasting union with Norway, prepared to accept a small measure of change, but convinced that extreme caution was essential. His ministry coincided with the final stages of the Union between Norway and Sweden, a period when Norwegian demands for complete independence had become so strident, not to say belligerent, that many Swedish Conservatives had become convinced of the necessity of a strong Swedish force, while many other Swedes were becoming increasingly persuaded that a dissolution of the Union was the only possible answer.

The Dissolution of the Union

Karl XIV Johan's hopes of an integrated Scandinavian peninsula had no doubt always been something of a castle in Spain, but by the 1880s it was obvious that a peaceful union on any terms was an impossibility, for by that time the two countries had developed very different social structures. Sweden still had a social hierarchy headed by the king and with many aristocrats occupying key positions in the community, while the Norwegians had evolved a more democratic system and were advancing more rapidly than the Swedes towards a real form of parliamentary government. If one adds to that their characteristic spirit of independence, it is hardly surprising that the Norwegians were anxious to terminate their association with Sweden. It is interesting to note that in Sweden the people who were fervently nationalistic held politically conservative views, whereas in Norway they were politically to the Left.

Trouble flared up in the 1880s over the king's right to veto the *Storting*. On the whole, the Norwegian Conservative government had accepted it, but the situation changed in 1883 when the party of the Left, *Venstre*, won the general election. In 1884 the *Storting* voted Prime Minister Christian August Selmer out of office, but Oscar II (who had succeeded his brother, Karl XV, in 1872) first refused his proffered resignation and then tried to form another Conservative government. Ultimately he had to give way and accept Johan Sverdrup as the leader of a *Venstre* government, but the situation remained uneasy.

Rumours were circulating that Oscar II was looking to Germany for military support should a solution to the Norwegian problem prove it necessary. Oscar had married a German princess, Sofia of Nassau, and had himself expressed his sympathy with Germany on a visit there in 1875. His Foreign Minister too, Oscar Björnstjerna, viewed Germany as Sweden's best ally. Oscar had in fact been given moral support by Bismarck in his stand against the Norwegian *Venstre* Party, but it went no further than that. The fact that the Norwegians believed the rumours, however, indicates their distrust of their monarch.

In 1892 the *Storting* decided to set up its own Norwegian consular service, a direct contravention of the Act of Union. Oscar and the Swedish Prime Minister, Boström, were willing to adopt a conciliatory attitude, but an increasingly voluble section of the *Riksdag* was becoming exasperated at what they termed a one-sided appeasement policy towards Norway and they urged the king to veto the *Storting* decision. By a coincidence Kaiser Wilhelm visited Stockholm that year and the more sabre-rattling of the Swedish Conservatives found comfort in this fact. The Norwegians were quiet for a while but were not to be intimidated. In the next skirmish, the *Storting* voted the erection of fortifications along their southern border with Sweden and the removal of the Swedish flag from the emblem of the Union.

A Norwegian–Swedish Committee proposed in 1902 that Norway should have her own consular service but on condition that the

Foreign Minister would control both the Norwegian and the Swedish consular services. Boström visited Norway in 1904 and put forward the committee's proposals, but they were rejected outright. King Oscar therefore declared negotiations at an end and there was general discontent on both sides of the border. Poor Boström was blamed both by the Norwegians and by the Liberal press in Sweden. Karl Staaff, the Liberal leader, demanded his resignation on the grounds that he stood in the way of an ultimate settlement. In April 1905 Boström withdrew and in his place was appointed Johan Ramstedt, a worthy civil servant, not a politician.

Meanwhile the *Storting* pushed ahead. In May 1905 it voted again to set up its own Norwegian consular service and when Oscar vetoed the decision, the entire Norwegian government immediately tendered its resignation. King Oscar refused to accept it on the grounds that he could not form another government in the circumstances. The *Storting* found this an indication that the king could no longer function as Norwegian monarch and declared the Union at an end forthwith.

The Swedes were wholly unprepared for this precipitous action and popular opinion in Sweden was outraged. Even those Swedish left-wing politicians who had hitherto sympathized with the Norwegians took exception to the way the *Storting* had humiliated the ageing King Oscar, who in all conscience had tried to be conciliatory towards Norway. It seemed obvious that there was no point in using force to keep the Union alive, but there was a reluctance to accept a dissolution solely on the *Storting*'s unilateral declaration. An extraordinary session of the *Riksdag* was called and a special committee under the Conservative leader Kristian Lundeberg was appointed. They listed Swedish conditions for a dissolution, which included an election or referendum in Norway to see if the people were behind the *Storting*, and if it should be proved that they were, then among other things they demanded the demolition of the border fortifications that the Norwegians had erected. Prime Minister Ramstedt thought that Lundeberg's committee were unduly harsh in their formulations. He resigned with his whole government and was succeeded by Lundeberg himself, who set up a coalition government. The situation is of special significance, for it was the first time since 1809 that a whole ministry had been replaced at once and the first time that the replacement had been dictated by the *Riksdag*–in other words, Sweden was for the first time being run on clearly parliamentary lines. It rates two other firsts: the government included Karl Staaff, the leader of the Liberal Party, and Alfred Petersson, 'the first peasant to sit at the King's council table'.

Meanwhile, the result of the Norwegian referendum showed 368,200 for and 184 against the dissolution of the Union. A clearer indication could hardly have been envisaged and on 31 August 1905 negotiations began in Karlstad between representatives of the two nations. They were far from amicable and both countries had mobilized their armies, but fortunately no outside power was eager to lend assistance. Wilhelm II had let King Oscar know that he wanted the matter settled as quickly as possible, while the Norwegians realized that they wouldn't receive the military aid that they had hoped for from Britain, nor could they expect much sympathy from Karl Staaff and his fellow-Liberals. Finally, in October 1905, the Karlstad Convention was approved by the *Storting* and the *Riksdag*. Oscar abdicated as king of Norway and the Union, after ninety troubled years, was terminated. A referendum in Norway showed a clear preference for a monarchy and King Oscar was asked if he would propose a Bernadotte prince as candidate for the throne. His ministers advised him against this offer, however, and instead Prince Karl of Denmark, Edward VII's son-in-law, was elected. He assumed the Norwegian name Håkon, became King Håkon VII of Norway, the first monarch of an independent Norway since the Kalmar Union.

The Forming of Political Parties

The internal political situation in Sweden was meanwhile changing too. After the question of tariffs had lost some of its political sting, the two factions of the Farmers' Party reunited in 1895 to form a large party with conservative leanings, and in 1896, partly as a reaction, *Folkpartiet*, a Liberal Party, was formed: a small party aiming at a broader franchise, a peaceful settlement with Norway, better education for the masses, and the spread of total abstinence. A feature of this party was its readiness to deal with forces outside the *Riksdag*. Such a force was the Universal Franchise Movement, which was formed in 1890 and worked for universal suffrage, by such means as distributing leaflets, helping to form associations, and arranging lecture tours. Among its effective ideas were the two so-called 'people's *Riksdag*', organized in 1893 and 1896 by means of 'a general election'. It was a mock parliament run on the same lines as the *Riksdag* and with representatives elected in the same way. It had the desired effect of engaging the interest of many adults both with and without a vote in the orthodox election. The Liberals co-operated, too, with the Social Democrats who were so far hardly represented at all in the *Riksdag*, but on certain issues they disagreed, in such matters, for instance, as the use of violent means to gain political aims and the political strike.

In a way, the defence issue, which in turn was affected by the Norwegian question, helped the move towards universal suffrage. If a man had a duty to defend his country, then surely he should also have the right to vote, and the slogan 'one man, one gun, one vote', was adopted. Verner von Heidenstam, an intensely patriotic poet, took up the point in his cycle of poems *Ett Folk* (One Nation), published in *Svenska Dagbladet*, where he declared in a poem entitled 'Medborgarsång' (The Song of the Citizen): 'It is true that we own a fatherland, we all equally inherited it with the same rights and the same obligations for both poor and rich . . . It is shame, it is a blemish on the Swedish flag that citizens' rights are called *money*'.

In 1900 the different liberal groups in the *Riksdag* joined together to form the Liberal Coalition Party, which had universal suffrage as one of its main aims. In the election of 1902 this Liberal Party, led by the gifted lawyer Karl Staaff, emerged as the largest in the Lower House, holding 104 seats as opposed to the Farmers' Party's 91; the Social Democrats had gained 4 seats, but the Upper House was still solidly Conservative and in a combined vote the Conservatives could still easily carry the day. However, the Conservatives too were gradually coming to the conclusion that reform was necessary, although their proposals contained built-in guarantees that people with wealth would outweigh those without it. The Conservative government put forward such a proposal in 1904, but the Liberals had it rejected because it embraced a system of proportional representation. The ensuing election took place during the negotiations in Karlstad between Norwegian and Swedish representatives. It was different from previous elections in many respects. The political parties were becoming organized in the modern sense of the word: the Liberal and Social Democratic parties had behind them national party organizations and the Conservatives had for the first time followed suit, forming in 1904 their 'National Constituency Party Association'; two Liberal representatives, Karl Staaff and Johan Widén, were actually members of the government, serving in Lundeberg's coalition; and because workers' incomes had been rising steadily, many of them had annual incomes above the stipulated 800 *kronor* and were thus entitled to vote. The result was a clear victory for the more radical parties at the expense of the Conservatives (the Liberals went from 104 to 106 seats, the Social Democrats from 4 to 13) and King Oscar was faced with a problem. With a clear Conservative majority in the Upper House and a Liberal majority in the Lower House–who should form the government? After fruitless attempts at a coalition and then a Conservative government, Oscar and Crown Prince Gustav (who was taking an increasingly active part in the country's affairs as his father grew old) accepted the only other alternative and asked Karl Staaff to form a government, which he did in November 1905.

Staaff quickly put forward proposals for the reform of the franchise and these were approved by the Lower House, but rejected by the Upper House, whereupon Staaff asked the king to dissolve the *Riksdag* and put the issue to the electorate. His request was refused and in May 1906 he resigned. Rear Admiral Arvid Lindman then formed a minority Conservative government and drew up his proposals for reform, based on the idea of universal suffrage to the Lower House for all taxpayers, proportional voting for local government bodies, and a system of proportional representation. There would still be plural voting in local government elections, but the maximum number of votes held by one individual would be reduced to forty (as opposed to one hundred in the towns and anywhere up to 5,000 in rural districts). Both Houses were tired of the seemingly endless squabbling over this question and accepted Lindman's proposal with only minor modifications. As it was a constitutional change it had to be accepted by two successive parliaments in order to become law. In the 1908 election the Liberal Coalition Party won 98 seats, the Conservatives 83, and (a remarkable increase) the Social Democrats 34. The new *Riksdag* accepted Lindman's proposal, and his Reform Bill was passed in 1909.

The first election to the Lower House after the franchise reform vote was an obvious setback for the Conservatives, who won 64 seats, a vote of confidence in the Liberals who obtained 102, and a great rise in the fortunes of the Social Democratic Party, who obtained 64. The Liberals had a clear majority, Lindman resigned, and Karl Staaff formed his second government. He then had the Upper House dissolved and its composition too as a result of the 1909 Reform Bill was changed, although here the Conservatives retained their majority with 86 seats as opposed to the Liberals with 52 and the Social Democrats with 12.

Modern party alignment had been established – the Conservatives drew their support from the large farmers, industrialists, and the upper-middle classes; the Liberals derived theirs largely from the old radicals, the temperance and Free Church movements, small farmers, and tradesmen; while the Social Democrats were supported by industrial workers, trade unionists, and some radical intellectuals.

The General Strike

Although there was generally a decided upward trend in the Swedish economy throughout the period, there were many fluctuations, and since Swedish workers were becoming more organized into trade unions and consequently more powerful, they were becoming less willing to accept an automatic worsening of their conditions of employment whenever a recession loomed.

As we have seen, LO, the Swedish Confederation of Trade Unions, was formed in 1898. Many Swedish employers recognized the right of the trade unions to negotiate for their members and for their own protection decided to form *Svenska Arbetsgivareföreningen* (Swedish Federation of Employers) in 1902. There were many bitter labour disputes in the first decade of this century, with disagreements on wages leading to strikes and lockouts. Although strikes were not illegal, a law passed in 1899 forbade even peaceful picketing. This did not prevent incensed strikers from turning on blacklegs and there were many violent exchanges. One of the most notorious was the so-called Amalthea Incident of 1908, when strikers in Malmö bombed a ship with English strike-breakers on board, killing one and injuring twenty people. These extreme actions were perpetrated by a young socialist faction of the Social Democratic movement, led by Hinke Bergegren, and disapproved of by Hj. Branting and the main body of the party. However, the distinction was not always appreciated by the general public.

The worst crisis started in 1908, when the international economic situation led to a reduction in Swedish wages, which triggered off a wave of strikes and lockouts. This time the employers decided on concerted action and in 1909 effected a large-scale lockout which was countered by a general strike. The strike failed, for after a month union funds gave out and the workers had to return to work without having their demands met, and membership figures for both LO and the Social Democratic Party declined. And yet some 300,000 men had come out on strike, had conducted themselves in an orderly fashion, and had demonstrated their potential strength to the Employers' Federation. Things would never be quite the same again.

Social Reforms

The nation's social conscience had been stirring since the turn of the century and with the Norwegian crisis safely out of the way, successive governments, Conservative, Coalition, and Liberal, introduced some measure of reform. The Norrland small farmers, who had been ruthlessly exploited by large timber companies during the last thirty years and were in danger of losing their land and livelihood, were protected in 1906 by a law severely restricting the acquisition of land by private enterprise. In 1907 the Lindman government bought half the shares of the Grängesberg iron-mining company in Lapland with an option lasting twenty-five or thirty-five years on the remaining half.

Lindman was shrewd enough to recognize the enormous importance of iron-ore for the Swedish economy. He realized too the great potential of hydro-electric power. In 1906 the state had built a plant at Trollhättan, north-east of Gothenburg, and in 1909 the Lindman government set up the Waterfall Board to supervise the development of Sweden's vast hydro-electric power. It is interesting to note that in the supply of these essential commodities, as with the building of the railways, there evolved a unique combination of state and private ownership.

At this period the committee looking into the causes of emigration produced its recommendations, one result of which was a system of home loans. A committee to examine the question of old-age pensions had been set up by Lindman's government as early as 1907 and studied carefully schemes operating in Britain, Germany, and Denmark. By 1913 its recommendations were accepted and a state pension scheme introduced for the payment of small pensions to citizens over sixty-seven years of age. Meanwhile other social measures had been introduced: teachers' salaries were improved, in the hope of raising the prestige of education generally; the penal code was improved; firms were forbidden to employ women on nightwork; and shop hours were limited by law. Laws on industrial safety were consolidated and brought up to date in 1912.

The Defence Issue

Conservatives still profoundly distrusted all that socialism stood for, while the Liberals were often suspicious of the methods that Socialists adopted to attain their objectives; but given the great differences in their respective political views, there was a reasonable amount of compromise. One issue which it proved impossible to solve by compromise was defence. Many Liberals belonged to pacifist organizations, while the Social Democrats were opposed on principle to the army and there was a lot of anti-military propaganda within radical circles. Many other Swedes, however, were concerned at the European situation, felt that Sweden was too vulnerable and that her military force could be increased. Lindman belonged to the latter group and during his ministry he had increased expenditure on defence. In 1911 he obtained the *Riksdag*'s approval for a new type of warship, the F-boat, but before work had started on it a general election intervened. One of the planks in Staaff's Liberal platform had been a reduction in defence in order to pay for social reform and when Staaff became Prime Minister, he promptly set up a defence committee, but meanwhile cancelled the F-boat. There was a strong immediate reaction in the country and a campaign was launched by the famous explorer Sven Hedin,

G

a staunch Conservative (and incidentally the last Swede to be created a peer), to raise funds to buy the vessel. Hedin also published a sensational pamphlet called *Ett Varningsord* (A Word of Warning; 1912), in which he gave a dire warning of the potential Russian threat. Seventeen million *kronor* were realized within a few months and the ship, the *Sverige* (i.e., Sweden), was launched in 1915.

Several of the members of the Defence Committee, not least Staaff himself, had become convinced of the need to strengthen the country's defences and to increase the period of military service, but while acknowledging this in December 1913 Staaff also stated that such a programme was contrary to the Liberal election programme and that action could be taken only after an election.

By now most Conservatives and many Liberals wanted a full and immediate reform of the army, a view shared by King Gustav V (who had succeeded his father in 1907). It was an open secret that King Gustav was not on good terms with Staaff, who had strong parliamentarian views, who thought that in a true democracy the monarch should be little more than a figurehead, and who helped to bring about such a situation by failing to consult the king before laying his proposals before the *Riksdag*. Those who wanted a strong defence force turned to King Gustav for help. On 6 February 1914, 30,000 farmers from all parts of the country assembled before the royal palace in Stockholm (the so-called *Bondetåget*, i.e., Farmers' Procession) bearing their banner 'with God and the Swedish people, for King and Fosterland', and appealed directly to their king. It was a piquant situation: the king, throughout the ages turned to by the ordinary people for protection against the nobles, was now being asked for help against the most democratically elected government that Sweden had enjoyed so far. King Gustav delivered his famous Palace Yard Speech (*borggårdstalet*), the rhetorical cadences and the patriotic style of which revealed the connivance of Sven Hedin. Using phrases like 'my army' and 'my navy', King Gustav declared that he shared the views of those assembled before him. The monarch had thus expressed a political opinion which conflicted with that of his government. Moreover, he had not told Staaff in advance of the speech he had intended to make. Staaff protested, but the king insisted on his right 'to communicate freely with his people'. Would the king promise to refrain in future from making political statements without first informing his government? No, the king would not. Staaff felt obliged to resign; Hjalmar Hammarskjöld, a moderate Conservative, complied with King Gustav's request to form a government at that point, but he had to face an election almost immediately. The Liberals found that they had to pay dearly for their attitude on defence, for they lost almost one-third of their strength (32 seats), some to the Social Democrats, but most to the Conservatives, and Hammarskjöld's party was the largest in both Houses. He proposed an increase in military service to 340 days and the commissioning of five new warships. There seemed little likelihood of this being accepted, but international affairs took command of the situation, World War I broke out, and in the ensuing feeling of urgency the Liberals agreed to vote for Hammarskjöld's proposal in return for minor concessions, and a special tax was levied to cover the costs.

The Cultural Scene

The cultural scene reflected the vast political, economic, and social changes that had occurred during these years. After the realistic novels of the mid-nineteenth century Swedish literature was strangely becalmed for some years, however, and the only author of stature to emerge was Viktor Rydberg (1828–95), poet, novelist, and essayist. He supported the new theological liberalism which began to oppose the Lutheran Church in the middle of the century and helped to warm up the campaign with his novel *Den siste Athenaren* (The Last Athenian; 1859), an attack on religious intolerance. He put the cat among the pigeons in 1862 with his controversial work *Bibelns lära om Kristus* (The Bible's Doctrine of Christ), where he demonstrated that the concept of the Holy Trinity and the divinity of Christ were a direct contrast to the message contained in the Bible. Lutheran ministers were not accustomed to having their authority challenged in this way and were outraged. Rydberg was aware of changes being wrought in his own country, but his reaction was basically pessimistic. His poem *Den nya Grottesången* (The New Song of Grotte) gives imaginative description of the potential evils of industrialization and the miseries it can inflict on man; but it offers no hope that, properly harnessed, the new forces could improve man's lot. In many respects Rydberg seems a man born out of his time, a writer whose sources of inspiration were the ancient classical world and Goethe.

Scandinavian culture was being shaken out of its lethargy by external events, however. Denmark was the first to be rudely awakened when her people discovered that despite the stirring ultra-nationalistic expressions of Scandinavian fortitude and Viking heritage, they were no match for the Prussians in war. Roused from their romantic dreams, they took stock of their real position. The outstanding Danish cultural personality of the time, Georg Brandes, a dynamic well-informed critic and popularizer, worked hard to introduce into Denmark the ideas of English and

European philosophers and scientists who were refashioning popular concepts. Largely through him the works of John Stuart Mill, Auguste Comte, Taine, Darwin, Feuerbach, and Strauss became known and assimilated. In his famous lectures in Copenhagen in 1871 on 'The Main Streams in Modern European Literature' he heralded what has become known as the 'Modern Breakthrough'. He declared himself to be against authority, tradition, and prejudice–a cultural radical in fact–and he urged authors to take an active interest in society and to debate social problems. Many gifted Scandinavian authors–Ibsen, Jonas Lie, and Alexander Kielland in Norway; Johannes Jørgensen, J. P. Jacobsen, Henrik Pontoppidan in Denmark–all complied. The outstanding writer who introduced the Modern Breakthrough into Sweden was August Strindberg (1849–1912), dramatist, novelist, poet, sometime journalist, civil servant, photographer, painter, pseudo-historian, and scientist. Few men had seen from the inside so many aspects of Swedish society and none was so able and willing to expose its defects. His novel *Röda rummet* (The Red Room; 1879), an amusing but biting satire on the class-ridden Swedish society of the period, struck out in numerous directions: bureaucracy; the publishing world; the business world; charity organizations with their condescending Lady Bountiful attitude; the *Riksdag* which, dominated as it was by conservative farmers, had dashed so many hopes after the 1866 Reform Bill; society's philistine attitude towards the arts–all came under attack. There was also a chapter devoted to the degrading social conditions in the slums of Stockholm. Strindberg's novel, with its outspokenness, realistic style, and recording of unsavoury details, was something new in Swedish literature. In his own admittedly unpredictable way Strindberg was, like Brandes, opening the minds of his fellow-countrymen to new European ideas. He wrote in 1882 a satire entitled *Det nya riket* (The New Realm) which goes much further than *The Red Room* in its social criticism. The ruling classes in Oscar II's Sweden, the royal family, the Church, the civil service, the military, and the bourgeoisie are all the subjects of Strindberg's bitter attack.

A group of writers who acquired the name of *Unga Sverige* (Young Sweden) began to look to Strindberg as their leader and inspiration. They too had been influenced by the Modern Breakthrough and like Brandes adopted realistic, questioning attitudes to society. Some of them were social radicals in close contact with the left-wing students' organizations *Verdandi* (at Uppsala) and *De Unga Gubbarne* (at Lund). Gustav af Geijerstam, Tor Hedberg, the young Oscar Levertin, Axel Lundegård, and the women novelists Anna-Charlotte Leffler, Alfhild Agrell, and Ernst Ahlgren (pseudonym of Viktoria Benedictsson) all took courage from Strindberg and followed Brandes's advice to debate social problems in their work.

One could not always criticize the Establishment with impunity. Hjalmar Branting, for instance, was condemned in 1889 to over three months' imprisonment for an article satirizing society and he was fined 500 *kronor* in 1895 for too pointed a criticism of Oscar II during the Union crisis. Strindberg himself was subjected to a charge of sacrilege, brought against him by the Church on the publication in 1884 of his collection of short stories *Giftas* (Married). The ensuing court case was followed with great interest and emotion by large sections of the community and when Strindberg was acquitted, he was hailed as a great champion by 'Young Sweden' and many other radicals. It was no doubt a criticism of Swedish society at the time that a writer like Strindberg with an uncontrollable urge to speak his mind felt obliged to spend much of his life abroad. The naturalistic plays which helped him to win international fame, works like *Fadren* (The Father), *Fröken Julie* (Miss Julie), and *Fordringsägare* (Creditors), were written abroad. Perhaps it is also indicative of social conditions that Strindberg felt able to return to Sweden by the turn of the century and it was there that he wrote *Till Damaskus* (To Damascus), *Ett Drömspel* (A Dream Play), and his *Kammarspel* (The Chamber Plays), which introduced a new concept in European drama, the symbolic expressionistic play, and pointed the way towards surrealist drama. One must not overstate a case of conciliation, however, for Strindberg always remained the young rebel and indeed only two years before his death in 1912 he had sparked off the 'Strindberg Controversy' with his articles in the radical papers *Aftontidningen* and *Social-Demokraten*, attacking the political, literary, and religious scene in Sweden. A few reforms had been effected since *The Red Room* had first appeared, but not nearly enough for Strindberg's liking.

The literature of the 1880s was socially involved, indignantly drawing attention to the flaws in society and chronicling changes brought about by industrialization. A change of mood became discernible, however, towards the end of the decade. The next generation of writers seemed afraid that Swedish society was being transformed too rapidly and that they must help preserve it in some way. There is a strong flavour of patriotism and provincialism in Swedish culture in the 1890s and an interest in Swedish history. Heidenstam wrote his celebrated poem 'Sverige' in 1899, set to music by the Swedish composer Wilhelm Stenhammar. The song rings out like an invocation with almost religious fervour: 'Sverige, Sverige, Sverige, fosterland'. Heidenstam also wrote a prose work entitled

Karolinerna (The Charles Men; 1897–98), depicting the hardship endured by Karl XII's soldiers.

While Heidenstam's works often sing the praises of his native Lake Vättern, the beautiful province of Värmland found its champions in Selma Lagerlöf (1858–1940) and Gustaf Fröding (1860–1911), but in both cases it is the old Värmland with elegant manor houses served by quaint rustics. Erik Axel Karlfeldt (1864–1931) sang the praises of his native Dalarna, while Per Hallström (1866–1960) and Pelle Molin (1864–96) apostrophized Norrland.

The visual arts had a counterpart to this in the works of Anders Zorn, famous for his painting of Dalarna peasant scenes, and in Carl Larsson's rustic paintings of his beloved Sundborn.

As early as 1873 Artur Hazelius had started to build up the museum now called the Nordic Museum in Stockholm, where relics of peasant culture from different Swedish provinces are preserved. In 1891 he built on to it the famous open-air museum at Skansen where representative cottages from different parts of the country have been transported, fully equipped and complete with inhabitants in folk costume.

Seen in perspective the writers of the 1890s are perhaps an important interlude in the general development of Swedish literature. They were followed by Hjalmar Söderberg (1869–1941), a *fin de siècle* writer who created sensitive, gifted, but essentially lonely, passive characters who observed the suffering of man, sympathized, but were unable to effect any amelioration of the situation. Söderberg is acknowledged as one of Sweden's best stylists, but he is perhaps too unique to be emulated and no schools have been formed round him.

Intrinsically less gifted but more indicative of the social scene were a group of novelists who began their literary careers in about 1910: Sigfrid Siwertz (1882–), Gustaf Hellström (1882–1953), Elin Wägner (1882–1949), and Ludvig Nordström (1882–1942). To this group could be added Hjalmar Bergman (1883–1931), a greater genius than the others who had nevertheless his points in common with them. They had almost all been journalists, they were trained observers, and were interested in the transformation of the Swedish social scene and hoped to chronicle it in their novels, which quite often followed the fortunes of a particular Swedish family through two or three generations. Hellström's novel *Snörmakare Lekholm får en idé* (Lacemaker Lekholm has an idea) serves as a good example. Lekholm, a simple working-class craftsman, is inspired to allow his intelligent son to take the *Studentexamen*, the equivalent of a Higher School Certificate. Hellström follows the fortunes of the Lekholms from the time that the Lacemaker decides to educate his son and in so doing produces a broad analysis of changing Swedish society.

There was much room for criticism of the Swedish political, economic, and social scene, but if one compares the situation in 1866 with that of 1914, there can be no doubt that Sweden had taken tremendous strides forward. She was well on the way to becoming a true parliamentary democracy; she was at least beginning to realize the vast potential of her forests, waterways, minerals, and her people's technological genius; and with the emergence of strong Liberal and Social Democratic political parties, was beginning to accept the desirability of some form of social justice in the emerging industrialized state.

Chapter 5

1914–1939

The Road to Prosperity–the Middle Way

World War I

IN AUGUST 1914 Norway and Sweden declared jointly their neutrality, and on the initiative of King Gustav V of Sweden the monarchs of Denmark, Norway, and Sweden met in Malmö in the autumn of that year to demonstrate their united intention of remaining neutral. These Nordic meetings were continued at a high level throughout World War I, the three Scandinavian Prime Ministers and Foreign Ministers meeting at frequent intervals, and the monarchs themselves meeting again in 1917, this time in Oslo (or Christiania as it then was). Sweden was no longer a self-sufficient country with a primitive agricultural economy, however, but an international trading country whose lifeline was her overseas trade, and although she was able to stand by her declared intention to remain neutral, this did not mean that she could remain aloof or could escape severe physical hardship and emotional strain.

With the exception of an extreme right-wing activist group (encouraged by Sven Hedin and with the blessing of the German-born Queen Viktoria,[1] who wanted Sweden to enter the war on Germany's side), there was widespread agreement with the policy of neutrality. Hjalmar Branting and Karl Staaff, the leaders respectively of the Social Democrats and the Liberals, both assured Hjalmar Hammarskjöld, the leader of a moderate Conservative government, that they would support him in this. Sympathy for the belligerents was divided, however. King Oscar II had been impressed by the strength and the pomp and circumstance of the new Reich, and had considered the Kaiser as his ally. His son Gustav V, whose mother, Queen Sofia, and wife, Queen Viktoria, were both German, was inclined to hold similar views. Although Sweden had declined to join the Triple Alliance of Germany, Austria-Hungary, and Italy, both the court and many leading

[1] Daughter of Grand Duke Frederick of Baden and Louise, daughter of Kaiser Wilhelm I.

Conservatives were drawn towards Germany, a country that they considered a bulwark against Slavonic barbarism, and were inclined to consider Britain's association with Russia as a betrayal of European civilization. The Liberals, on the other hand, felt more closely aligned with Britain, whose parliamentary democracy Karl Staaff had always admired. The Social Democrats had adopted many of their ideas from German Social Democracy, felt closer to the German than to the British Social Democrats, and had received assistance during the General Strike from the German Workers' Movement. In the end, however, it was the *Entente*, not Germany, that gained their sympathy. This point was emphasized in 1915 when a book entitled *Sveriges utrikespolitik i världskrigets belysning* (Sweden's foreign policy in the light of the World War) was published by a group of writers of widely different political views. The writers emphasized the qualities that the Germans and Swedes had in common and urged on their countrymen 'a courageous participation on Germany's side'. Staaff reacted to this 'activist' document by emphasizing on a lecture tour the dangers of giving in to Germany and urged strict neutrality. Branting did likewise, and his colleagues showed their strength of feeling by expelling the two Social Democrats who had contributed to the book, Otto Järte and Yngve Larsson, and another Social Democratic activist, Gustaf Steffen.

In the first year of the war the Germans made several attempts to activate Swedish pro-German views, making much of the close ties between the Swedish and German royal families. Prince Max von Baden, Queen Viktoria's cousin, visited Stockholm to suggest a German–Swedish alliance; they dangled the prospect of handing over to Sweden the Åland Islands as a reward for helping Germany. They bought majority shares in the newspaper *Aftonbladet* (the money coming from the German Ministry of War) and tried to influence Swedish public opinion. So too did some officials at the German Legation in Stockholm – indeed baron von Reichenau did it so hamfistedly that he had to be recalled to Berlin – while the Swedish minister in Berlin, Arvid Taube, convinced of a speedy outcome of war in Germany's favour, did his best to bring about an alliance between the two countries. Sweden did not enter into such an alliance, however, and the most the 'activists' achieved was that the neutrality was occasionally prejudiced in Germany's favour.

Sweden's agriculture had taken on an international character. She did not grow enough grain for her requirements and she also imported maize and concentrated cattle foods to further her dairy farming and artificial fertilizers for arable farming. To keep her other industries going she needed also to import machines, oil, coal, and raw materials for the textile and other industries. It was equally important for her to export her timber, pulp, engineering products, and iron-ore to pay for essential imports.

In her attempt to choke off imports to Germany, Britain was anxious to prevent neutral states from re-exporting important raw materials to her enemy and exercised considerable pressure on Sweden to join the blockade. Hammarskjöld, who had German sympathies and was, moreover, an outstanding expert on legal matters, considered that a neutral state had both a right and a duty to prevent its trade from being controlled by a belligerent, which did not improve the already difficult relations between Britain and Sweden. First Britain and then Germany, too, seized Swedish ships on the high seas, searched and often confiscated their cargoes. Britain was particularly anxious to prevent goods from America reaching Germany via Sweden. She kept a blacklist of Swedish firms with special contacts with Germany, and blacklisted firms were shunned by British firms.

In the first few months of the war Swedish exports to Germany increased. Not only iron-ore, that particularly desirable Swedish commodity in a modern war, but even foodstuffs found their way to Germany. When British coal imports dropped, this was compensated by German coal and so this vital commodity was assured for Sweden. But as Swedish imports from the West diminished, serious shortages of grain, oil, paraffin, and animal foods began to be felt. Poor harvests exacerbated the situation, prices rose sharply, and soon the cost of living soared. The government adopted various measures to counteract this, but to little effect. The importing of corn was taken over by the government in 1914 and food could be exported only on licence. In 1915 maximum prices were laid down for wheat, rye, and oats, but this simply led to grain being used for other purposes and crops without price controls were grown instead. Nor could the government contain large-scale blackmarketing and profiteering. By October 1916 sugar was rationed and in January 1917 bread- and flour-rationing was introduced too.

On 1 February 1917 Germany began her policy of unrestricted submarine warfare which caused many Swedish deaths (280 Swedish ships and 800 lives were lost at sea during World War I) and lost Germany the sympathy of many Swedes. The United States then came into the war, which increased the pressure the *Entente* countries were already putting on Sweden's trade with Germany.

New trade negotiations had been started with Britain, but Hammarskjöld was dragging his feet. Vital imports were not reaching Swedish harbours, the food situation was becoming desperate, and there was widespread dissatisfaction with 'Hunger-skjöld', as the Prime Minister was nicknamed. The truce observed by all the Swedish political parties at the outset of the war was becoming untenable and from 1916 there had been dissension within the government itself, for the Foreign Minister, Knut Wallenberg, unlike Hammarskjöld, considered a trade agreement with Britain to be of the utmost importance. In March 1917 the government was defeated in the *Riksdag*, ostensibly over a defence issue but in effect as a result of its whole trade policy. Hammarskjöld offered his government's resignation, although he appears to have considered himself indispensable to the country in the present crisis. The Liberals and Social Democrats were firmly united against him by this time, however; the Conservatives would not back him up in a parliamentary struggle; and King Gustav was obliged to accept the proffered resignation. He then turned to the right-wing Conservative Ernst Trygger, who eventually had to admit with annoyance that he was unable to form a government. It was the moderate Conservative Carl Swartz, with Arvid Lindman as his Foreign Minister, who became the next Prime Minister. Swartz's sympathies were not very different from Hammarskjöld's, but he was much more flexible in negotiations with Britain. In May 1917 he reached an agreement which allowed nineteen Swedish ships being held in American and fourteen in British ports to return home with their cargoes, while a number of Allied vessels with timber on board, trapped in the Baltic, were escorted by Swedish warships through minefields in the Sound. This brought some slight relief, but soon the bread ration had again to be reduced and rationing was extended to include potatoes.

The political situation was changing both at home and abroad. The Revolution in Russia strengthened support for the *Entente* in most Swedish circles. It also encouraged left-wing circles in Sweden already incensed by the acute food shortages which affected above all the industrial workers in urban areas. There were protest marches and demonstrations, the most threatening of which coincided with the Prime Minister's reply on 5 June to a question put by Branting concerning votes for women and the abolition of plural voting in local elections. Some 20,000 workers had gathered on Norrbro and Gustaf Adolfs Torg (Gustavus Adolphus's Square) near the *Riksdag* building in Stockholm and had to be dispersed by the police. The election campaign in the autumn of 1917 took place in the shadow of these political disturbances and focused attention once more on the quest for real political democracy. The political temperature was raised another degree by the so-called Luxburg Affair. It was revealed in September that Count K. L. von Luxburg, the German chargé d'affaires in Buenos Aires, had been using Swedish diplomatic channels to send coded telegrams to Berlin about shipping movements. It also transpired that Luxburg had used Mexican and even American channels too in the past, that the British knew about them and had been extracting important information from them; but these facts were not allowed to detract from a good scandal, which added further embarrassment for an already harassed government.

By the time of the election there had been a certain re-forming of political groups. The once powerful *Lantmannapartiet* (Farmers) had gradually been absorbed into the Conservative Party in the Lower House, but the Farmers had now begun to re-form into two different parties: *Bondeförbundet* (the Agrarians' Party), mainly representing smallholders, and *Jordbrukarnas riksförbund* (the Farmers' Union), representing large farmers. The Social Democrats had been suffering from criticism from within, a left-wing contingent maintaining that the party was too accommodating towards the bourgeoisie. This led in May 1917 to an open split when a left-wing splinter group including Zeth Höglund and Fredrik Ström formed Sweden's left-wing Social Democratic Party. It had its own daily paper, *Folkets Dagblad Politiken*, in which it put forward a doctrinaire Marxist view and demanded that the masses should seize power by revolutionary means. In the election the Conservatives won only 57 seats, the Liberals 62, the Social Democrats 86, the left-wing Socialists 11; and in addition the Agrarians' Party won 9 and the Farmers 5. There was clearly a large majority against the Conservatives and Swartz resigned. King Gustav found it impossible to form a coalition and was obliged to ask the Liberal leader to accept office. Karl Staaff had died in 1915 and the Liberals were led by Nils Edén, a professor of history at Uppsala University who, although a capable politician, never commanded the affection and authority enjoyed by his predecessor. He was astute enough to learn by Staaff's experiences in dealing with the king and before forming a government he submitted his proposals, which King Gustav accepted. His other condition before taking office was that the king would no longer allow unofficial advisers to come between himself and his Cabinet. In other words, King Gustav was tacitly accepting that Sweden was a parliamentary democracy and that his own powers were severely limited. As though to emphasize the point, Edén appointed Hjalmar Branting, a Social Democrat and a republican by conviction, as Finance Minister and included three other Social Democrats in his Cabinet.

The new government had to deal with a crisis situation. The cost of living had doubled since 1914; there was an acute shortage of fuel, dairy produce, and meat; ruthless speculators were making fortunes out of the shortage; Swedish ships were being torpedoed; and an unusually dry summer had caused a poor harvest in 1917. These matters obviously had to be given priority over parliamentary reform. Edén negotiated with the Allies and by the terms of an agreement reached in May, grain, fertilizers, oil, and coffee were imported into Sweden on the strict understanding that they would not be re-exported to Germany. Swedish iron-ore exports to Germany were considerably reduced, the surplus finding its way to the Allies. Almost one-half of the Swedish merchant fleet was also leased out to the Allies. These measures had scarcely begun to have an effect by the time of the armistice in November 1918.

Sweden was affected in a number of ways by the Russian Revolution. One outcome of the October Revolution was that on 6 December 1917 Finland declared her independence and by 4 January 1918 the Swedish government had recognized the new state. When civil war broke out in Finland between the Reds and the Whites, Edén was in a quandary. The Finnish (White) government requested Swedish aid and Swedes of right-wing persuasions demanded active Swedish participation on the side of the Whites, while the more militant Socialists in Sweden sympathized with a Red government that had been formed in Finland in January. In the end the Edén government refused to be drawn into the conflict, although arms to the Whites were allowed to pass through Sweden, as were Finnish volunteers who had been in Germany for military training. About a thousand Swedish volunteers were also given permission to go to Finland where they joined the White army.

The Åland Islands

Relations between Sweden and Finland were complicated further by the question of the Åland Islands whose inhabitants were almost all Swedish-speaking. In 1917 the Åland Islanders expressed a wish to be reunited with Sweden, but there were still Russian troops on the islands in February 1918. Seven thousand islanders appealed directly to the Swedish king and his people, and the Swedish government sent two warships to evacuate those who wished to place themselves under Swedish protection. The Russians withdrew and a Swedish force took their place, but by now the Finns were suspicious of Sweden's motives. German troops who were helping White Finland relieved the Swedish forces on the islands, but they too withdrew as the World War ran its course. Finland was reluctant to lose the Åland Islands, the Swedish-speaking Finns particularly feeling that the loss of so many linguistic allies would worsen their own position. A referendum was organized on the islands in June 1919, when over 95 per cent of the voters declared their wish to be reunited with Sweden, but it was ignored by the Finnish government in Helsinki. The islanders then tried to have the matter brought up at the Peace Conference in 1919, but the Powers were too occupied with weightier matters. The Swedish government then appealed in 1920 to the League of Nations to mediate. A three-man International Committee studied the question and in 1921 found in Finland's favour. They also recommended guarantees to the islanders that their language and culture would be protected. Sweden (under protest) and Finland both accepted the committee's findings and in 1922 Finland legally granted the Åland Islands a large measure of self-government.

Parliamentary Reform

The Revolution in Russia indirectly affected Swedish internal politics too. Edén's government had tried to push constitutional reform through the *Riksdag* in spring 1918, but the Upper House had thrown out his proposals. Left-wing militants were becoming more voluble in Sweden, however, and many, including Per Albin Hansson, wanted a showdown with bourgeois society by means of a general strike. With Russia as a warning to their immediate east and under the threat of a general strike and even a revolution, the Conservatives were more susceptible to reasonable reform, and Edén pushed home his advantage. An extraordinary *Riksdag* had been called to deal with some economic measures and the government used the opportunity to put forward a reform programme which was accepted in essence by both Houses. Plural voting in local elections was abolished. This was not a constitutional matter and could therefore come into operation immediately. An extraordinary *Riksdag* had no powers to change the constitution, however, and the government could merely give warning of its intention and then wait until the next session of the *Riksdag* to put forward proposals for lowering the voting age from twenty-four to twenty-three; the abolition of property qualifications; votes for women; and women's right to stand for election to the *Riksdag*. These were approved and confirmed by the following *Riksdag* and thus became law in 1921, the year in which Sweden could be said to have become a true parliamentary democracy.

In order to put the new reforms affecting local government into effect the whole of the Upper House was dissolved in 1919; there were local elections, followed by elections to the Upper House. The result was a reduction in the Conservative seats from 86 to 38, and an increase for the Social Democrats from 19 to 49; the Liberals won 41 and the Agrarians won 19, while the left-wing

Socialists won 3. An essential function of the Upper House, as conceived in the 1866 Reform Bill, had been to act as a stabilizer and to provide continuity in the *Riksdag*, but its composition was now almost the same as the Lower House and for the first time the Social Democratic Party was the largest in the *Riksdag*.

The coalition between the Liberals and Social Democrats had had one specific aim, to push through parliamentary reform, and to this end the two parties had glossed over essential differences in their philosophies. Now that they had accomplished their aim, co-operation became increasingly irksome. Edén was still able to lend his support to the Social Democrats in 1919, when a 48-hour week for all workers except farmworkers was introduced, but he disagreed fundamentally on issues like nationalization and taxation, and in March 1920 he resigned, the Liberal–Social Democratic coalition came to an end, Hjalmar Branting became Prime Minister, and for the first time in her history Sweden had a wholly Social Democratic government in power.

It was short-lived, for in the autumn elections both the Social Democrats and the Liberals lost seats to the Conservatives and Agrarians, almost certainly because of a middle-class fear of socialism and annoyance at the Liberal support of the Social Democrats. Branting resigned, neither the Right nor the Left was prepared to take up the reins of office, and a non-party ministry of officials led by Louis De Geer and then Oscar von Sydow steered the country through the final stages of the electoral Reform Bill. The Lower House was dissolved to allow the new laws to be put into effect. The Social Democrats made substantial gains and Branting formed his second ministry, but his government did not command an overall majority in the *Riksdag*. It began indeed a twelve-year period of frequent changes of government when no one party could gain a dominant position and there seemed little likelihood of a coalition. The new electoral reforms had also included the introduction of proportional representation, which helped the growth of new parties. The two Farmers' parties merged into the *Bondeförbundet* (Agrarians), but most moves were in the opposite direction—a Communist wing emerged from the left-wing Social Democrats, which split into a Moscow group and an Independent group in 1924.

The First Post-War Depression

The period 1920–33 is characterized partly by industrial expansion, a time when many Swedish products (Electrolux, SKF, Swedish matches, etc.) entered world markets, when Sweden instead of depending on foreign capital for her expansion began instead to export capital; it was the age of Kreuger, the Swedish Match

King, who not only acquired control of several Swedish companies, including Cellulosabolaget and L. M. Ericsson, but built up an international financial empire. By the end of the 1920s, writes K. Samuelsson, 'Kreuger started to act as a vehicle for international transfers of capital and gradually did so on a scale that bears comparison with Marshall aid'.[2]

The period is also punctuated, however, by depressions, serious labour disputes, squabbles between trade unionists, Communists, and syndicalists, and unemployment. The first post-war depression was at its worst in 1921–22, when approximately one-third of trade union members were unemployed, and although the Commission on Unemployment, set up at the outset of the war to organize public work and to dispense emergency relief, continued to function, its ameliorating effects were limited, partly because of its directive that members of unions involved in labour disputes were not to be given employment and that payment for the work that it did organize had to be kept under the normal wage levels for manual workers. Å. Elmér writes that

> In January 1922 there were probably over 200,000 workers unemployed, which means that some million people lacked means of support if the families are taken into account. Of these 32,000 were given public relief work, mainly roadbuilding, while 64,000 were given financial support through local government unemployment committees. In addition many unemployed, especially those with families to support, were granted local relief, but a large group of unemployed simply had to manage themselves by some means or another.[3]

The emergency employment often took the form of building roads in desolate areas.

> For a craftsman who would normally earn 12.50 *kronor* a day it was not exactly pleasant to have to go off to some desolate spot far from home and build roads for wages lower than the lowest wage for manual work, live in primitive barracks, and eat wretched food while the poor relief had to support one's family at home.[4]

Elmér's picture contrasts vividly with the gay picture of the 1920s conjured up by Samuelsson:

> Many people reaped quick fortunes from Kreuger shares and debentures and many were willing to stake their all in the expecta-

---

[2] Samuelsson, op. cit., p. 230.   [4] ibid, p. 58.
[3] Å. Elmér, *Från Fattigsverige till välfärdsstaten* (Stockholm, 1969), p. 57.

tion of big new profits. The corks of champagne bottles popped, caviar abounded in profusion and cabarets and revues enjoyed a golden age. At the Vasa Theatre, Margit Rosengren and Lars Egge sang 'The Last Waltz'; Gösta Ekman and Tollie Zellman acted out *A Comedy at the Castle*, from the stage of the Oscars Theatre; and a film with Lars Hansson, *Sin*, was playing to packed houses at the Röda Kvarn cinema. The first 'talkie' was shown at Children's Day celebrations in October 1928. Riches so quickly earned had to be ostentatiously exhibited. In a setting of widespread poverty, large-scale unemployment, political deadlock and general gloom, the diamond rings shone so much more brightly, the black muskrat fur looked so much warmer and more genuine on the older ladies, and the minivers and silver foxes so much more becoming on the younger women. The swallow-tailed coat and high hat were in fashion, and their wearers would drive between parties in a Daimler-Benz, Oldsmobile or Buick . . . The 1920s were a wonderful time to live in for the very few, an oligarchy that looked forward to a future where stocks kept eternally rising in value and never ceased to pay handsome dividends.[5]

Branting's government rode the worst of the first post-war depression, but was toppled in 1923 over its attempt to alter the directives of the Commission on Unemployment. It was succeeded by a minority Conservative government headed by Trygger who remained in office until autumn 1924. This Conservative ministry came to grief over the defence issue. Sweden had joined the League of Nations in 1920 and, represented by respected men like Hjalmar Branting and Östen Undén, had worked for international justice and international disarmament. This was an article of faith for the Social Democrats. The war to end wars had been fought, an international organization had been set up to tackle the problem of world peace, and Swedish taxes could therefore be channelled from defence to social improvements. Trygger had no such faith and wanted no running-down of Swedish defences. The *Riksdag* threw out his defence proposals in autumn 1924, however, and Branting became Prime Minister for the third time. He was an ailing man by this time and soon had to resign, the premiership being taken over by his party colleague Rickard Sandler.

There was soon almost a repetition of the 1923 *Riksdag*. Sandler's government wanted to revoke a decision made by the Commission on Unemployment that unemployed men should be sent to the Stripa mines in Västmanland where there had been labour disputes.

To a Social Democratic government it smacked of blacklegging. However, the *Riksdag* upheld the commission's ruling and Sandler resigned.

Weigh-master Parliamentarianism

A key figure in the *Riksdag* was Carl G. Ekman, the Liberal leader who became known as the 'Weigh-master'. The Liberal Party had split into two groups in 1923 over the prohibition issue, one group, the *Folkfrisinnade* (Independent Liberals), supported largely by country districts, being in favour of total prohibition, the other (called simply Liberals), supported by the old-fashioned intelligentsia in urban areas. The Independent Liberals had 35 seats in the Lower House in 1924, the Liberals had only six. Thus the votes that Ekman, an Independent Liberal, could be sure of in the *Riksdag* were extremely few, but in a parliament without a majority party he was able to manoeuver so skilfully that many major political issues became dependent on his support. When Sandler's government resigned in 1926, King Gustav asked Ekman to form a government on as broad a basis as possible. It was a difficult task, for both the Agrarians and Conservatives had decided not to co-operate and so Ekman's ministers were all either Liberals or Independent Liberals. In both Houses of the *Riksdag* the Independent Liberals had some 51 seats, the Conservatives 115 seats, and the Social Democrats 148, but although on a knife edge, Ekman's first ministry lasted two years, finding support now from the Right, now from the Left, depending on the issue involved. At its party conference in 1928 the Social Democratic Party, by far the largest party in the *Riksdag*, showed its frustration at this 'Weigh-master Parliamentarianism, this damned system, where one links arms one day with Admiral Lindman and the next day with Per Albin Hansson and not a single Swedish citizen knows what's going to happen'.

Two important pieces of legislation are associated with Ekman's first government. In 1927, with the support of the Social Democrats and Agrarians, a school Reform Bill was passed, making a six-year basic schooling compulsory for all social classes and allowing girls to attend grammar schools on the same basis as boys. In 1928, against a background of fluctuating world markets, the increasing strength of the trade unions, wildcat strikes, and boycotts, Ekman gained support from the Conservatives and Agrarians for a law on collective agreements and the setting-up of arbitration tribunals with three representatives appointed by the government, two by the Federation of Swedish Employers, and two by the trade unions.

The Second Post-War Depression

In the elections to the Lower House in 1928 the Conservatives gained 73 seats, the Agrarians 27, the Liberals 32; the Social Democrats lost 15 (4 to the Communists). The composition had thus changed, Ekman resigned, and Arvid Lindman again formed a Conservative government, which was soon faced with a formidable economic situation as the second post-war depression began to be felt in Sweden. The farmers were particularly hard hit as agricultural prices slumped, and they demanded protective measures. Lindman proposed higher tariffs on grain imports and an order compelling flour-mills to accept a minimum quota of home-grown grain, but increased tariffs were rejected, Lindman resigned, and Ekman formed in June 1930 his second ministry. But by now the country was in the throes of an industrial as well as an agricultural crisis. Sweden went off the gold standard, the slump continued, unemployment figures soared, wages were depressed, and Ekman's only weapons seemed to be the old tested Commission on Unemployment and strict government economies. Unemployment in 1931 had reached 89,000, an increase of about 180 per cent on the 1930 figure. By December 1932 it had reached 161,000.

The situation grew ugly in 1931 when wage reductions led to conflicts and outbreaks of violence, often Communist-inspired. The worst of these were undoubtedly the riots at Ådalen in Norrland in that year. A local strike within the pulp industry had led to a sympathy strike at the Graninge Company's sulphate and sulphite factories. The company retaliated by employing strike-breakers who were attacked by strikers, at which point troops were brought in. The strike then spread to the whole of the Ådalen district and a protest march was staged. When the demonstrators ignored the military commander's order to disperse, he ordered his troops to fire; five people were killed and five wounded. (The incident was the subject of a publication, *Ådalen 31*, by Birger Norman in 1968 and a touching film by Bo Widerberg made in 1969.) A wave of protest swept the country as the deaths were reported and although Ekman's government was not responsible, it bore the brunt of public criticism.

What finally brought Ekman's political career to an end was Kreuger's suicide in Paris in March 1932 and the collapse of his empire, which caused a wave of suicides in Sweden. In the course of the investigations into Kreuger's affairs it was disclosed that Ekman's Independent Liberal Party had secretly received contributions from Kreuger and that Ekman had tried to conceal the fact. Ekman resigned and although his party remained in office under

Felix Hamrin, it had forfeited public support and in the ensuing elections in 1932 the Social Democrats and the Agrarians made substantial gains, while the Conservatives and Independent Liberals lost heavily.

The Foundation of the Welfare State

Per Albin Hansson formed a Social Democratic government with Sandler as Foreign Minister and Ernst Wigforss as Minister of Finance. Per Albin Hansson, known affectionately by his countrymen simply as 'Per Albin', was a bricklayer's son from Malmö. He had only four years' formal schooling, started work as a messenger boy when he was only twelve years old, and worked his way up through the Social Democratic Party, helping to form the Social Democratic Youth Organization in 1903. Although he became a brilliant parliamentarian and tactician, remained the undisputed leader of his party from 1928 until his death in 1946, and was Prime Minister for fourteen years, he was always a man of the people with the common touch. Perhaps his one affectation was his continuing lack of affectation, for even as a hard-pressed Prime Minister he continued to live in a modest apartment in Stockholm and to use public transport, and indeed he collapsed and died one October evening after alighting from a tram-car on his way home from a meeting of Scandinavian ministers.

He and Wigforss were men of vision, Hansson looking beyond political-party allegiances to what he called 'Folkhemmet' or 'Home of the People', a welfare state where all members of the community could live in security, in his own words 'a policy without regard to class or group, a policy for the whole people'; and Wigforss looking for a way out of the cycle of economic crises that had punctuated the last two decades, and for the means to finance the 'Home of the People'. Wigforss, who was attracted by some of J. M. Keynes's theories on political economy, believed that the country's economic problems were the result of under-consumption and that the answer lay not in ever-increasing cheeseparing by the state, but in stimulating the economy. The government should invest in large-scale useful projects (building houses and hospitals, for example) and should pay reasonable wages for the work done, which in turn would create further demand and lead to full employment. Expenditure on social welfare would become a stimulus to demand and investment, and would boost production. The investment programme could be paid for by loans and higher taxes.

The Social Democrats had pledged themselves, as part of their election programme in 1932, to create more employment and Per Albin Hansson's government put forward a proposal in 1933 to invest some 200 million *kronor*, a vast sum at that time, in public works, mostly in the building of houses. The discredited Commission on Unemployment would be folded up, the emergency work (often pointless and miserably remunerated) organized by the commission would go, and a state unemployment insurance scheme be introduced. A special committee was set up to examine the proposals, while hard bargaining went on between the government (which lacked an overall majority in the *Riksdag*) and the non-socialist parties to try to reach a compromise. Hansson's proposal seemed doomed, but in May 1933 he surprisingly made a pact with an Agrarian, Axel Pehrsson-Bramstorp, behind the back of the Agrarian leader, Olof Olsson. Most of the party members supported Pehrsson-Bramstorp, Olsson resigned, and Per Albin Hansson was assured of the necessary majority to push through his proposals. His deal with the Agrarians, soon christened the *kohandeln*, a pun on coalition ('cow-lition') and implying 'horse trading' (literally 'cow dealing'), included protective measures for farmers, which led to increased food prices. This aspect was severely criticized by many Social Democrats who asserted that when some of the people who had voted them into office were living barely at subsistence level, it was unethical to slap taxes on margarine in order to make butter more competitive and to retain import levies on food. Hansson, however, was prepared to sacrifice the sprat if he was sure of netting his mackerel.

In June 1933 the government's unemployment and agricultural policies were accepted by the Social Democrats, the Agrarians, and some Independent Liberals. There were serious misgivings in large sections of the community, expressed for instance in the Liberal paper *Dagens Nyheter*, by no means the government's harshest critic:

> At a time when the economy is becoming poorer and incomes in all directions are being cut down, our governing powers are preparing . . . to put into operation the building of great new hospitals, road works, and the electrification of the railways, to sink tens and tens of millions into improving housing conditions in the country districts . . . what consequences this will have in the coming years if the crisis lasts one dare hardly consider.
> (3 March 1933)

However, the crisis didn't last and fears proved unfounded. There was internationally a general economic improvement and it is still a moot point to what extent state intervention caused the improvement in Sweden's economic fortunes in 1933. In any case, with an assured majority Per Albin Hansson was able to launch his social plan that gained for Sweden a reputation for being a model welfare state.

Wigforss's budgets showed where the state would seek the means to finance the project. A progressive income-tax scheme was introduced which put income tax up by some 20 per cent; limited companies were taxed twice: the company paying first, then the shareholders being taxed on their dividends. Indirect taxes were also raised, duty on spirits, coffee, and tobacco rising sharply (which led to many caustic comments on the fact that Wigforss himself was a teetotaller). The Social Democrats' crisis programme did not include state ownership, however. They had, as Marquis Childs emphasized, chosen the middle way.

Soon the unemployment figures began to drop rapidly and Sweden's trading position improved. The *krona* was deliberately kept 7 per cent under parity with the pound sterling; imports were therefore expensive, which helped Swedish textile and metal industries, and exports were relatively cheap. Swedish iron and steel exports rose rapidly, due sadly in part to the rearmament programmes of Germany and other European countries, but a lot of the steel found its way to the home market too and improved living standards in many ways. The government's building programme was showing results and the serious overcrowding resulting from rapid urbanization abated. Real wages began to rise and people had proof all round them of a palpable improvement in their living standards.

It was a good climate for the introduction of social policy. In 1934 a state-supported unemployment insurance scheme was introduced. The following year old-age pensions were raised appreciably. When Gustav Möller, the Social Minister, tried to introduce a scheme whereby pensions would be based on local costs of living, however, he met Agrarian opposition. Meanwhile a defence committee, set up at the beginning of 1930, had put forward its proposals by 1935. All its members were agreed that rearmament was necessary, the Agrarians and Liberals proposing a defence budget of 148 million *kronor* per year, the Conservatives wanting more, and the Social Democrats less. The government tried to arrange a deal in 1936: if Möller's local cost-of-living pensions were accepted, the Social Democrats would vote for increased defence. The *Riksdag* refused and Hansson resigned. Pehrsson-Bramstorp formed a minority government, but the autumn elections intervened before he had put forward any proposals to the *Riksdag*.

The elections were an endorsement of the country's support for Hansson's 'Home of the People'. The Social Democrats, with their election slogans 'Welfare Policy', 'Remember our poor and our old people', and 'Per Albin again', won 112 seats out of 230 in the Lower House; the Agrarians won 37; the Conservatives only 44 (a loss of 12); the Liberals (the Independent Liberals and the Liberals had reunited in 1934 calling themselves *Folkpartiet*) won 27 seats, an increase of two. There was still no overall majority, however, and after some hesitation Hansson again invited the Agrarian leader, Pehrsson-Bramstorp, to join in a coalition government. This meant that they had a commanding majority in both Houses and could continue their social reform. It also meant that some measure of real power was transferred from the *Riksdag* to *Kanslihuset*, the Swedish Whitehall.

Möller's social policy included a new item from 1936. Gunnar and Alva Myrdal had pointed out in their study *Kris i befolknings-frågan* (The Population Crisis; 1934) that the Swedish birth-rate had become dangerously low and stressed that the working classes must be persuaded to abandon their newly-formed habit of raising their living standards by practising birth control. The means of persuasion would be a system of welfare measures which the Myrdals outlined in their book. In 1935 the government set up a committee to review the situation and it was largely as a result of its recommendations that Möller drew up a bill, passed in 1937, for family allowances and small government loans to married couples setting up house. By the end of the 1930s the birth-rate had risen again, but how much credit the new legislation can take for that is, of course, impossible to establish.

Other social measures introduced in the immediately pre-war years included (in 1937) the extension of legislation on the 8-hour working-day to include farm labourers and (in 1938) the introduction of two weeks paid holiday for all workers and regulations governing the hours worked by merchant seamen.

It was also in this period that the Saltsjöbaden Agreement, which has had such a beneficial effect on Swedish labour relations, was reached. It was essentially an agreement between LO (the Confederation of Trade Unions) and SAF (Swedish Federation of Employers'). Both sides were aware of the government's intention to intervene in labour disputes that were damaging to the nation and it was partly this latent threat that led to what is now referred to as the 'spirit of Saltsjöbaden'. In 1938, at the Baltic resort a few miles out of Stockholm, both sides bound themselves to procedures regulating collective bargaining and industrial action. Despite initial misgivings on all sides, it led to an unparalleled degree of harmony in labour relations and reduced considerably the damage to the national economy caused in the past by strikes and lockouts.

In the period from World War I until the outbreak of World

War II, there seemed hardly any aspect of Swedish life that had not changed. In his autobiography E. Wigforss called the years from 1933 to 1939 the 'Years of Success',[6] and in many ways his boast is justified. Industrial production was rising, wages were improving, there was a growing feeling of security among the workers, children of all classes were assured of a basic education, the humiliating Poor Relief was being replaced by National Insurance.

Even physically the face of Sweden was changing. In the 1933–37 budget the *Riksdag* assigned 23 million *kronor* to housing (18 million for rural and 5 million for urban dwellings) and it became easier to obtain state and local council loans to finance residential building. Sweden was blessed with sufficient land, timber, steel, and good craftsmen and she was uncluttered with dense slum areas found in countries with an earlier industrial development. Architects and planners now put this great potential to effective use and in both town and country, new houses, apartment blocks, and public amenities went up which drew admiring architects from many other countries. A great Stockholm exhibition was staged in 1930 where 'Functionalism' was a key feature of model dwellings and Swedish architects like Gunnar Asplund and Sven Markelius, who had gained international reputations, displayed their art.

Swedish design embraced a variety of objects. At the Paris Expo in 1925 Swedish architects and designers showed off their use of glass, pewter, and textiles. They had a common theme–'Vackrare Vardagsvaror', i.e., 'more beautiful everyday things'–and this too can be seen as part of the democratization process going on in Sweden. Beautifully designed objects were not to be the prerogative of the idle rich, but reasonably priced everyday objects found in every home.

Well-designed public as well as private buildings went up in this period, Ragnar Östberg's City Hall (*Stadshuset*) in Stockholm was completed in 1923; many towns acquired their 'People's House' (*Folkets Hus*), a meeting place where local organizations could meet and entertainment and study courses could be laid on, and their People's Park, a public park often with an open-air theatre. The emphasis was on design, not only of buildings like the Concert Hall in Gothenburg by N. E. Eriksson in 1935, the Museum in Linköping by Ahrbom and Zimdahl in 1937, Bromma Airport by P. Hedqvist in 1936, and the 'Gondolen' Restaurant in Stockholm by O. Thunström in 1935; but also of wholly functional buildings like Trelleborg Public Baths, designed by E. Fehling in 1939, and even the Refuse Incinerating Plant in Lövsta by H. Blom in 1939.

The process of democratization was revealed in many ways. The

[6] E. Wigforss, *Minnen* (Stockholm, 1950–54), III.

development of clothing and shoe factories, coupled with the rise in wages, meant that many more people began to dress well, and the poor members of society were no longer immediately recognized by their homespun suits and cloth caps. Organizations started earlier in the century grew in strength: trade unions, the temperance and Free Church movements, and the consumer co-operatives. The latter organization played a large part in setting high standards in retail trade and seeing that the consumer was fairly treated. Marquis Childs describes (in *Sweden: The Middle Way*) how under the inspired management of Albin Johansson and with the faithful support of its members, the *Kooperativa Förbundet* (KF; the Co-operative Societies) succeeded in breaking price-rings and cartels and preventing excess profiteering. Its first outstanding success was in 1909 when a margarine cartel tried to prevent wholesale merchants from supplying KF. KF bought its own factory, produced its own margarine, and forced the cartel to lower its prices. In 1922, for the same reasons, KF bought the flour-mill *Tre Kronor* just outside Stockholm and broke the flour-milling cartel that had been operating since 1914. Galoshes and electric-light bulbs were other commodities that KF began to manufacture itself in order to break monopolies and prevent excessive profit-making.

The 1920s, and particularly the 1930s, were years of enthusiasm—people of a later, more cynical, generation might even say naïve idealism. Educational facilities became available to an unprecedented degree: the ABF (*Arbetarnes Bildningsförbund*; the Workers' Educational Association), Folk High Schools, correspondence courses, libraries built up by the different organizations—all offered, almost free of charge, sustenance for the enquiring mind from whatever social stratum.

Communications continued to improve during this period: the electrification of the railways was extended; the humble bicycle had already had an effect on the country; and now the motor-car was introduced. The first automobile was used in Gothenburg in 1891 and by 1939 there were 250,000 cars registered. The aeroplane was introduced into Sweden in 1910 and by 1924 there were regular air flights.

Even the remote villages were equipped with electric lights, telephones, and the wireless. National radio transmission was started in 1922 and became a state-controlled monopoly in 1924. Cinemas sprang up in all parts of the country and Swedish films were made from 1907. 1914–1920 were successful years for Swedish film-makers, the great Victor Sjöström and Mauritz Stiller completing some fifty films between them in those years. By 1925 they and their great discovery, Greta Garbo, had gone to Hollywood and the Swedish film industry went through a lean period, although still capable of producing people of world renown—for instance the director Gustaf Molander and the actress Ingrid Bergman, who enjoyed her first major success in the Swedish film *Intermezzo* (1936), starring Gösta Ekman. But whether showing indigenous or imported films, cinemas continued to attract a large public and opened up new worlds to people in remote areas.

The Literary Scene

The literature of the period not only reflected many of the changes in society, but by gaining a stronger voice in the community began to fashion some of those changes. Better education, not just in schools but by adult education movements, increased the potential number of readers, and newspapers began to carry short stories and serialized novels. This whetted the appetite, helped the publishing world, and led to the Swedish best-seller. E. Hj. Linder points out[7] that whereas *Hans Alienus*, a prose-work by Heidenstam, a well-known figure in the 1890s, sold 2,500 copies in 1900 and was considered successful, the novels of G. Hellström, V. Moberg, and O. Hedberg ran into editions of tens of thousands in the 1930s. Swedish professional writers came into being, authors whose works sold well enough for them to live by their pen.

Sweden was a non-belligerent, but the war had an indirect effect on Swedish literature, with Pär Lagerkvist (1891–) conveying in expressionistic verse and drama the desperation of Man caught up in a brutal situation, having lost his religious faith and unable to find a reason for existence. This desperate mood resolved in the 1920s into an acceptance of life, but Lagerkvist, like several of his contemporaries, including Erik Blomberg, Hjalmar Gullberg, and Johannes Edfelt, has continued to express compassion for Man who is born with a need for a faith and yet has had his traditional beliefs swept away.

Swedish writers also responded quickly to the influence of important authors in other countries, for example Kafka, Proust, Gide, D. H. Lawrence, T. S. Eliot, Walt Whitman, Ernest Hemingway; but perhaps the most striking feature of the period was the emergence of working-class authors who described realistically and movingly the conditions they had experienced in their youth. The first generation of these authors, people like Martin Koch (1882–1940), Dan Andersson (1888–1920), and Gustav Hedenvind-Eriksson (1880–1967), led the way. They used a technique reminiscent of Zola and the naturalistic school of writing but were unique in that they had personally experienced the working-class

[7] E. Hj. Linder, *Svensk illustrerad litteraturhistoria* (Stockholm, 1964), V, 2.

conditions that they described. Hedenvind-Eriksson, for instance, had been a forestry worker and plate-layer and knew the physical and emotional hardships endured by the manual workers in the north of Sweden. They were followed by a group of proletarian authors who have become acknowledged masters in their own country and beyond. Vilhelm Moberg, a soldier's son from Småland, based his *Knut Toring* trilogy (1935–39) on his childhood memories. He comes of sturdy Småland peasant stock who for many generations eked out a meagre living on stony smallholdings. Moberg has identified himself with these peasants and portrays them as individuals who have struggled not only for their livelihood but for their independence.

The Swedish peasant's life was difficult, but he was still a rung higher on the ladder than the *statare*, landless agricultural workers paid in kind. They worked long hours, were housed in ramshackle, notoriously bug-ridden cottages, and were grossly exploited by the large landowners. Many of them were illiterate and as a class they were the unrepresented, forgotten underdogs of society. Even they, however, produced imaginative authors whose autobiographical novels laid bare the evils of the system. Ivar Lo-Johansson (1901–), whose parents had been *statare*, had a succession of labouring jobs before becoming a journalist. In 1925 he started a European journey which he financed by writing articles on what he had seen. It was the proletariat version of the Grand Tour, resulting in descriptions of conditions endured by workers in several countries, including coal-miners in England. More than most of his contemporaries Lo-Johansson had a social message. In his novel *Godnatt, Jord* (Goodnight Earth; 1933) and his short stories *Statarna I and II* (1936–37), all based on his childhood experiences, he gives a detailed study of the *statare*, their history and culture, with the ultimate aim of helping to abolish the system.

Jan Fridegård (1897–1968) came from a similar background, was a soldier, an odd-job man, a travelling salesman, and a second-hand bookseller before making his name as an author. The eponymous hero of his autobiographical trilogy, *Lars Hård* (1935–37), a man at odds with society, is the sensitive son of a *statare*, and the story of his development contains bitter satire on society and realistic descriptions of Fridegård's own home background.

Another aspect of the Swedish working classes is shown in the autobiographical tetralogy *Romanen om Olof* (The Novel of Olof; 1934–37) by Eyvind Johnson (1900–), who was born in Boden in the north of Sweden. Johnson too travelled widely and had a variety of menial jobs before finally becoming established as an author. Against a realistic background of the Norrland forests, sawmills, and developing railways he traces the fate of the young boy Olof battling against not only the appalling outward hazards and hardships experienced by Norrland workers but also the pathetic inner problems of puberty. Olof's struggle for independence, for an education, and for human dignity achieved universal stature in Johnson's sensitive study.

The same is true of Harry Martinson's autobiographical work, *Nässlorna blomma* (Flowering Nettles; 1935). Martinson (1904–   ) was very young when his father, a sea captain, died and his mother ran off to America. He experienced the humiliation of being a child 'on the parish' in a country district, farmed out to families prepared to keep him cheaply and forced to participate in the manual work on these farms from an early age. He was, among other things, a farm labourer and a merchant seaman, reading widely when he could, educating himself as he went along; and he made his mark on Swedish literature in 1927 when, together with four other budding authors, he published an anthology of verse called simply *Fem unga* (Five Young Men) and a cycle of his own poems entitled *Spökskepp* (Ghost Ship). In his novel *Flowering Nettles* his raw material is his own childhood experiences. It seems remarkable that in this book, with its inventive language and rich vein of humour, Martinson is able to portray the child Martin, his *alter ego*, without self-pity and to show generosity and to find some goodness in most of the characters.

What all these authors had in common was the ability to project characters in the round – not the faceless proletariat that instilled fear in the hearts of the settled middle classes, but sensitive, often intelligent, human beings who had the right to be treated with some measure of dignity. They helped to change society's attitude to the working classes and it was largely due to them that the pernicious *statare* system was abolished by law in 1945.

Sweden had emerged as a country where the sons of the lowliest farmhands could become respected authors, where a bricklayer's son could rise from messenger boy to Prime Minister, where a foreman's son could work his way up from messenger boy to Managing Director of the Co-operative Society. She seemed to offer a reasonable standard of living to all and unlimited opportunity to those prepared to work their way up. As it happened, she wasn't on the way to becoming an egalitarian paradise, but considering the great changes wrought between 1914 and 1939, it is perhaps not surprising that there were those, both Swedes and foreign visitors, naïve enough to think that she was.

Chapter 6

1939–1945
The Problems of Neutrality

THE SWEDISH SOCIAL DEMOCRATIC PARTY had always been traditionally opposed to huge defence budgets. In the 1920s it chose, like so many others, to put its trust in the League of Nations and to apply its means to the building-up of the welfare state. The Swedes were not blind, however, to the rise of totalitarian forms of government in Europe, to large-scale rearming, and to the resultant threat to world peace and to Western culture generally. Many Swedish writers drew attention in the early 1930s to the gathering forces of evil in Europe. Pär Lagerkvist's prose-work *Bödeln* (The Hangman), published in 1933, the year when Hitler came to power, compares a group of simple-minded superstitious craftsmen in a medieval tavern with sophisticated customers in a modern dance restaurant and demonstrates in a horrifying climax that in his bestiality and worship of violence man has regressed since the Middle Ages. The book castigates violence generally, but it also contains a specific reference to Nazism at one point when 'a young man with an energetic childish face stepped in front of him [i.e., the executioner] and stood to attention with his arm raised high in the air. "Heil!" he said, and stood a moment, rigid'.

In 1934, when journeying through Europe to Greece and Palestine, Lagerkvist wrote an essay entitled *Den knutna näven* (The Clenched Fist) which appeared in *Dagens Nyheter* on 18 March. Here he states that 'the newspapers from Europe stifle me with their stench of blood, confusion, and darkness'. He warned his readers that all that Western culture had struggled for was in danger.

Lagerkvist's weapon as a writer is a Swiftian irony. In 1935 he published *I den tiden* (In Those Days), a collection of short stories set in the future. The story *Det lilla fälttåget* (The Tiny Tots' Campaign) satirizes bitterly both the militaristic training of youth as organized by the Fascist and Nazi movements, and exaggerated nationalism and war hysteria. In *Det märkvärdiga landet* (The Strange Country) a tourist from a well-established totalitarian state describes a visit to a quaint anomalous country called Liberien which has many puzzling features, including freedom of the press, the rights of citizens to develop naturally and express views fearlessly, and the absence of racial prejudice and hatred.

Lagerkvist was not alone in seeing these threats. One of the targets in Hj. Gullberg's cycle of lyric poems *Att övervinna världen* (To Overcome the World; 1937) is Nazism and doctrines based on violence. Eyvind Johnson's novel *Nattövning* (Night Manoeuvres; 1938) demonstrates the way Nazism appeals to, and exploits, the base elements in man and shows that it could happen in Sweden as well as any other country.

Swedish newspapers and periodicals, too, carried criticism of Nazi methods and after 1933 the new German regime often expressed annoyance at the anti-Nazi attitude of the Swedish press.

Nazi sympathizers did exist in Sweden, although the numbers were very small. The Swedish National Youth Union, a Conservative youth group, wanted the Conservative Party to develop closer affinities with Nazism, but the Conservative leader, Lindman, rejected such demands and by 1934 the Youth Movement had broken with the Conservatives. The Swedish National Socialist Party was formed in 1930 under Birger Furugård, who had been active in introducing Nazism into Sweden since 1924, but in the 1932 election it commanded only 15,000 votes. In 1933 the breakaway National Socialist Workers' Party was formed under S. O. Lindholm, but they were defeated in the 1936 elections and faded out of political life. In 1934 three Conservative members of the *Riksdag* formed the National Group in the Lower House, but none of them was re-elected in 1936. Although the National Socialists never won as much as one per cent of the votes cast in general elections, their actions caused a ban on uniforms for political organizations to be introduced in 1933.

Swedish foreign policy in the 1930s shows a gradual realization of the impotence of the League of Nations and an attempt to find some other means of defence which would not encroach on what had become traditional Swedish neutrality. The situation was common to all the Scandinavian countries and from 1932 the Foreign Ministers of Denmark, Norway, and Sweden began to hold regular meetings to consider ideas on Nordic co-operation.

Meanwhile, despite growing scepticism, Sweden did not withdraw from the League and was consequently involved in the series of international crises. Swedish troops helped keep the peace in the Saar during the 1935 referendum. During the war between Italy and Abyssinia an Italian plane bombed a Swedish Red Cross ambulance in December 1935, which roused indignation in Sweden, solicited a forthright remark from her Foreign Minister, Sandler, that the League of Nations had a duty to defend states from aggressors, and led to Sweden's willingness to co-operate in economic sanctions against Italy proposed by the League of Nations.

Hitler had withdrawn from the League in October 1933 and had started rearming with impunity. The Scandinavian countries then learnt with dismay that a naval agreement had been concluded between Britain and Germany in 1935 providing that the German navy would not exceed one-third of the British. Hägglöf writes that 'Hitler could hardly conceal his glee. "The Baltic is now a bottle which we can close", he said in November 1935. "The British cannot exercise any control there. We are the masters of the Baltic" '.[1] When in July 1936 the German reoccupation of the Rhineland elicited nothing more effective than protests from France and Great Britain, it was obvious that the League was shipwrecked. The Scandinavian countries were among several that reasserted their neutrality.

There was at this point interest in some form of a Nordic defence treaty, with Sandler an enthusiastic advocate, but all that emerged was a good example of the Scandinavian paradox. Race, language, and culture bind the countries together emotionally, but geography and international politics often pull in the opposite direction. Sweden felt particularly close ties with Finland and saw possible danger in the Baltic; Norway relied on keeping contacts with the West; Denmark was anxiously viewing Germany's increasing strength, aware that Hitler was not inclined to accept the 1920 Dano-German border as binding. In Lund in 1937 the Danish Prime Minister, Thorvald Stauning, irritably declared that Denmark was not going to be cast in the role of Scandinavia's 'watchdog'. When in May 1939 Hitler offered the Scandinavian countries a pact of non-aggression, Denmark was the only one to accept.

There seemed more hope for a Fenno-Swedish plan for the defence of the Åland Islands, but this plan soon ran into Russian opposition and was abandoned.

When on 1 September 1939 Germany attacked Poland, a European war was obviously inevitable, and in October the kings of Denmark, Norway, and Sweden and the President of Finland publicly declared Scandinavian neutrality; but if this was meant to indicate Scandinavian solidarity, it was an empty gesture, as was very soon proved.

[1] G. Hägglöf, *Britain and Sweden. From the Vikings to the Common Market* (Stockholm, 1966), p. 31.

The Finnish 'Winter War'

Russia, which, with the signing of the pact with Germany in August 1939, had a free hand in the eastern Baltic, demanded that the Finns withdraw from the border area to allow a more effective Russian defence of the approaches to Leningrad. Finland refused to give way and looked to Scandinavia for help, but direct military aid was refused.

Sweden was in a quandary. By 1936 she had started to rearm, but on a very modest scale, and although by 1938 when war over Czechoslovakia seemed inevitable the *Riksdag* had approved a considerable increase in the defence budget, both civil and military authorities knew that P. A. Hansson's public statement in 1939 that 'our defence is in good order' was mere whistling in the dark. Even so, when Russia attacked Finland on 30 November 1939 and the Finns appealed directly for help, many Swedes wanted to go to Finland's defence. A National Coalition Government was set up in December 1939 under the premiership of P. A. Hansson, with Wigforss (who had helped build up the welfare state and had opposed all Sandler's efforts to deviate from strict neutrality) as Finance Minister. Sandler had resigned over what he considered Sweden's betrayal of Finland, particularly in the Åland question, and his place as Foreign Minister was taken by Christian Günther, a professional diplomat. All the other political parties except the Communists were represented in the Cabinet.

Sweden never came closer to entering willingly the arena of war than at this period. There was strong pro-Finnish sentiment in the country, especially among military leaders, the Conservatives, and academics, but evident too in most walks of life. In the end Sweden declared herself not neutral but a non-belligerent, sending money and shipments of arms to Finland, arranging credit for her, allowing Swedish volunteers to fight for Finland, but not entering the war officially.

The Finns fought a heroic but desperately uneven battle and by February 1940 could obviously no longer hold out alone. They made a dramatic plea to the Swedish government, which sparked off renewed pro-Finnish agitation in Sweden, with the slogan 'Finland's cause is ours'. A Finland Committee and an organization called Scandinavia's Freedom (*Nordens Frihet*), supported by many leading Swedish figures (including the writer Eyvind Johnson; the historian Nils Ahnlund; Ragnar Casparsson, head of the Trade Union information service; and Sandler, the former Foreign Minister), organized lecture tours, collected funds, won support for Finland, and roundly criticized the Swedish government. The

1 Contemporary sketch by Konrad showing the scene outside
Riddarhuset in Stockholm on 7 December 1865 when the Nobles
accepted by 361 votes to 294 the Parliamentary Reform Bill

2 Contemporary sketch by O. A. Mankell and A. G. Hafström
showing the ceremonial unveiling of the statue of Karl XII in
Stockholm on 30 November 1868

3 King Oscar II (1829–1907) and his queen, Sofia of Nassau (1836–1913), in 1907 – their golden wedding year

[*Opposite*]

4 The future King Gustav VI Adolf (1882–   ) in 1904

5 Crown Princess Margaret (1882–1920), first wife of Gustav VI Adolf, at a garden party in 1910

6 King Gustav V (1858–1950) delivering his famous Palace Yard Speech in February 1914. Crown Prince Gustav Adolf is standing on the king's left

7 Hjalmar Branting, the great Social Democrat leader, addressing a May Day crowd

8 Rickard Sandler (*third from left*) seen with cabinet colleagues after tendering his resignation in 1926. On his right is Per Albin Hansson and on his left Östen Undén

9 The Stockholm Conference of 1939. *Left to right*: Haakon VII of Norway; President Kallio of Finland; Gustav V of Sweden; Christian X of Denmark

10 Prince Gustav Adolf (1906–47) with his bride Princess Sibylla of Saxe-Coburg-Gotha (1908–   ) on their arrival in Stockholm after their marriage in 1932

[*Opposite*]

11 A patrol of Swedish army machine-gunners on skis in 1940

12 An armed Swedish soldier watches as German soldiers of the Engelbrecht division (transported in 106 trains) board a train while proceeding from Norway to Finland via Sweden in 1941

14 One of the Balt conscripts being dragged by force to Trelleborg in January 1946 when the refugees were returned to Russia despite vigorous public protest

13 Count Folke Bernadotte (1895–1948) with his wife (the former Estelle Romaine Manville of New York) in 1945

16 Colonel Stig Wennerstrom, arrested in 1963 on charges of spying for the Russians

15 Tage Erlander (*left*), Social Democrat Prime Minister, with Bertil Ohlin, leader of the Liberals, in 1954

18 Prime Minister Olof Palme with his wife on a visit to 10 Downing Street in April 1970

17 King Gustav VI Adolf and Queen Louise (1889–1965) in the grounds of Sofeiro Palace in southern Sweden

19 A poor quarter of Stockholm about the end of the First World War

22 Västgöta Bridge in Uppsala

[*Opposite*]
20 Slussen in Stockholm, a focal point connecting Lake Mälaren with the Baltic by water and Gamla Staden with Södermalm by land.

21 Underground heating being laid in the streets of Uppsala

23 A procession on its way to the American Embassy in Stockholm to protest against the Vietnam War

24 A modern student hostel of Uppsala University with the Cathedral in the background

25 View of Lake Mälaren showing the reed fringe associated with land uplift and sedimentation

26 The forestry industry in northern Sweden. Logs to be carried in spring to the sawmill

27 Kiruna, Sweden's northernmost city. In the background is Luossavaara mountain where iron-ore is mined

government stood by its policy of non-intervention, however, realizing that active participation could mean an open conflict not just with Russia but with Russia's ally, Germany.

For once Per Albin Hansson seemed to misjudge the mood of the people and gave such a cool account of his government's decision that he angered even the non-activists, and King Gustav V felt obliged to intervene by expressing his own views publicly. These views were basically the same as Hansson's, but he expressed them more eloquently and helped to pacify public opinion.

Finland then turned to Britain and France, who requested permission to send troops to Finland via Narvik and Lapland. Both Norway and Sweden refused, for both rightly feared that the Western Allies were more interested in preventing iron-ore mined in Lapland from reaching Germany than in helping Finland. These events had in any case little bearing on the 'Winter War', for the Finns capitulated a few days later and the Allies would have been too late to affect the outcome of the war.

With the help of Swedish mediation, the Peace of Moscow was signed by Russia and Finland on 12 March 1940. Finland lost a lot of territory to the Russians. Ivar Anderson, who was during this period editor of *Svenska Dagbladet*, a member of the Committee on Foreign Affairs, and a supporter of the Finnish cause, writes in his memoirs that

> the Soviet government's treatment of a defeated Finland did not surprise us; it was what we had expected, but right to the last had hoped to prevent by a fairly firm and bold Swedish attitude. The knowledge of the sacrifices we had made through the contribution of Swedish volunteers and material and economic aid could not at that moment dull the feeling that we had betrayed our duty to our brother country and to our own cause.[2]

Anderson's words are a comment on Sweden's role throughout World War II. Not being strong enough to engage in direct action, the Swedes offered what they could in material and diplomatic aid and emerged unscathed, but with an undefined feeling of guilt.

Sweden Isolated

The next blow Scandinavia sustained followed closely on the Peace of Moscow. Stockholm had been picking up warning signals from Berlin in the first week of April and it was realized that something was being planned in the Baltic area. The information was passed on to Norway, but was not taken seriously. Denmark too

[2] I. Anderson, *Från det nära förflutna* (Stockholm, 1969), p. 35.

I

had been warned of an impending German invasion, but had taken no action. Ivar Anderson tells us that 'Günther appeared calm as usual. The alarming German measures possibly indicated an attack on England via Holland and Denmark'.[3] The Foreign Minister was wrong: on 9 April Denmark and Norway were invaded. Denmark capitulated immediately, while the Norwegians made a desperate heroic stand; but by early summer they too were forced to surrender. Again Sweden declared her neutrality, but with Finland in the shadow of Russia and Denmark and Norway occupied by the Germans, her chance of remaining neutral seemed slender. She had already disappointed the Finns, and there now began a series of events that soured relations between Sweden and Norway.

King Håkon and his government had left Oslo before the Germans captured it and the Norwegian Foreign Minister, Halvdan Koht, enquired whether King Håkon, Crown Prince Olav, and members of the Norwegian government could enter Sweden, be allowed to move freely there, and return to Norway when circumstances permitted it. The Swedish government decided that to allow the Norwegians to conduct their government from Sweden would certainly provoke Germany, and so reluctantly gave Koht a negative reply. The exiled government made London its headquarters instead. Matters were not improved either when Carl J. Hambro, the President of the Norwegian *Storting*, arrived in Stockholm to solicit Swedish aid for Norway and was prevented by the Swedish Foreign Office from broadcasting. Hambro, a proud and influential man, never forgot the incident and was caustic about Sweden for many years to come.

There is still speculation on Hitler's decision to invade Norway and Denmark but not Sweden.[4] The key is almost certainly the iron-ore in Lapland. Denmark was a stepping-stone to Norway; Narvik was important because the ore was shipped from there and extreme measures were necessary to prevent it from falling into the hands of the Allies. Sweden was effectively encircled and her shipping was at the mercy of Germany. Provided she co-operated by continuing to supply Germany with the necessary iron-ore, there was nothing to gain by invading her and something to lose, for even if Sweden offered only a minimum amount of resistance, the iron-ore supply would be cut off for a while.

[3] ibid., p. 37.
[4] A committee set up by the Danish parliament after the war included in its report a German document dated Berlin, 26 February 1940, dealing with 'Politische und Verwaltungsmassnahmen bei einer Besetzung Norwegens, Dänemarks und Schwedens' and with a subsection 'Schweden. Hafen Lulea und Bahn Lulea-Narvik müssen sicher zur Verfügung stehen. Sonst keine Besetzung'. On 1 March 1940 Sweden was crossed out. (The document is reproduced in C. Wahlgren's *På skilda fronter* (Malmö, 1970), p. 80.)

The Swedish government assessed the situation realistically and decided there was no point in indulging in heroics, but that did not absolve them from criticism from the Norwegians, the British, and indeed many of their own countrymen. While the Norwegians kept up their organized resistance to the Germans, the Swedish government rejected German demands for the transit of troops through Sweden to Norway. One hardly envied the Swedish minister in Berlin, Arvid Richert, his task, for he was called to the German headquarters in Belgium and subjected to Ribbentrop's direct threats against Sweden. By May the Swedes allowed what they called 'humanitarian' transport (mainly medical personnel and supplies) to pass through Sweden to German troops in Narvik and some 800 German sailors, civilians, and wounded soldiers to return to Germany by the same route.

After the Finnish 'Winter War', during which Swedish troops had been called up and massed along the border, the Swedish army had been demobilized again and despite pleas at the beginning of April by the chief of the Swedish armed forces, General Olof Thörnell, to start rearming quickly, the government had refused to act, basically because, like Norway and Denmark, they did not believe Germany would invade. After 9 April they saw the wisdom of Thörnell's demands, but by then were afraid of provoking Germany, who had insisted that Sweden should not start mobilizing her forces. The operation had therefore to be done stealthily without German knowledge. Certainly in the first few weeks of the German invasion of Scandinavia there was little hope that Sweden would have been able to withstand a German attack for long.

By June Norway's resistance had collapsed, France had capitulated, Holland and Belgium were in German hands, and Britain's ability to withstand a German invasion seemed in question. Sweden was completely hemmed in by German–Soviet forces and could see no sign that the situation would be likely to improve. Swedish memoirs from this period by such leading figures as Ernst Wigforss and Ivar Anderson stress the psychological effect on the Swedish coalition government of the unbroken series of German victories. When at this juncture Germany stepped up her demands for permission to send troops and supplies to Norway through Sweden, there was little resistance. There were rumours that Halifax, the British Foreign Minister, was planning to negotiate with the Germans and that he was advocating 'commonsense and not bravado', a motto guaranteed to appeal to the Swedish mentality. Only Sandler and Undén on the Foreign Affairs Committee voted against compliance, the rest bowing to circumstances, and so began the notorious 'transit traffic' which was to last for three bitter years.

Munitions and a continuous stream of uniformed but unarmed German soldiers travelled by rail from southern to northern Norway via the provinces of Värmland and Dalarna, and Norrland. It is calculated that some 2 million men were transported that way.

The British government and the Norwegian government-in-exile sharply criticized this deviation from strict neutrality and so, to the obvious embarrassment of the government, did several articulate Swedes, including Torgny Segerstedt, editor of the Gothenburg paper *Göteborgs Handels- och Sjöfartstidning*, who bitterly attacked the pusillanimous way the government gave in to Germany. The weekly journal *Nordens Frihet* (Scandinavia's Freedom), run largely by academics in Stockholm, Ture Nerman's weekly journal *Trots allt* (Despite all), and *Arbetaren* (The Worker), a syndicalist publication, were all highly critical of the government. *Stockholms-Tidningen*, owned and edited by Ivar Kreuger's brother Torsten, and *Aftonbladet* advocated the opposite view, demanding increased co-operation with Germany, but Swedes holding such views were in the minority and became even fewer in number as reports reached Sweden of Nazi atrocities, especially in Norway. In Stockholm during the war the so-called 'Tisdagsklubben' (i.e., Tuesday Club), with Amelie Posse at its centre, was a meeting-place for Swedes who wanted to express their disapproval of Nazism and the way the Swedish government had given way to German demands. The various people who attended did not in any way form a homogeneous group and Tisdagsklubben had little political significance, but it at least gave a measure of release in the worst days of the war.

As a neutral country Sweden was something of a listening-post and a meeting-place for the belligerents. Among the most notable visitors were members of the German opposition, representatives of the 'other Germany' who cherished the hope that if by some means Hitler and his leading Nazis could be removed, there would then be a possibility of negotiating a peace settlement with the Allies. Many of these Germans were clergymen, and several of them went to the Nordic Ecumenical Institute at Sigtuna, the idyllic small town half-way between Stockholm and Uppsala, where the Director, Harry Johansson, was able to help them with contacts. It was there in May 1942 that the bishop of Chichester, Dr George Bell, met the German theologians Dr Dietrich Bonhoeffer and Dr Hans Schönfeld, Director of the Study Department of the World Council of Churches. They told Dr Bell about a strong, organized opposition movement inside Germany planning to bring down the Hitler regime, and asked him to convey the information to the British government. It would obviously have strengthened their hand if they could have been given a promise of a peace settlement with the Allies once Hitler was removed, and on their behalf Dr Bell pressed the point in England, but received little encouragement.

Several members of the German opposition visited Sweden in 1942 and 1943, desperately trying to transmit information and to find out the latest attitude of the Allies. A frequent visitor was Adam von Trott zu Solz, a member of the German Foreign Office who, by virtue of his position, was able to travel widely without arousing Ribbentrop's suspicions. He was an active opponent of the Hitler regime and so, it later transpired, were several members of the German Legation in Stockholm.

Another frequent visitor was Helmut von Moltke who, like Adam von Trott, was an active member of the Kreisau Circle (whose name derives from Moltke's Kreisau estate), a resistance group which had plans to set up an alternative form of government after the Nazis had been removed and which was in contact with other opponents of Hitler, including Dr Karl Goerdeler, former burgomaster of Leipzig.

Through Harry Johansson and the Sigtuna Institute several meetings were arranged. In December 1942 Dr Eugen Gerstenmaier and Dr Hans Schönfeld met the Swedish bishop John Cullberg and gave an account of the work of the German resistance which included many clergymen, both Protestant and Catholic. They were far from encouraged by what they had learnt about the Allies' call for unconditional surrender. Harry Johansson had received a letter from Dr Bell describing the attitude of the English Church, but it contained little comfort for the German opposition.

In January 1943 a further meeting took place, this time with the bishop of Stockholm, Manfred Björkquist, the Norwegian artist Henrik Sørensen, and Lt-Col. Theodor Steltzer present. Steltzer was attached to the German army in Norway and was dismayed at the brutality of the Nazis there. Like many of the German opposition he was a religious man and a patriot, and wanted to save his country both from Nazism and from destruction by the Allies.

Towards the end of January Sir Walter (later Lord) Monckton was in Stockholm, and at the British Legation he was able to meet Swedes who, through their Sigtuna contacts, were able to put forward the hopes and fears of the German opposition, but it was in that same month that Franklin D. Roosevelt and Winston Churchill met at Casablanca and declared that their aim was 'unconditional surrender'. In March the bishop of Chichester addressed the House of Lords and gave an account of the work of the German opposition. Although he was given a mildly sympathetic hearing, the government maintained its view that with or without Hitler, Germany must first be forced to capitulate before any peace negotiations could commence.

Despite this discouraging response the German opposition continued to hope for peace terms and to use Stockholm as a sounding-board. Moltke, von Trott, and Gerstenmaier all visited Stockholm during 1943. So too did Harold Nicolson, who was the guest of the British minister in Stockholm, Sir Victor Mallet, for a week in the autumn, but he bore the same message: total surrender and only then peace negotiations.

When the plot to assassinate Hitler misfired in the summer of 1944 several of the Germans who had visited Stockholm were among those convicted of complicity. Adam von Trott and Helmut von Moltke were both executed, Steltzer was condemned to death, but saved by the mediation of Felix Kersten, while Gerstenmaier was sentenced to six years imprisonment, but was freed by the Allies in 1945.

The German Foreign Office took a great interest in the Swedish press, and articles critical of Nazism, conditions in German-occupied countries, and especially of the Führer were reported by the German Legation in Stockholm and quickly led to official complaints and often implied threats. Hitler was excessively sensitive to adverse criticism and Gustav V himself, who was opposed to anti-semitism but not to Germany, tried on occasion to pacify him. The Swedish government felt compelled to introduce censorship and confiscated several editions of newspapers felt to carry offensive material. The offence was almost invariably against Germany. The frequency of these confiscations forms an interesting comment on German fortunes in the war:

1 September 1939–31 August 1940	17
1 September 1940–31 August 1941	64
1 September 1941–31 August 1942	178
1 September 1942–6 November 1943	60

After 6 November 1943 they ceased altogether[5]

If one discounts the unrelieved tension of living for almost four years on a powder-keg, Sweden fared much better in the Second than in the First World War. Her agricultural policy of the 1930s had already led to a greater degree of self-sufficiency, and several goods imported until the outbreak of the war began to be manufactured at home (e.g., fertilizers and combustible oils); substitutes were found for other commodities hitherto imported, cellulose, for example, replacing woollen fabrics and fodder. Distribution was much better organized too. Effective government control was

---

[5] Quoted in L. Furhoff and H. Hederberg, *Dagspressen i Sverige* (Stockholm, 1968), p. 57.

quickly introduced, a new Department of Economics being established in 1939 to control industry and agriculture. A fair system of rationing was introduced soon after the outbreak of the war, first of petrol in 1939 and subsequently in 1941 of coffee, tea, bread, bacon, and fats.

Even so, Sweden was still dependent on overseas trade which in effect meant dependence on Germany's goodwill after 9 April. Fortunately Germany needed Swedish iron-ore, timber products, and ball bearings, and was prepared to send fertilizers, solid fuel, synthetic rubber, and industrial products in return. Britain was not unsympathetic towards Sweden and had, moreover, an interest in keeping Sweden independent, for she derived essential products such as ball bearings and much information from Swedish sources. Gunnar Hägglöf, when Swedish ambassador in London, called on Winston Churchill in 1953 to inform him that he had been awarded the Nobel prize for literature. He quotes Churchill as saying on that occasion

> you were in a dangerous position. A very dangerous position. But you did right. You kept out of the war and you mobilised. Yes that was right. I did not press you too strongly. I didn't wish to. I understood your situation.[6]

Agreement was reached with Great Britain and Germany towards the end of 1940 to allow a number of Swedish merchant ships on specified routes to ply between Gothenburg and non-belligerent countries, including Latin America. This traffic was invaluable to Sweden's hard-pressed paper and pulp industries and also assured her supplies of rice, coffee, grain, cotton, and mineral oil. A State Commission was set up in Sweden to control prices and to align wages with the cost of living. This was taken further in 1942 when a price and wages freeze was imposed. Thus Sweden was spared the effect of the excessive profiteering and inflation that characterized World War I.

Gösta Bagge, leader of the Conservative Party and a member of the coalition government, said in a May Day speech in 1940: 'Like the hedgehog we have rolled ourselves up in the face of danger with our spikes facing in all directions', which seemed to sum up the mood of the country. The hedgehog was tempted to pop its head out in the summer of 1941 when Hitler changed the course of the war by turning on his former ally and attacking Russia. The Finns at this point sought German help in moving the Fenno-Russian border forced upon them in 1940. Once more Finland was at war and sought Swedish aid, and this time the situation was even more complicated

[6] Hägglöf, op. cit., p. 37.

than before, since the general Swedish mood was indubitably anti-Nazi. About one thousand volunteers went to Finland, but there was little genuine enthusiasm for the Finnish cause in this phase of the war.

Germany made new demands on Sweden in 1941, requesting above all that 18,000 men, the so-called Engelbrecht Division, be allowed to proceed from Norway to Finland via Sweden. Finland supported Germany's request. There was dissent in the Cabinet, with four Social Democrats, including Wigforss, unwilling to concur, but Günther and Per Albin Hansson convinced that Sweden had no choice. King Gustav V himself was said to have stated most strongly that he would not be associated with action likely to drag Sweden into a war with Germany, that he therefore wanted to comply with the German request, and was prepared to 'accept the consequences of his decision'. Per Albin Hansson interpreted this as a threat to abdicate, although it is doubtful whether that was what the king meant by 'the consequences'. It was finally decided that the Engelbrecht Division would be allowed transit, but that Germany was to be told categorically that it was 'a once only concession'. Despite their bravery the Finns once more found themselves in a hopeless situation. They had linked their fortunes to those of Germany and by 1944 the outcome was obvious. There was a real threat that Finland would be swallowed up by Russia like the other Baltic states, but partly through Swedish diplomacy a separate armistice was arranged between Helsinki and Moscow in September 1944. Finland remained independent but had to pay an enormous indemnity, which to her great credit she succeeded in doing.

As Germany's position deteriorated, her stranglehold on Sweden slackened and the threat to Swedish neutrality began to come from the other side. The agreement with Germany to allow German transit traffic was cancelled in August 1943. By early 1944 the United States ordered Sweden to go further than this and to cease trading with Germany and thereby prolonging the war. The supply of Swedish ball bearings to Germany was a particularly sore point, for after intensive bombings of Schweinfurt in Germany in October 1943 the Allies were convinced that they had crippled Germany's own manufacture of these vital components and that they had found her Achilles heel. By spring 1944 America and Britain were exerting enormous pressure on the Swedish government and on SKF, the Swedish Ball Bearing Company, to stop all supplies to Germany. America was even said to have hinted that the SKF plant in Gothenburg might be bombed 'by accident' if exports to Germany continued. The Swedes were in a dilemma, for even though Germany was by this time hardly likely to win the war, she was still capable of causing Sweden great hardship. They had also to consider the ethical question of their neutrality. If the matter had been dealt with more discreetly, the Swedish government might well have phased out supplies to Germany fairly quickly and quietly, but the Allies caused such a furore that international attention was focused on the whole affair and it became difficult for anyone to back down. However, trade between Sweden and Germany was reduced during the second half of 1944 and ceased altogether by the beginning of 1945.

The Flow of Refugees

In the last phase of the war thousands of refugees were able to benefit from Swedish neutrality. Norwegian aid, a scheme for feeding Norwegian children and aged, had been in operation since 1942. The following year the Nazis had hardened their policy towards Denmark. In the contest between the Himmler and Ribbentrop factions among the German authorities, as Glyn Jones points out,[1] the former gained the upper hand and the order came that Danish Jews were to be deported. The decision was leaked in advance, the Danish Jews were forewarned, and most of them escaped before the German arrests were made. They were hidden by friends and smuggled across to Sweden in what became a well-organized operation. Of some 7,000 Jews in Denmark it was estimated that well over 6,500 escaped that way. In all about 11,000 Danes fled to Sweden in the autumn of 1943 and by 1945 the number had swelled to 15,000. Similarly, as German atrocities against academics, trade unionists, and other intractable elements in Norway increased, the smuggling of Norwegian refugees across the border into Sweden which had been going on to some extent since April 1940, was intensified and the number of Norwegians in Sweden reached 36,000 by 1945.

Unofficially Sweden was active in other ways, too, in helping Norway and Denmark. From 1943 many of the Norwegian and Danish refugees in Sweden were given what was termed 'police training', but was in fact ordinary military instruction. Weapons and other goods were also smuggled from Sweden to the resistance movements in Norway and Denmark.

There was a point beyond which Sweden would not go, however. In February 1945 the Norwegian government-in-exile contacted the Swedes concerning what would now obviously be the final phase of the Norwegian occupation and expressed their fears that the retreating Germans might in desperation create havoc. By April they were asking Sweden if she would be prepared to take military counter-measures amounting in effect to total mobilization, a request

---

[1] W. Glyn Jones: *Denmark* (London, 1970), p. 177.

which was shortly afterwards made by the Danes too. The Swedes rejected the request, partly because they were afraid it might provoke the Germans and partly because they had reason to believe that the German forces in Norway would lay down their arms without any trouble when Germany officially surrendered. This view was based on information gleaned a few weeks previously when Himmler had tried to ascertain via Sweden what possibility remained for a peace settlement with the Allies. Even so, Swedish plans were drawn up for military action in Norway and Denmark if it were to prove necessary and the Swedish Prime Minister let the Germans know that the Swedes would not stand idly by if their Scandinavian neighbours were subjected to pointless destruction. In the event, the German surrender in Norway and Denmark did not realize the fears expressed by the Norwegians and Danes.

When Finland withdrew from the war after the truce with Russia in 1944, German troops were evacuated and began to return from northern Finland to Norway, ravaging as they went. Fifty-five thousand Finns with 32,000 cattle fled from Finland to Sweden during the autumn of 1944. The Russians advanced into the Baltic states at this time and well over 30,000 refugees from these states found their way into Sweden too.

As the German Reich crumbled and the fate of many captives lay in the hands of a few desperate men, Sweden did what she could to save Scandinavian lives. Her most successful spokesman was Count Folke Bernadotte, who won over Himmler, not so much apparently as Vice-Chairman of the Swedish Red Cross but in his personal capacity as the nephew of Gustav V. Seven thousand Danes and Norwegians were assembled at a camp near Hamburg and then allowed home via Sweden. Other nationalities also benefited and in all about 19,000 people, including Jews and Frenchwomen, escaped the chaos of Germany by this means.

An Aliens' Commission had been set up in Sweden in 1944 to deal with the refugee problem and by the end of the war it was estimated that there were over 300,000 refugees in Sweden who were all cared for. Some of the refugees who reached Sweden were German soldiers who had fought on the Eastern front, and these were returned to the Russians without any complications arising. One group which arrived from the Baltic states in May 1945, however, caused considerable friction. There were seven Estonians, eleven Lithuanians, and 149 Latvians, and they arrived in German uniforms and were said to have fought against the Russians, who now demanded their return. The refugees protested that they had been forced to enlist (some were only boys) and begged for asylum. The king of Sweden sent a telegram to Stalin asking for clemency, but this was refused. By

November the Swedish government announced its irrevocable decision that the 167 men concerned would be handed over to the Russians. This led the internees to protest by hunger strikes, self-inflicted wounds, and even suicide. On 25 January 1946, when they were taken on board a Russian vessel at Trelleborg, a Latvian lieutenant made his final dramatic protest by stabbing himself in the neck and bleeding to death on the quay rather than be taken to the Soviet Union.

The affair became something of a political scandal, and it is still brought up periodically, most recently in a 'novel' by the Swedish writer Per Olov Enquist called *Legionärerna* (The Legionaries; 1968). The affair is perhaps a microcosm of Sweden's role in World War II. The lives of well over 30,000 Balts had been saved, but because the Swedish government bowed to Russian demands–partly it must be said because they feared the Russians might again invade Finland– 146 were abandoned, the remaining twenty-one having either died or being considered too ill or weak to be transported. From a purely legal aspect the government was perhaps justified and seemed to have little choice, but public opinion was outraged and the Swedish conscience is still uneasy. Whatever the official attitude, one encounters occasionally remarks in casual contexts that show a guilty conscience–such as, for instance, in Hans Krook's article on Estonia in *Svenska Dagbladet* on 19 September 1971, where he states that 'We in Sweden feel a sense of shame generally as soon as the Baltic is brought up in one form or another. A heavy feeling of shame has also lain over the whole complicated question of the handing over of the Balts'.

The Political Situation

Party politics played little part in Swedish life during most of the war years and the National Coalition Government established in December 1939 remained in office until July 1945. Per Albin Hansson symbolized Swedish neutrality and enjoyed the confidence of the nation. Ivar Anderson, a Conservative member of parliament and editor of a Conservative newspaper, writes quite freely that

indisputably Per Albin Hansson was through his position in the Labour movement and his political talents the man the country needed in the post of Prime Minister. He had authority and inspired confidence . . . I, together with most Conservatives, looked upon Per Albin Hansson during the war years as a great national asset.[8]

[8] Anderson, op. cit., p. 162.

This was borne out in the 1940 elections when the Social Democrats under Per Albin Hansson took 58 per cent of the votes to the Lower House and had a majority in the Upper House. It was considered a vote of confidence in Hansson as leader of a coalition.

One result of the coalition, the absence of an organized parliamentary opposition, plus the emergency situation caused by the war, was that many important decisions were taken outside the *Riksdag*, which consequently lost much of its authority. The Cabinet made vital decisions on foreign policy, while all important economic questions were decided through negotiations between government and the important economic organizations in the country. The rights of the citizen were infringed in many ways: the government had set up a secret police organization (*säkerhetstjänsten*) which collected secret information on several activities and kept some political organizations under constant surveillance; the press was censored; taxes both direct and indirect were increased, purchase tax was introduced in 1942, prices and wages were frozen, and rents controlled. There was a Board of Information which in the interests of national security was not above manipulating public opinion rather than informing the public. The annoyance and fears registered at the growing power of the government indicated the degree of free speech and genuine democracy the Swedes had come to take for granted. Official reports which were known to be false angered the public— such as, for example, a news item that a German plane had crashed into a mountain in the province of Bohuslän in 1940 when in fact hundreds of witnesses had seen it being shot down by Swedish anti-aircraft guns because it was violating Swedish territory. Most Swedes sympathized with the unpleasant measures the government often had to take, but they were indignant at what seemed an obvious attempt to misinform. It was this trend as much as the yielding to German pressures that incensed people like Torgny Segerstedt.

By 1944, when the international situation was no longer so acute, the coalition was beginning to chafe and several cabinet ministers of different political parties began to express the need for a new form of government. The 1944 election showed too that the public was beginning to think in terms of party politics again, for the Social Democrats lost the absolute majority they had gained in 1940, although they held exactly half the seats in the Lower House. It was with a sense of relief on all sides that a Social Democratic government was formed under Per Albin Hansson in July 1945 and political life could return to normality.

The problems confronting the new government were real enough even though Sweden was not faced with the tremendous task of building on ruins, as were so many European countries. The *Riksdag* had approved in 1942 a five-year defence plan and embarked on it at full speed. Aircraft and tanks were developed and a large part of Swedish industry had been turned over to the manufacture of munitions; there was an acute housing shortage; the national debt, despite the imposition of the defence tax, increased income tax, and purchase tax, was enormous. From the beginning of the war to 1945 it had risen from 4,000 to 11,000 million *kronor*. The Social Democrats, while saddled with these problems, wanted to get on with the furthering of their social policies, while the opposition wanted to restore the freedom of the individual and to prevent any further erosion of it by state control.

Literature of the 1940s

Once Lagerkvist and several writers of his generation had found their fears to be well founded they tended to adopt an exhortatory style, encouraging their readers not to lose heart or their belief in the ultimate victory of a humane civilization. Eyvind Johnson, who had been extremely active in the 'Finland's cause is ours' campaign, depicts in his novel *Krilon* (1941–43) a Stockholm craftsman called Krilon and his opposition group in World War II. This ironic, allegorical, parodying, and very complex work criticizes doctrines based on violence and states Johnson's genuine belief in democracy. Harry Martinson had gone even further than Johnson and had enlisted as a volunteer in the Finnish 'Winter War'. His literary contribution to the cause was *Verklighet till döds* (Reality to Death; 1940), containing impressions from the front line and a severe criticism of the industrial giant Russia crushing her small Finnish neighbour. Vilhelm Moberg's novel *Rid i natt* (Ride this night; 1941; filmed in 1942) has an historical setting, dealing with the Swedish peasants' revolt against their overlords in the 1650s, but its central theme is man's struggle for freedom against repression, and the immediate popularity of the novel showed that the public were quick to see the parallels with the contemporary situation. Pär Lagerkvist himself published two cycles of poems during the war, *Sång och Strid* (Song and Strife; 1940) and *Hemmet och stjärnan* (Home and the Star; 1942), which contain stirring patriotic invocations, the *patria* being Scandinavia rather than just Sweden. The first of these was sold surreptitiously in Norway during the occupation and was said to have afforded many Norwegians strength and comfort.

The generation of authors that began their literary careers round about the beginning of the war presented in their work a much more disillusioned and pessimistic world. They had been born too late to participate in the development of the Labour movement, the campaign for universal suffrage, and all the other enthusiastic movements that had helped to bring about a more egalitarian society. Many had had left-wing sympathies, but after Russia's attack on Finland, Stalin's purges in the 1930s, and the occupation of the Baltic states their faith in communism was shattered. With mounting frustration they saw Sweden standing impotently by while violence was perpetrated all around. They also began to lose faith in their own government as more control and censorship was introduced and some of them became syndicalists, wanting a new society but one without state power. Their views were expressed in their journal *Arbetaren*.

The release gained from action, the relief derived from being able to take positive action however dangerous, was denied to these young Swedes. Their war was a war of nerves, of monotonous months guarding borders but not being allowed to act; of a black-out literally and, as censorship of the press increased, metaphorically; of trains rattling through Sweden by night containing representatives of a regime they hated and yet could not combat. The Swedish watchword during the war, *tystnad, vaksamhet, samhällsanda* (i.e., silence, vigilance, community spirit), suggests the isolation and introverted tendencies in Sweden at this period.

Many of the young intellectuals were admirers of Albert Camus, Jean-Paul Sartre, and French existentialists. They were also drawn to the Danish philosopher Kierkegaard and his views on the concept *Angst* which seemed to them the condition that allowed man to be aware of his spiritual existence and of life. Kafka's work, too, was popular among them.

These writers, who were given the name *Fyrtiotalisterna* (i.e., The Forties Group) attempted to open man's eyes to his desperate position. They were notoriously difficult to interpret, often employing in their lyric verse the imagery of the French surrealists and of T. S. Eliot.

The writer who epitomized the '40s Group was the playwright and prosewriter Stig Dagerman (1923–54). From 1941 he contributed to the syndicalist paper *Arbetaren*. The theme of his first novel *Ormen* (The Snake; 1945) is fear and the means of conquering it by admitting its power. In *De dömdas ö* (The Island of the Dead; 1946) he evokes a nightmarish, terrifying landscape and propounds his concept of *Angst*, that fear must be kept alive, as it is man's only means of proving that he is living. His play *Skuggen av Mart* (The Shadow of Mart; 1948) makes a case for the anti-hero, the man who has always been pushed into the background by the hero and who struggles for the right to be afraid. Dagerman was extremely prolific for five years, but then went through a period of literary sterility that led to his suicide.

Other leading writers of the period–Karl Vennberg (1910–   ), Lars Ahlin (1915–   ), and Erik Lindegren (1910–68; known to operagoers for his libretto *Aniara*, based on Harry Martinson's space poem of that name)–have also expressed the same desperate determination not to accept comforting illusions, but to see the human condition as it is, even though, as Vennberg expressed it in one of his poems:

> to live is to choose
> o blessed choice
> between the indifferent
> and the impossible.

Unlike Dagerman, however, they did not take the situation to its awful ultimate conclusion, but have gradually learnt to resign themselves to life. This too is no doubt in many ways a reflection of the social and political climate. Tensions relaxed after 1945 despite the Iron Curtain, Sweden became part of the mainstream of Western civilization again, and there were once more grounds for optimism.

Chapter 7

1945–
The Social Democrats' Harvest

WITH WORLD WAR II at an end and the national crisis over, the reason for a coalition government had disappeared, and a purely Social Democratic government was formed in July 1945. For a brief spell there seemed a preponderance of familiar faces in the top posts, for Per Albin Hansson remained Prime Minister, Gustav Möller continued as Minister of Social Affairs, and Ernst Wigforss remained Finance Minister. The wartime Foreign Minister, Christian Günther, was replaced by Östen Undén, but this was hardly an innovation, for Undén had held this post in Branting's third ministry and had held other government posts before that.

The sudden death of P. A. Hansson in October 1946 brought about a change in the chairmanship of the Social Democratic Party and the premiership. He had no obvious successor, but one popular candidate was Gustav Möller, who had done so much to steer the Social Democrats' social policy in the 1930s. Möller, however, was already sixty-two and many thought a younger man ought to be chosen. E. Wigforss, himself sixty-five and aware that he was not going to be elected,[1] urged the adoption of someone from the younger generation. The choice was Tage Erlander, forty-five years old and a graduate (after ten years as an undergraduate at Lund University, studying first mathematics and physics and then social sciences). Erlander had been Under-Secretary to G. Möller at the Department of Social Affairs, but his cabinet experience in October 1946 comprised only one year as Minister of Education.

Succeeding P. A. Hansson was a formidable undertaking. The Swedish workers had identified themselves with 'Per Albin' in a very special way and had approved of his simple, direct approach and his unaffected manner, while the nation as a whole saw him as the man who had brought them through the war unscathed.

---

[1] This perhaps avoided a delicate constitutional issue, for according to Ö. Undén, King Gustav was resigned to accepting the choice of the parliamentary Social Democratic Party, but stated: 'But I won't have Wigforss!' (Ö. Undén, *Minnesanteckningar*, Stockholm, 1966, p. 165).

Erlander, on the other hand, was not well known and his personality had made no impression on the population. There were stories that the old King Gustav did not know his name and had difficulty afterwards in remembering it. The trade unions were wary of the tall academic from Värmland who was not a good public speaker and had peculiar mannerisms. Gradually, however, Tage Erlander established his own style–a mixture of irony (often self-irony), dry humour, earnestness, occasional anger, and a competent grasp of his brief. His popularity grew and by the time he relinquished the office of Prime Minister in 1969 he was known affectionately as Sweden's 'längsta statsminister' a pun meaning both the longest and the tallest prime minister. 'Längsta' is justified on both scores, for he had by then been Prime Minister for twenty-three years and he is several inches over six feet tall.

On his death on 29 October 1950 King Gustav V had also broken two records, for he was ninety-two and had ruled for forty-three years, longer than any previous Swedish monarch. He was succeeded by his eldest son, Gustav VI Adolf, then sixty-eight years of age. The Bernadottes had had close ties with Germany–both Oscar II and Gustav V had German consorts–but Gustav Adolf had close affinities with Britain. He first married Princess Margaret of Connaught (daughter of Queen Victoria's third son), who died in 1920, and then Lady Louise Mountbatten (sister of Earl Mountbatten of Burma), whose death occurred in 1965. Gustav VI Adolf, a popular monarch and respected humanistic scholar, has the reputation of holding truly democratic views, and he accepted wholeheartedly the constitutional limits that his father had obviously resented. Many Swedes hold republican views and indeed republicanism is an official plank in the Social Democrats' platform; but until recently little has been done about it, and Tage Erlander himself is on record as saying, 'Yes, I'm a republican, of course. But no, I don't think I want a republic'. And as long as Gustav Adolf reigns the monarchy seems assured. His eldest son, Prince Gustav Adolf, who was married to Princess Sibylla of Saxe-Coburg-Gotha, was killed in an air-crash in 1947, leaving four daughters and an infant son, Carl Gustaf (born in 1946). The republicans' hand was thus strengthened, for with a gap of over sixty years in the ages of the crown prince and his grandson, who was next in line of succession, a regency period was a strong probability and this could be a transition from monarchy to republic. King Gustav Adolf's robust health and longevity have altered the situation, however. He is still in possession of his faculties and his grandson is of age and already deputizing for him in the performance of certain official duties. However, a Constitutional Committee has recently put forward

K

proposals concerning the monarchy, and the signs are that these will be laid before the *Riksdag* in 1973. They include the proposals that the king will become known as the Head of State; that the present weekly sessions with the king and his Cabinet will be replaced by a meeting only once a quarter; that the government and not the Head of State will be chief of the armed forces; that the Speaker of the *Riksdag* in consultation with the deputy speakers and the leaders of the political parties will decide who should be asked to form a government. If these proposals are accepted (which is not certain, for the popularity of the royal family is generally acknowledged), the last vestiges of royal power will have been removed. At all events, it is universally accepted that no changes will be implemented during Gustav VI Adolf's lifetime.

Swedish Neutrality

Since the war all the major political parties in Sweden have agreed that neutrality must be Sweden's guiding principle and that Sweden must avoid joining any power bloc. Defining the form Swedish neutrality takes is not so simple, however. The Swedes themselves like to describe their foreign policy as freedom from alliances in peacetime, aiming at neutrality in the event of war. They do not want a rigid form of neutrality on Swiss lines, however.

This was obvious in 1946, when by an overwhelming majority the *Riksdag* voted to join the United Nations. Although an apparent departure from neutrality, since they were committing themselves to participation in economic sanctions and even military action decided on by the Security Council, the *Riksdag* knew that the veto would always be their safeguard. Sweden is geographically caught between East and West, and with representatives of both having the power of veto, it was inconceivable that the Council would place Sweden, as a member of the United Nations, in the position of supporting one against the other. Indeed leading Swedish politicians have said since that without this obvious neutralizing effect of the United Nations in the tension between East and West, they would not have voted for Sweden to join.

When tension began to build up and the Iron Curtain was becoming an unpleasant fact of political life, it became impossible for Sweden to remain wholly independent. She hesitated when offered Marshall Aid in 1947, for Russia and her satellites had declined; but basically she had become too dependent on foreign trade to remain isolated, and finally accepted Marshall Aid, went on to co-operate in the OEEC, and in 1949 joined the Council of Europe, showing that her sympathies were with the West. She would not go beyond these economic ties, however. When in March 1952 Sir Anthony

Eden proposed that the Council of Europe should embrace defence too, Ö. Undén made it known that Sweden would in that case have to withdraw.

But while honouring the inviolate principle of neutrality, the Swedes were well aware of the increasing dangers of the Cold War. Russia had emerged from World War II as master of the Baltic, controlling Poland, East Germany, and the Baltic states and menacing Finland. Sweden's position was obviously precarious. So too was that of Denmark and Norway if Russia should decide to attack the West and need air-bases. In the face of this threat and on Sweden's initiative, Norway, Denmark, and Sweden began tentatively in 1948 to consider the possibility of a Nordic defence treaty. Once more one comes to the Scandinavian paradox. There was a lot of goodwill, the representatives recognized the affinities between their peoples, they were all really kinsmen-but their geographical positions and their political views were not wholly compatible. The Norwegian Foreign Minister, Halvard Lange, had no faith in the security of a defence union and was inclined to consider America as his country's insurance. The Danish Prime Minister, Hans Hedtoft, tried to bring the Norwegian and Swedish views closer together but with little success. It had been assumed that the United States would supply a Nordic defence bloc with arms, but when America intimated that this would not be the case, the joint Scandinavian scheme fell through and Norway decided to join NATO. Hedtoft suggested a bilateral defence treaty between Denmark and Sweden, but Sweden declined and the Danes therefore decided to give up their neutrality and follow Norway's example.

The possibility of Sweden joining NATO sparked off a lively debate in Sweden, with Professor Herbert Tingsten, editor of *Dagens Nyheter*, a Liberal newspaper with the largest circulation in the country, and Dr Knut Petersson of the *Göteborgs Handels- och Sjöfartstidning* urging the Swedish government to follow the lead given by Norway and Denmark and to join NATO. However, the debate on the whole was extra-parliamentary, most members of the *Riksdag* being determined to hold to their non-alignment policy. An important part of their argument was that Finland, who had had to sign a Treaty of Mutual Assistance with the Soviet Union in 1948, was in a very delicate position and that if Sweden were to become a member of NATO, Russia might well feel justified in occupying Finland and placing strategic weapons there against the West to 'protect' her.

Neutrality has become something of a religion in Sweden and it has its credo. Gunnar Hägglöf reminds his readers that at the point where East and West directly confront each other, danger may well occur. 'Only a few years ago American tanks were confronting Russian tanks in Berlin muzzle to muzzle. We all agreed, I think, that this was a dangerous state of affairs'.[2]

Since then neutral countries have been allowed to act as buffer states, Austria and Yugoslavia, for instance, helping to ease tension further to the south. Gunnar Hägglöf goes on:

> more than half of the East–West line across Europe is covered by the Baltic Region. . . . Denmark and Norway have joined NATO, but with the important reservation that they don't accept foreign bases in peacetime. . . . In the eastern part Finland cultivates a close relationship to the Soviet Union but maintains with great conviction her independence and her integrity. In the centre of this Scandinavia between East and West lies Sweden, pursuing her traditional policy of neutrality . . . this system, this Nordic arch, has a great deal of inherent logic.

It is the same view stated in different words by Wigforss, who says that if one accepts that Russia as well as the West has after all a security problem, fearing the West as much as the West fears her, then Sweden 'could make a better contribution if as an island of neutrality she reduced in some measure the tension by reducing the immediate friction areas' than if she joined a Western defence alliance.[3] One must admit that it has indeed inherent logic.

Although Sweden finally decided to remain outside NATO, there were several incidents that caused anti-Russian sentiment in the post-war years. Russia's insistence on the custody of the Balts who had fled to Sweden (see above, p. 138) was one pointer. The Wallenberg affair was another. Raoul Wallenberg, a secretary at the Swedish Legation in Budapest, disappeared in January 1945 when Russians took the city; the Russian authorities admitted that they had taken him in 1945, but they offered no further information of his whereabouts. The matter was brought up periodically by the Swedes until in 1957 it was finally admitted that according to available documents Wallenberg had died in a Moscow prison in 1947. Before the Wallenberg affair was settled, the so-called Catalina affair had started. Two Swedish air force Catalina planes were shot down over the Baltic by the Russians in 1952. Swedish indignation was nationwide and the government sent a sharp note to Russia asking to have the whole matter brought up before the International Court at The Hague. When Russia refused, many Swedes demanded that the matter should be discussed by the United Nations. Undén, the Swedish Foreign Minister, wanted to treat it as a legal, not

[2] Hägglöf, op. cit., p. 39.   [3] Wigforss, op. cit., p. 439.

a political, matter. The issue was eventually taken to the United Nations and the anger died down, but there was no doubt where Swedish sympathies lay in the Cold War.

Although Sweden had decided to remain neutral and not to join NATO, the situation was not the same as in the 1930s. As Wigforss expresses it in his memoirs, two things had changed: 'Social Democracy had been converted to a faith in the value of military defence and the Conservatives to a hope of an international peace organization'.[4] Neither side was unrealistic. If Sweden was to be alone outside NATO, then it was necessary to spend more and not less than Norway and Denmark on defence. As the Norwegian Eivind Berdal, Briefing and Programme Officer within NATO, puts it: 'we should not make the mistake of thinking that the Swedes are getting a free ride. The Swedes are indeed paying for their defence. I'm told that they spend on average 85% more per capita for defence than for example the Norwegians'.[5] In fact over 13 per cent of the national budget is spent on defence, with the bulk of it used on air power. The Swedish air force, the third strongest in Europe, uses the SAAB J 35 Draken, an all-weather fighter, and is now buying in quantity the SAAB 37 Viggen all-weather attack aircraft, which carries an air-to-surface guided missile under the fuselage. It is also equipped with J 32-B Lansen fighters and Bloodhound 2 surface-to-air missiles.

The army is supplied mainly with weapons from Bofors, the Swedish munitions firm, although British Centurion tanks also form part of their equipment. Training in general is geared towards speedy mobilization and the defence of Swedish territory. The role of the navy, too, is primarily defensive and for this it has anti-submarine frigates, torpedo-boats, submarines, minesweepers, minelayers, and destroyers, some of which are equipped with Seacat surface-to-air missiles and R6-308 ship-to-surface missiles. Coastal artillery is strategically placed and is served by naval helicopters.

Swedish men between the ages of nineteen and forty-seven are conscripted for a basic ten months' training and then for refresher courses of fifteen to forty days.

A great amount of planning has gone into civil defence too. Plans exist for the evacuation of about one-third of the population from the urban areas at short notice, and shelters have been blasted out of solid rock for those in the towns who will remain to keep essential services and industries running. These shelters are used as underground garages, sports-halls, etc., in ordinary conditions – the Katarina underground garage near Slussen in Stockholm, for

---

[4] ibid., p. 436.
[5] E. Berdal, 'The Defence of Scandinavia', in *Scandinavia and European Integration*. Conference held at University of Aberdeen, 1971.

instance, could shelter thousands in an emergency. There is a civil defence organization in which citizens from sixteen to sixty-five are liable to serve. They are organized into local reserve corps and mobile relief units.

Sweden also realizes that as a member of the United Nations she must accept the responsibility involved. She has sent civil and military personnel to United Nations peace-keeping operations in Korea (1953), the Middle East (1956–67), the Congo (1960–66), and Cyprus (1964). Swedish neutrality also played a part, no doubt, in the appointment of the Swede Dag Hammarskjöld as Secretary-General of the United Nations in 1953 and Gunnar Jarring as United Nations mediator in the Israel–Arab conflict.

The Nordic Council

Even though the Nordic defence treaty had foundered, official committees had been set up to consider the possibility of a Nordic customs union and this work continued after 1949, since some definite form of pan-Scandinavian co-operation still seemed desirable. On Danish initiative the Nordic Council was established in 1952, a consultative body built partly on the pattern of the Council of Europe. Its 78 elected members, members of parliament from Denmark, Norway, Sweden, and Iceland (and from 1956 from Finland too), meet annually for one week in each of the Scandinavian capitals in turn, and although their role is only consultative, they have through their recommendations to their respective governments effected a move towards common Nordic policy on many vital issues. There is now a free labour market for Scandinavians within Scandinavia; passports are no longer necessary within the Scandinavian area; a common Nordic social security system is evolving; common laws in the different Scandinavian countries are being integrated; the Nordic Research Institute has been established; Nordvision arranges the production and exchange of TV programmes; the Scandinavian Airlines System (SAS) comprises the national Danish, Norwegian, and Swedish Airways.

The Council avoids defence and foreign policy, but has evolved the 'Nordek' plan, a form of Nordic common market which would create a pan-Scandinavian system of taxes, customs, trade and industry, and finance. It seemed likely to succeed until it collided with the EEC, but now its future is uncertain.

Sweden and the EEC

The EEC has proved a complicated issue for Sweden and there is still no obvious solution in sight. When a free-trade area was proposed to help European countries outside the EEC to negotiate more effectively with 'the Six', Sweden was willing to join it. EFTA came into being in 1960, with Sweden as one of its member countries, together with Great Britain, Denmark, Norway, Portugal, Switzerland, and Austria. Finland was given associate membership, and Iceland joined too in 1970. EFTA was not conceived as an alternative to the EEC, and several attempts were made to amalgamate the two in some way. When in 1961 Britain, followed by Denmark and Norway, sought full membership of the EEC, Sweden, Switzerland, and Austria, the neutral countries, applied for associate membership. President de Gaulle exercised his veto and the attempt was temporarily abandoned. On a renewed attempt by Britain, Denmark, Norway, and Ireland in 1967, Sweden also asked to negotiate, and this time, although she made no specific mention of the form of membership she required, the possibility of full membership was now not ruled out. De Gaulle again made it an academic question and the matter was in abeyance for a while.

The situation changed when President de Gaulle relinquished office, and by 1970 negotiations had started between Britain, Denmark, Norway, Ireland, and the Community. In November 1970 Sweden too had to decide what form of membership she wanted, but with a positive outcome now likelier than it had been for a decade, the Swedish government became increasingly aware of the dangers. In their application they left the form of membership open until practical questions had been dealt with, but emphasized that they must be allowed to preserve their traditional neutrality.

In some respects Sweden would have fewer difficulties than the rest of Scandinavia in adapting to the EEC, for she is not largely dependent on fishing, her farming policy over the last few years fundamentally follows the same line as that of the EEC, she is not fettered with a 'special arrangement' with Russia; nor need she fear competition, for her industry is modern and efficient. But the basic problem is always there: full membership would be at odds with her accepted policy of freedom from alliances. The Werner Plan for a gradual economic and monetary union worries the Swedes, but even more of a threat, they think, to their neutrality policy is the D'Avignon Plan which aims at co-operation among EEC countries on foreign policy.

In March 1971 the Swedish Prime Minister, Olof Palme, Erlander's successor, abandoned the idea of full membership and gave the D'Avignon report as one of his reasons. He pointed out that questions of defence could not be excluded from the kind of co-operation envisaged by the D'Avignon report and that all the EEC countries are members of NATO. Swedish membership would therefore not be compatible with Swedish neutrality.

Sweden's whole economy is based on a healthy export market and it has also become closely woven into the whole Scandinavian pattern–Sweden has invested in all the Scandinavian countries (Norwegian firms, for instance, produce components for Swedish firms) and there are thousands of workers from other Scandinavian countries at present resident in Sweden. What will happen if Norway and Denmark join the Community and Sweden does not?

Some form of association would seem to be the only solution, but neither the Swedes nor the Commission have so far succeeded in formulating satisfactory terms. Sweden is unwilling to accept the rulings of a body on which she is not represented, but she can hardly be represented if she is not able to abide by the Rome Treaty. The suggestion of a special free trade agreement with each side fixing its own tariffs, quotas, and trade policies has not found favour with the Community. The possibility of a preferential trade agreement has been aired, but other countries outside the Community, especially the United States of America, could justifiably raise objections to this.

At a recent conference on the subject Anthony Morris, of the Information Section of the European Communities in Brussels, said that 'The Community's view is that some arrangement with Sweden is essential';[6] and H. E. Leif Belfrage, the Swedish ambassador to the United Kingdom, was confident that 'if approached in a positive spirit of co-operation a way would be found'; so there would appear to be sympathy on both sides, but so far the conundrum is unsolved.

Since the war, therefore, Sweden has successfully pursued her own brand of armed neutrality and preserved the Nordic Arch, and has found this compatible with membership of the United Nations and of international cultural, altruistic, and trade organizations. The process has sometimes been something of an international tightrope walk. In early 1972 it looked as though Denmark would join the EEC. A public opinion poll in Norway showed 32 per cent for the EEC, 45 per cent against, and 22 per cent, 'don't know'. There will be an advisory referendum in both Denmark and Norway in September 1972. Unless an overwhelming trend is then shown against entry, the respective governments will presumably follow their own inclinations and join.

The Development of Social Welfare

During the war the development of the social welfare programme was in abeyance, but in 1944, when it looked as though the war would soon be over, a twenty-seven point post-war programme was

[6] *Scandinavia and European Integration.* Conference held at University of Aberdeen, 1971.

drawn up under the guidance of Ernst Wigforss. He himself has stated since that the experience of the war years helped fashion his thoughts. If Swedish society could support the kind of defence burden never dreamed of in the 1930s, then it could surely exert itself for peaceful purposes. The programme aimed at full employment, a rise in real earnings, increased old-age pensions, unemployment and sickness benefit, financial aid to help children, equal educational opportunities for all, and a shorter working week. It had a strong socialistic flavour–there was to be an 'industrial democracy' and the state was to have increased control of the economy.

In the election to the Lower House in 1944 the Social Democrats had lost ground, but still held exactly half of the seats, i.e., 115 out of 230, and had a majority in the Upper House. Per Albin Hansson was not averse to some permanent form of coalition, but many of his colleagues were impatient to embark on their new social programme. In July 1945 they had their way and a purely Social Democratic government was formed under Per Albin Hansson. Gunnar Myrdal was appointed Minister of Commerce and said exuberantly that 'the labour movement is now approaching its harvest'.

In matters of doctrinal socialism, nationalism, and a wholly planned economy the harvest was a lean one. The government set up a series of committees to examine the possibility of nationalization or rationalization of several vital industries and commodities, for example insurance, combustible oils, and the shoe industry, but this led to very little. S. Carlsson writes that 'it is remarkable that in practice the Social Democratic government in Sweden was less socialistic than the contemporary Labour Cabinet in Great Britain in 1945–1951'.[7] They may well have taken their losses in local elections in 1946 as a broad hint and decided to leave well alone. The Swedes are essentially pragmatists in politics and if a private industry is doing well, the tendency is to leave it alone, provided that through taxation a reasonable share of the profits is made to serve the general weal.

In terms of social benefits and sharing the country's wealth more evenly, however, Myrdal's 'harvest' was a bumper crop. Indeed, there was general agreement in the *Riksdag* on many of the reforms introduced in the immediate post-war period, although the parties divided sharply on how the reforms should be paid for. In 1946 all parties agreed to the raising of the old-age pension and the removal of any form of means test in connection with it. Professor Bertil Ohlin, by that time leader of the Liberal Party (*Folkpartiet*), urged that the pension should be geared to the cost of living index, a sign

[7] S. Carlsson and J. Rosén, *Svensk historia* (3rd ed., Stockholm, 1970), II, 588.

of the already incipient danger of inflation. His proposal was not accepted until 1950, but has been an important factor in preserving the standards of old people in Sweden ever since. A child allowance scheme had been in existence since 1937, but it had been granted after a means test. In 1947 a new scheme was introduced, whereby all mothers received an allowance for each child, including the first. It was actually a means of regulating incomes, for there had been up to this point tax relief for each child in proportion to the total sum paid, a system benefiting most those with high incomes. The new scheme meant that those in the high-income bracket now paid more tax, while the large, poor families benefited the most. To the Child Allowance Scheme were added free school meals for all schoolchildren and free school books.

Equal opportunity for all children was the ultimate aim of the *Riksdag* and towards that end a School Commission was appointed in 1946 to examine the educational system. Four years later its proposals led to the experimental establishment of the comprehensive school system. After a further ten years the nine-year basic comprehensive school was established in every district throughout the country (cf. below, p. 191).

A national compulsory health insurance scheme was also accepted in principle almost unanimously by the *Riksdag* in the first years of this 'harvest' period. In 1946 the *Riksdag* gave its blessing to a free health service for all citizens and state subsidies to cover the cost of medicines, and sickness benefit for all wage-earners temporarily indisposed. Time was needed to build up resources before introducing the scheme and there was disagreement in the *Riksdag* over numerous technicalities concerning methods of assessing sickness benefit, with the result that it was 1955 before the National Health Service actually came into operation.

The government was largely supported by the non-Socialist parties when putting its social reforms through the *Riksdag*, but met fierce opposition in other fields. The threatened nationalization programme was not pursued, but opposition parties were afraid of increasing state control under the protection of wartime regulations still in force. Food-rationing was not abolished until 1949 and rent controls remain to this day, and are still considered by the opposition to be the main cause of Sweden's housing shortage.

Above all the opposition feared the government's tax policy. Both direct and indirect taxation during the war had risen sharply with the levying of a special defence tax and a 5 per cent purchase tax. The public now expected that the first post-war budget would offer tax relief. Wigforss, however, had to finance a costly social programme and although the special wartime taxes were abolished, the money still had to be found. He wanted, moreover, to see wealth distributed more evenly in the country. This his proposals in 1947 did. Income tax on low incomes was reduced but raised considerably on large salaries on a steeply graduated scale; corporation tax was raised from 32 to 40 per cent; capital over 30,000 *kronor* was taxed, again on a graduated scale. Death duties already existed, but now an extra estate duty was levied on undivided estates of 25,000 *kronor* or above on a steeply graduated scale up to 60 per cent of the total. The opposition to this budget was among the most acrimonious the Swedish parliament had known and revealed one feature uncharacteristic of Swedish politics – a personal attack on Wigforss himself, who was accused by non-Socialist parties of being a fanatic in his dealings with the richer members of the community.

Tage Erlander's first period of office was difficult and his government's whole economic policy was noisily attacked. A post-war depression had been predicted and an economic planning committee set up in 1944 under Gunnar Myrdal had considered ways of stimulating the post-war economy and offsetting the expected fall in prices. In the event post-war trends were in the exact opposite direction and Myrdal's carefully planned measures to combat a depression were hastily superseded by anti-inflationary measures. In the period 1946 to 1947 imports were dangerously high and Swedish gold reserves were drastically reduced. By 1947 restrictions had to be imposed on many goods, especially cars, petrol, and coffee; controls on building, investment, and prices were increased and coffee-, tea-, and cocoa-rationing (and in 1948 petrol-rationing) were reintroduced.

The troubled history of Myrdal's trade agreement with Russia was already causing the government considerable discomfiture. Partly because good relations with Russia seemed desirable at the end of the war and partly because potential Russian markets would help to counteract the putative post-war inflation, a special trade agreement was signed in Moscow in October 1946, offering Russia credit up to 1,000 million *kronor* for the purchase of Swedish goods over a five-year period. The opposition attacked not the principle but the extent of the agreement, a credit of 200 million *kronor* annually and up to 20 per cent of Swedish exports. The government's defence, that it would counteract the depression in Western countries, became increasingly untenable. Herbert Tingsten, no friend of the Soviet Union, carried in his paper *Dagens Nyheter* reports of Myrdal exerting pressure on ASEA when that firm refused to meet Soviet requirements. It was maintained that Myrdal threatened to allow General Electric access to the Swedish markets, thus destroying ASEA's virtual Swedish monopoly if ASEA did not co-operate.

Myrdal denied the charge, while admitting plans concerning General Electric had been discussed; Tingsten for his part said he had got the information himself from Thorsten Ericson, the head of ASEA. In the event, the Russians made little use of the advantages being offered and by April 1947 Gunnar Myrdal had been appointed head of the United Nations Economic European Commission; but the affair had affected the public's faith in the government.

In the 1948 election campaign the vigorous new leader of the Liberals, Bertil Ohlin, supported by *Dagens Nyheter*, criticized the government for its 'misrule', its love of controls, its economic blunders, and its tax policy. The Socialist paper *Morgon-Tidningen* rounded on the Liberals by reporting that the Liberal Party in Stockholm had used between 3½ and 4 million *kronor* donated by 'big business' on their campaign. The figure had been supplied by Seth Molander, a Social Democratic member of the *Riksdag*. Ohlin insisted that the real sum was only 300,000 *kronor*, *Morgon-Tidningen* was sued for libel, Molander reported a conservative paper to the Press Council for describing the affair falsely. Two lawyers were appointed by Ohlin and Erlander to examine the evidence and they reported the day before the election that Molander had used misleading figures. The poll was very high (82·7 per cent) and the Liberals doubled their votes, emerging as the largest non-Socialist party in the *Riksdag*, but not at the expense of the Social Democrats so much as of the Conservatives. The Communists lost through events in Czechoslovakia at this time. The Social Democrats retained 112 seats (a loss of three), the Liberals 57, the Agrarians 30, the Conservatives 23, and the Communists 8. Thus the Social Democrats still had more seats than the combined non-Socialist parties and the real losers were the Communists and the Conservatives.

The election marked the end of a noisy period by Swedish standards, the Socialist 'harvest', the period of threatened increased nationalization, and state controls. Erlander's second term of office began on a quieter note. There was in 1949 a temporary respite in the post-war inflationary tendencies, Ernst Wigforss resigned after seventeen years as Finance Minister, and the government accepted a more pragmatic form of Social Democracy and concentrated on consolidating reforms they had already set in motion.

The dangers of inflation have never been removed in the post-war period, however, and a critical period followed hard on the Korean War in 1950, the cost of living rising in a few years by between 25 and 30 per cent. Yet it was a period of economic expansion, with a steady rise in industrial output and with the use of regulating price indices, real wages and pensions rose so that the improved standards of living were shared by most people to at least some extent.

The government was not in a secure position, however, having a very slender majority, and in 1951 Erlander successfully wooed the Agrarian Party, now led by Gunnar Hedlund, into joining a coalition. Erlander, Ö. Undén, and Per Edvin Sköld remained as Prime Minister, Foreign Minister, and Finance Minister respectively, but the Agrarians were given four cabinet posts, with Gunnar Hedlund himself as Minister of Internal Affairs and Sam Norup as Minister of Agriculture. The coalition ensured office for the Social Democrats and gave a measure of power to the Agrarians they would not otherwise have commanded, but the two parties were not ideally suited to work together. The respective Social Democrat and Agrarian supporters were obviously not enamoured of the coalition either, for in the 1956 elections both parties lost seats. The Social Democrats held 106 seats, the Conservatives, under their energetic new leader Jarl Hjalmarsson, won 42, the Liberals 58, the Agrarians only 19, and the Communists 6. It looked therefore as though the non-Socialist parties could oust the Social Democrats at long last if the Agrarians would abandon their already precarious support of the Socialists.

The Compulsory Pension Scheme

The issue that gave the Agrarians their chance to leave the coalition was a compulsory pension scheme which the Social Democrats decided to introduce in 1957. Ironically it also dashed the opposition parties' hopes of defeating the Social Democrats and forming an alternative government, for although Agrarians could not agree with the Social Democrats' scheme, neither could they accept an alternative favoured by the Conservatives and Liberals, and so they put forward their own. Even within the parties opinions were divided and Bertil Ohlin proposed a national referendum. (The consultative referendum had been written into the constitution in 1922, but hardly ever exercised.)

In October 1957 the nation went to the polls to vote on three alternative pension schemes. The first, supported by most Social Democrats and Communists, was for a compulsory superannuation scheme to be paid via the employers, which would guarantee at the age of sixty-seven (the normal retiring age in Sweden) a pension equivalent to at least 65 per cent of one's average wage calculated on the most productive fifteen years of one's working life. The pension would be guaranteed by the state against inflation. The opposition disliked the element of compulsion in the scheme and were also afraid of the economic power it would put into the government's hands, for the contributions, calculated to reach 50,000 or 60,000 million *kronor* by 1990, were to be placed in a state fund, and by skilful investment of such a vast sum the government could obviously manipulate the economy. A leader in the Independent Liberal paper *Sydsvenska Dagbladet* which spoke of 'a state fund running into thousands of millions of *kronor*, the most important purpose of which seems to be to help the government out of its perpetual economic troubles and to make an inroad into a socialization of economic life'[8] was no doubt expressing the fears of many people.

The second alternative, supported by the Agrarians, was for a voluntary superannuation scheme. A farmer would instinctively secure his old age by investing in property, and disliked being compelled to join a scheme involving large contributions. The third alternative, backed by, among other organizations, the Conservatives, the Liberals, and the Swedish Federation of Employers, was also a voluntary scheme, but with emphasis on agreements reached by large employers and union organizations.

The result of the referendum, 46 per cent for alternative one, 15 per cent for alternative two, and 35 per cent for alternative three, could be interpreted in many ways, but in no way could the Social Democrats claim an overall majority for their scheme. The coalition government was replaced by a wholly Social Democratic one (with Erlander, Undén, and Gunnar Sträng as Prime Minister, Foreign Minister, and Finance Minister respectively, and Torsten Nilsson being appointed as Minister of Social Affairs) which prepared a modified version of its original proposal. When it was obvious that this would not be accepted by a *Riksdag*, Erlander called for the dissolution of the Lower House.

In the ensuing election the Liberals unexpectedly lost 20 of their 58 seats – mostly to the Agrarians.[9] The final results were Conservatives 45, Agrarians 32, Liberals 38, a total of 115; the Social Democrats won 111 and the Communists 5, a total of 116. The Speaker was a Social Democrat and the result was therefore stalemate. It was at this point that Erlander showed his skill as a parliamentary tactician and the opposition demonstrated why it has remained the opposition for so many years. A compromise between all parties on the pensions issue might have been possible, but the Liberals refused to abandon their scheme, even though both *Dagens Nyheter* and *Expressen*, traditionally their supporters, urged them to do so and the local elections continued to show a fall in their popularity. Several individual members of the Liberal Party were turning against its official line to the point when in January 1959 one Liberal

---

[8] Quoted C. Wahlgren, op. cit., p. 260.
[9] This party, *Bondeförbundet*, changed its name to *Centerpartiet*, the Centre Party, in 1957.

member of the *Riksdag*, Ture Königson, let it be known that the dictates of his conscience would not allow him to vote against the government's proposal. In May the government's pension scheme was therefore accepted by 115 votes to 114. Although by far the largest single party in the Lower House, the Social Democrats had nevertheless no overall majority, but by skilfully playing the non-Socialist opposition parties off against each other Erlander had saved his position.

He again took advantage of the opposition parties' weaknesses in dealing with taxation. State expenditure was extremely high and the Conservatives in 1959 wanted to abolish child allowance for the first child, free school meals and textbooks, but the Liberals and Agrarians would not go this far. Meanwhile, in his 1959 budget Sträng wanted to introduce purchase tax. The Communists objected to indirect taxation and were prepared to vote against it, but Erlander threatened in that case to resign, which would have meant a non-Socialist government. The Communists accepted purchase tax as the lesser of two evils, in the combined voting of both Houses of the *Riksdag* (the normal procedure in financial matters) Erlander's government received 185 votes against 178, Sträng's budget was balanced, and Erlander had weathered another storm.

In the 1960 elections he secured his party's position. The Liberals were not enjoying cordial relations with *Dagens Nyheter* and *Expressen*, and in 1956 LO, the Swedish Trade Union Confederation, had bought *Stockholms-Tidningen* and *Aftonbladet* from Torsten Kreuger, an arch-Conservative, for 25 million *kronor*. Thus the press was not slanted in favour of the non-Socialist parties. Even more to the Social Democrats' advantage, the Conservatives stood firm on their measures to reduce public spending and insisted, moreover, that if they came to power, they would rescind the newly-initiated pension scheme. The Agrarians preferred to leave that issue dormant, while the Liberals had accepted the scheme as a *fait accompli*. The Agrarians, on the other hand, rejected the Conservatives' 'anti-social' measures and in that they were joined by the Liberals. In the election campaign Bertil Ohlin and Gunnar Hedlund made a joint declaration supporting the Social Democrats' social policy and deploring the Conservatives' 'extreme' policies. All Erlander needed to do was to point to the open rift and suggest that the opposition parties were too divided to offer a credible alternative government. The election results–Conservatives 39, Agrarians 34, Liberals 40, Social Democrats 114, and Communists 5–changed the knife-edge 115–115 into a comfortable 119–113. They also led to recriminations among the non-Socialist parties (one result of which was that in 1961 Jarl Hjalmarsson was succeeded by Gunnar Heckscher as the

Conservative leader) and thus assured the Social Democrats office for many years to come.

The Social Democrats reasoned that the 1960 election results demonstrated that the public wanted to retain the pension scheme and the social services they were now enjoying, even if it meant paying purchase tax, and their new policies went further in the same direction. Purchase tax was raised to 6 per cent; in 1962 the nine-year compulsory comprehensive school was definitely introduced; child allowances were improved; and in 1963 a statutory four-weeks holiday with pay was introduced.

Tage Erlander was never more firmly in control than during this period. Harpsund, an estate some eighty miles from Stockholm, had been placed at the Prime Minister's disposal in 1953 and from the late 1950s until 1964 Erlander often invited to this Swedish Chequers or Camp David representatives of various important pressure groups to sound out their views. These meetings were salutary in that different organizations were able to put their point of view directly to the Head of Government, but they had the more dangerous consequence in a democracy that when legislation was presented to the *Riksdag* by the government, agreement had already been reached unofficially between the Social Democrats and the organizations most closely concerned. Gunnar Heckscher objected strongly to this 'Harpsund democracy' which he thought could lead to a one-party system in Sweden, with power concentrated in perpetuity in the hands of the Social Democratic Party. Criticism mounted, and by 1964 the Harpsund meetings had been drastically reduced.

Despite their fears of a one-party system, the opposition parties proved incapable of sinking their differences, although certain changes were taking place in party formations. Heckscher wanted some form of united non-Socialist front, but in the 1964 election campaign he and his party projected their view that those too old to qualify for the new superannuation scheme (i.e., those born before 1896) should be allowed benefit, the Agrarians and Liberals didn't agree, and the Conservatives refused to abandon the point. Once more, therefore, the Conservatives were the odd-man out in an election campaign and lost seats. In 1965 Heckscher resigned over the lack of non-Socialist support and was succeeded by Yngve Holmberg.

In 1964 a political group called *Medborgerlig Samling* (i.e., Citizens' Assembly) was started in Malmö with the ultimate aim of uniting all three opposition parties. By capturing three *Riksdag* seats from the traditional non-Socialist parties in 1964 and thus splitting the vote, it had perhaps the opposite effect, and it has made little headway since; but its very existence in 1964 was symptomatic. A similar attempt was made in Gothenburg in 1966 when a group called *Samling 66* (Assembly 66) was launched with the specific aim of uniting the opposition parties.

The Liberals and Agrarians made a more obvious move in 1966 to establish formal co-operation, but the 1968 election campaign demonstrated that they had not yet evolved a united front. In 1969 the Conservative Party changed its name from *Högern* (i.e., Right) to *Moderata samlingspartiet* (i.e., Moderate Party), a sign that they are more amenable to co-operate with the two Centre parties.

While the right-wing party was moving further Left the Swedish Communists were moving slightly Right. In 1964 C. H. Hermansson was appointed leader of the Communist Party and helped change its direction. It has freed itself from any dependence on Moscow and international communism and, accepting the principle of parliamentary democracy, has set itself the task of socializing Sweden by peaceful constitutional methods. In 1967 it changed its name to *Vänsterpartiet Kommunisterna* (i.e., Left-party Communists) and for many Swedes of left-wing persuasions who consider that the Social Democrats have lost their reforming zeal, it has become more attractive and less menacing.

The local election results in 1966 worried the Social Democrats, for they showed a move towards the non-Socialist parties, with the co-operation between Liberals and Agrarians proving attractive to the electorate. The general election in 1968 restored their confidence, however, for they won 125 seats in the Lower House, a gain of 12, and so once more had a majority in both Houses. Almost certainly external events affected the results, for the Russian invasion of Czechoslovakia started during the election campaign, and although Hermansson was the most vociferous of the party leaders in condemning Russia, his party still lost many votes; and in time of crisis there is a tendency to retain the government already in office. When, therefore, Tage Erlander retired as Prime Minister in 1969 and handed over office to Olof Palme, he seemed to be leaving a party firmly in the saddle. Palme's situation was a difficult one, however, partly because the 1968 results were not necessarily a true reflection of Sweden's political mood, partly because the *Riksdag* was on the point of a major upheaval, and partly because there were genuine signs of unrest in the country.

As early as 1954 a Constitutional Commission under Rickard Sandler had been set up and in 1963 its recommendations were put forward, the most important of which was a proposal for a unicameral parliament. The reaction was a mirror picture of British politicians' attitudes to the reform of their Upper House. The Conservatives, Liberals, and Agrarians were in favour, but the Social

L

Democrats dragged their feet, for ever since the 1940s, they had been assured of more support in the Upper House than in the Lower House. In 1966 a committee was appointed to examine the process of government and to take into account all the arguments that had been put forward since the commission had first reported. By 1967 agreement was reached to institute a unicameral system and to hold both local and general elections every three years. Proportional representation would be retained, the number of *Riksdag* members was fixed at 350, of which 310 would be appointed by direct voting in the constituencies, while 40 'national seats' would be divided among the parties to ensure exact proportional representation. To gain a 'national' seat a party would require a minimum of 12 per cent of the votes in a constituency or 4 per cent in the country as a whole.

The first general election following this new pattern was in September 1970 and the result was a slight drop in the Social Democrats' percentages of votes. Of the 350 seats in the new *Riksdag* (which, incidentally, had moved from the old *Riksdaghus* opposite the Royal Palace to a new building near Sergels Torg) the Conservatives won 41, the Liberals 58, the Agrarians 71, the Social Democrats 163, and the Communists 17; thus the Social Democrats have formed a minority government, while the Communists have an extremely advantageous position and could bring down the government.

Olof Palme's Premiership

Olof Palme's record as Prime Minister has been a troubled one. Born in 1927, Palme is of distinguished birth.[10] He has an American as well as a Swedish degree, a keen mind, and the reputation of being go-ahead, forceful, ruthless, or opportunist, depending on one's point of view. Anthony Howard, who interviewed him in May 1971, writes: 'in this previously least doctrinaire of socialist countries, Mr Palme represents that most unsettling phenomenon, a left-wing politician who prides (almost preens) himself on having a philosophy'.[11] In February 1968, when still Minister of Education, he joined in a demonstration against the American presence in Vietnam and was photographed marching through Stockholm by the side of the North Vietnamese ambassador to Moscow, which won for him the support of many young radicals, but caused many others to question his judgement – or at least prudence.

Relations between the United States and Sweden became very strained when Palme first came to power. American deserters from

[10] His father, Gunnar Palme, a member of a comfortable upper middle-class family; his mother, née Elisabeth von Knieriem, an aristocrat.
[11] A. Howard, 'Sweden: The Fading Dream', *New Statesman* (June 1971).

the Vietnam War were given asylum in Sweden and there are still some five hundred of them in Sweden today. Matters were at their worst in 1970 when young Swedish members of left-wing political groups threw eggs at the American ambassador, Jerome H. Holland, 'the representative of the American oppressors in Vietnam', the ambassador was recalled to Washington for consultation, and the Swedish government received an indignant protest from America. (The situation was not without irony, for the Swedish left-wing groups are also vigorous supporters of the world's coloured population and Ambassador Holland is coloured.) The gradual withdrawal of American forces from Vietnam has helped to improve the situation, Holland has returned to Stockholm, and normal courtesies have been restored. No doubt the Swedish authorities are not sorry to see a reduction in the number of deserters reaching their country, for many of them have helped to finance their stay by illegal sale of drugs to young Swedes, and indeed several of them have been prosecuted and deported for such offences.

In 1967 a State Investment Bank was set up, and this was followed in 1969 by the Department of Industry, with Krister Wickman as its first minister. Thus before Olof Palme was ever in command, the government was being accused of increased interference in large business concerns. His political persuasions are left of Erlander's and as Prime Minister he has increased, not reduced, his opponents' fear of socialism. He has inherited the problems of the sparsely populated areas (cf. below, pp. 178f.), but his tendency to speak in terms of the national economy and large-scale planning has not won the confidence of the individuals who feel they have already been sacrificed to the planners.

In the last years of Tage Erlander's premiership state expenditure had risen on an unprecedented scale. In 1956–60 the amount was barely 14,000 million *kronor*, whereas in 1968 it was 35,000 million. This was acquired by both direct and indirect taxation; but the latter method was increasingly used in the late 1960s, with purchase tax reaching 10 per cent. In 1969 purchase tax was replaced by value-added tax.

Another trend manifest before Olof Palme took office was a rise in unemployment–admittedly a relative phenomenon, for Sweden has had a remarkable post-war record of full employment and 2 per cent is considered a worryingly high figure. Similarly, while the growth in economic output from 1960 to 1965 was 5·4 per cent, it dropped to about 4 per cent from 1965 to 1970; moreover, Sweden has had a deficit in her balance of payments, the current account showing in 1969 a deficit of over £49 million and in 1970 of over £126 million.

Before retiring as Prime Minister, Erlander set up a commission to inquire into low incomes, and although a final report was not published, the preliminary findings show that about one-third of the working force and some 60 per cent of pensioners are below what the Swedish Trade Union Confederation considers the poverty line. Again this is relative, for in Sweden the poverty line is higher than anywhere in Europe; but the report demonstrated that the gap between the low-paid workers and the middle and upper brackets is widening despite the social welfare and tax policies of recent years. Olof Palme's reaction to the report was to initiate a campaign for 'equality', with all future wage settlements having what he called a 'low-income profile'. Erlander admits that it was perhaps an ill-judged moment to introduce such a campaign, however worthy it may be. Palme follows two lines: extremely high taxation on even relatively moderate incomes, and a boosting of the lower-paid workers in wage agreements. This has already led to unrest and strikes, a most unusual phenomenon in Sweden. Swedish employees are almost all organized into large effective unions which by means of free collective bargaining reach binding wage settlements without state interference. This has applied equally in the past to the public sector, and the government has its own bargaining office to negotiate wage settlements with its own employees. With his 'low-income profile' philosophy, however, Palme's desire to influence wage structures becomes more marked. One important cause of the un-official strike that broke out in the state-owned LKAB mines in 1970 was that highly paid skilled workers were trying to retain their wage differentials. Trouble erupted again early in 1971 when members of two large white-collar unions, SR (the Federation of Government Employees) and SACO (the Central Organization of Swedish Professional Workers), refused the offer made by their employer (i.e., the state) and withdrew their labour, throwing the country into chaos for six weeks. Their point was that the increase offered to them was not enough to offset the rise in the cost of living, and their living standards were therefore being eroded by Palme's policy. In other words, they would have nothing to do with an equal-ity that reduced the standards of the higher-paid members of the community.[12] University students, whose numbers have increased enormously in the post-war period, watched uneasily, for unemploy-ment is beginning to affect graduates, and most of them are studying with the hope of enjoying a high standard of living afterwards. They

[12] R. Huntford, writing in *Sweden Now* (May 1971), called the strike 'that un-likely phenomenon, the militant bourgeois revolt . . . When Mr Bertil Östergren, secretary-general of SACO, reiterated . . . that his members would not tolerate a reduction in the real buying power of their salaries and hence in their standard of living, he meant that the middle classes wanted to survive'.

are potential members of SACO and are anxious about Palme's desire to remove differentials in wage structures.

In dealing with unemployment Gunnar Sträng, the Minister of Finance, wants to leave taxation at its present level and dole out selective direct aid where it is most needed. The non-Socialist parties, on the other hand, want him to stimulate demand, reduce value-added tax, and cut employers' contributions, thus helping industry to expand. The present leaders of the opposition parties, Gösta Bohman (Conservative), Thorbjörn Fälldin (Agrarian), and Gunnar Helén (Liberal), actually united in putting forward in November 1971 an economic proposal to this effect, which was hailed as a sign that they were on the way to presenting a united front and a moderate alternative government. The Communists are in a difficult position, for they have always deplored indirect taxation and are particularly unhappy about tax on food. It will be difficult for them to vote against opposition proposals for the reduction of taxes they consider pernicious, and yet not doing so could bring down the government. Political commentators draw parallels between this situation and the crisis in Norway and Denmark that brought down the governments of Gerhardsen and Krag in 1965 and 1968 respectively.

It is difficult to judge whether the Social Democrats would be replaced after some forty years in office. Evidence shows that half the voting population want some form of Socialist government, but the question is how far to the Left they want such a government to go. All political parties in Sweden accept the concept of a mixed economy and they all accept the welfare state. Disagreement arises over the proportions of the public and the private sectors, the level of taxation, and the amount of state control governing the life of the individual. The Social Democrats under Olof Palme are showing signs of becoming more doctrinaire Socialist than ever before. An article in *Tiden* (a Socialist periodical) in November 1971, headed 'What do the Social Democrats want?', stated that the present confusion in the party is caused by the old 'practical pragmatic methods' which no longer work, and what is now needed is a 'radicalization of the party's policy'. It may be that too radical an approach would alienate more than half the electorate and that a working union of the non-Socialist parties would prove an acceptable alternative. Certainly, one cannot mistake a strong current of discontent and one frequently reads articles expressing fears of increasing government control. However, in the last forty years the Social Democrats have weathered many political storms and may well do so again in 1973.

Chapter 8

The Modern Scene – Debit and Credit

'It seems to me', writes Gunnar Hägglöf,

> that Sweden's important contribution to history has been to have cultivated a vast country in Northern Europe and to have maintained against a harsh climate and an equally harsh nature a relatively high level of European civilization. Scandinavia could well have been one of the wastelands of the Northern and Arctic hemisphere.

As we have seen, the process of cultivation has been in progress for thousands of years, but the remarkably high material standards pertaining in Sweden today are of recent origin and result mainly from the development of Swedish industry.

Because Sweden has a relatively small population (even now only some 8 million people live there) there is a tendency to think of her as a small country, but the fact is that this elongated land is one thousand miles long and covers over 170,000 square miles, which means that in Europe only Russia, France, and Spain are larger. If one considers the Swedish terrain and Sweden's geographical location, however, one realizes why it took the settlers so long to overcome the natural difficulties in large parts of this country. Sweden lies between the Northern latitudes 55° 20′ and 69° 04′, which fact comes more clearly into focus if one notes, for example, P. O. Sundman's remarks that Moscow straddles the same degree of latitude as Smygehuk (Sweden's southernmost point) and Archangel is some 435 miles further south than Treriksröset, Sweden's northernmost point;[1] or Professor O'Dell's orientation:

> If the 60° N. latitude line is followed on a globe, the line passes through the centre of Sweden across the Shetland Islands, Cape Farewell in Greenland, north of Juneau in Alaska, across the neck of the Kamchatka peninsula and north of Tobolsk in Siberia.

---

[1] *Sweden in the Sixties*, p. 25.

About three-twentieths of the area of Sweden is north of the Arctic Circle.[2]

The Swedish climate is considerably warmer than the latitude would suggest because of the warm currents carried to Scandinavia by the Gulf Stream, and the average mean temperature ranges from 27° F in the north to 45° F in the south. There is a great variation of temperature between north and south in the winter, with the south having on average some 56 days per year below freezing-point, while in the north the comparative figure is 217. The north enjoys a short spring that is little more than a thawing period and then a hectic summer. Within the Arctic Circle the sun never actually sinks below the horizon for over seven weeks and even further south in the country it never seems to grow really dark in June. Nature exacts payment in the winter when there is a corresponding period of darkness. Before man had learnt to harness hydro-electric power and to light and heat his home efficiently, large parts of the extreme provinces of Sweden were hostile to Western man, with only the nomadic Lapps tending their reindeer herds able to cope adequately with the harsh prevailing conditions.

There are two rich agricultural belts, the plains of Skåne in the south and the Central Plain–actually three large lowland plains, Mälaren-Hjälmare, the Vänern Plain, and the Östgöta Plain. Only 10 per cent of the Swedish land area is arable, 8 per cent is covered by water (there are estimated to be some 96,000 lakes), much of the 1,500 miles of coastline is indented by archipelagos, the north-west of Sweden bordering Norway has barren mountains, while much of the vast Norrland area is covered by dense coniferous forests. Lapland, one-seventh of which lies beyond the Arctic Circle, is the most northerly province and covers over a quarter of Sweden's total area. It embraces vast rivers and lakes, mountain heather, and primeval moss-covered fens. Many of these landscapes are spectacular and beautiful to behold, but they were daunting to a small population before the technological age. When Linnaeus, the famous Swedish botanist, set out for Lapland in May 1732 with his pens and ink, a microscope, 'perspective glass' (telescope), papers for pressing botanical specimens, his diary, a gun, and a wallet containing his travel permit issued by the provincial governor, he was about to explore uncharted territory and remarked on leaving Gävle that here was the last apothecary and general medical practitioner in the north– and yet almost two-thirds of Sweden lies north of Gävle.

[2] *The Scandinavian World* (London, 1963), p. 110.

Swedish Industry

There was great potential wealth in the north, with its vast store of virgin forests and, to carry the felled logs, mighty rivers flowing swiftly from north-west to south-east into the Baltic; great waterfalls to be harnessed; and large mineral deposits; but as late as the mid-nineteenth century Sweden was still one of Europe's poorest countries. In the next fifty years, however, the process of industrialization was rapid, and by the early years of this century the Swedish growth-rate was well above the international average. The depressions of the 1920s and 1930s restricted progress, but Sweden was not so adversely affected as more highly industrialized countries, and could quickly reverse the trend once the international situation had started to ease. Escaping the direct destruction of World War II, Sweden was able to forge ahead by the mid-1940s and has now caught up with–and in many cases overtaken–the highly advanced industrial countries. Post-war Sweden has emerged, in fact, as the country with the highest standard of living in Europe.

The development of Swedish industry began with the exploitation of raw materials, and here Sweden was fortunate, for she was rich in minerals and timber, the very products in demand by countries at a more advanced stage of industrialization, and was thus able to attract large capital investment from abroad. Then the engineering industry was developed, relying heavily on Swedish inventions such as ball bearings, telephone equipment, separators, etc. The trend now is towards industries that are technologically well advanced and that require large-scale capital investment. To hold their own in a competitive international market Swedish companies have had to streamline, specialize, merge, and expand, and it must be said that they have succeeded remarkably well.

Sweden's most important natural resource is timber. She is traditionally a land of lakes and forests, and 55 per cent of the country's total area is forest land–about 55 million acres of forest in all. It is, moreover, on the increase, for as Swedish agriculture becomes more streamlined small farms are sold off and the arable land is planted with trees. For centuries the dark mysterious forests enriched Swedish folk-tales and legend with stories of trolls and sprites, but otherwise provided only domestic fuel, tar, and charcoal for the iron and steel industry. From the late nineteenth century, however, with the setting-up of steam-driven sawmills and the heavy demand from abroad, timber became the largest single Swedish export, and when the demand for timber slackened off at the turn of the century, the demand for wood fibre for paper soared and Sweden became the world's largest pulp exporter. Her pulp industry is still growing, and is the sector of the forestry industry that is expanding most.

Both in location and method the emphasis is changing. In the past the forestry industry was associated with the north of Sweden and conjured up a picture of logs floating along great Norrland rivers down to sawmills on the Gulf of Bothnia. The trees would be felled in the winter, taken out to the frozen rivers, and then transported naturally with the arrival of the spring thaw. The picture is still valid up to a point, but the method is now outmoded, being considered slow and wasteful. Now it is cheaper and quicker to use motor haulage. And owing to the great climatic variations in Sweden, the annual growth-rate of trees in the south is two or three times greater than in the north, and there has therefore been large-scale afforestation in southern and central Sweden, where more timber is now felled than in the north. The sawmills are still almost exclusively on the north-east coast, but pulp- and paper-mills are found as far south as Skåne. Technological progress is in evidence throughout the industry, with felling, floating, barking, and snedding, once the province of muscular lumberjacks, now performed by machines. The heart of the dark, silent forest, that cliché of Scandinavian lyric poets, is nowadays assailed by the drone of machinery, ranging from the handy portable electric saw to the heavy all-purpose forest tractors.

Developments within the forestry industry are typical of Swedish industry as a whole. Small uneconomic sawmills have been squeezed out by larger, highly mechanized sawmills, which in turn have gradually embraced all stages of operations from the management of forest land to logging, joinering, the manufacture of pulp and paper, and more recently the production of such products as plywood and fibreboard. Some of these large firms have continued to develop from large national companies into international ones. Svenska Cellulosa AB and Mo och Domsjö AB, for instance, have acquired paper-goods factories in Europe, while others have gone as far afield as Canada.

As in most other Swedish industries, figures over the last decade are impressive. Mechanization and automation have reduced the number of workers, while production figures have risen steadily. Sweden is second only to America in the production of fibreboard and her 700,000 tons per annum amount to 12 per cent of the total world output; she is the world's foremost pulp exporter, providing 25 per cent of the world's export of pulp; she also sells 13 per cent of the total world exports of paper and board.

Like forestry, Swedish mining has a long tradition, but production was on a modest scale until late in the nineteenth century. The development is similar, with the emphasis first on semi-manufacture, but gradually shifting to processing and manufacturing, and forming a sound foundation for the modern engineering industry. The most important deposits are at Kiruna and Malmberget (i.e., 'The Ore Mountain') in Lapland and at Grängesberg in central Sweden, which among them produce 85 per cent of the annual total of some 28 million tons. LKAB (Luossavaara-Kiirunavaara AB), 95 per cent of which is owned by the state and 5 per cent by Grängesberg, is responsible for the greatest amount of iron-mining in Lapland. It has the greater part of the ore transported by rail to Narvik and exported from there. The Bergslagen district in central Sweden has long been famous for its ore, which is of low phosphorus content and contains no sulphur, and is used to produce high-quality Swedish steel.

Laisvall in the north is the largest lead-mine in Europe, while a new copper-mine has recently been started at Aitik and currently produces about $3\frac{1}{2}$ million tons per annum.

Iron- and steel-works occupy their traditional sites near forests, although electricity has long since supplanted charcoal in the metal processing. Both mining and the iron and steel industry have gone through a process of concentration and rationalization in recent years, so that, for instance, eleven mines closed or were amalgamated in central Sweden in the mid-1960s, and LKAB and Grängesberg now operate a joint sales company, Malmexport AB. The process is perhaps even more marked in the case of Uddeholms AB and Stora Kopparbergs Bergslags AB which now own iron-mines, steelworks, sawmills, pulp- and paper-mills, forests, farmland, and even generate electricity. In the steel industry manufacture has been increasingly concentrated on a few large companies, the three largest–Stora Kopparberg,[3] Grängesberg-Oxelösund, and Norrbottens Järnverk–covering 64 per cent of the total output of commercial steel.

The most impressive industrial developments of all are in the engineering industry which in the period between the wars increased production at double the national average and in the 1960s had kept up an 8 per cent increase per annum. It is now the largest section of industry in the country, employing about 40 per cent of the country's total work force. It is mainly located around the three largest cities, Stockholm, Gothenburg, and Malmö. The main theme in this industry's development, too, has been standardization, concentration, and precision, and the result has been the emergence of some of the largest Swedish firms, turning out extremely sophisticated products. As other industries have developed, the demand for machines has

[3] Stora Kopparberg has a charter dating back to the thirteenth century and is said to be the oldest limited company in the world.

increased, and the engineering firms have responded – the chemical industry and paper and pulp industries, for example, have invested heavily in equipment, while the building industry needs pneumatic machines, air-conditioning equipment, roadbuilding equipment, etc. There has been a corresponding increase in demand for office equipment and, with the constantly rising standard of living, for domestic appliances. Some of the Swedish engineering firms concerned have become known internationally – SKF (Swedish Ball Bearing Company), second on the list of Swedish top manufacturers in 1969, Alfa-Laval, Atlas-Copco, and Aga, fourteenth, fifteenth, and twenty-first on that same list respectively.

One of the most spectacular increases has been in the motor-vehicle industry which in 1969 showed a 10 per cent increase in production. The largest manufacturer is Volvo, which accounts for over 75 per cent of the total national output of vehicles and now tops the list of Swedish manufacturers, with a turnover of 4,400 million *kronor* and export sales of 2,071 million *kronor*. Apart from private cars, Volvo also produces lorries and tractors. Fourth on the list of top Swedish manufacturers is Saab-Scania, which makes automobiles, lorries, buses, aircraft, and electronics. More than one-half of the industrial mergers in the mid-1960s were in the engineering industry, and both Saab and Volvo were involved. Saab merged with Scania-Vabis in 1968: Saab concentrating on aeroplane manufacture, missiles, data systems, and private cars; and Scania-Vabis specializing in lorries and buses. The following year Volvo took over Olofströms, which had been previously subcontracted by Volvo to produce tools and spare parts.

In electrical engineering output has increased by 7–8 per cent per annum in the 1960s and demand has been for consumer goods such as refrigerators, vacuum-cleaners, washing machines, etc., which the internationally known firm Electrolux has eagerly coped with. In the field of telecommunications L. M. Ericssons Telephone Co., fifth on the list of Swedish manufacturers, takes the lead, specializing particularly in telephones and telephone equipment. ASEA, the third largest Swedish firm, manufactures electrical motors and deals in particular with power transmission. This firm also has an interest in atomic power, forming, together with the state, Asea-Atom to produce atomic reactors.

In shipbuilding Japan heads the international table, with Sweden and West Germany jostling for second place. Swedish shipyards produce about 10 per cent of the world's annual output and 75 per cent of this production is for export. In the face of the keenest international competition Swedish shipbuilding firms have had to invest on a large scale and rationalize their production methods as never before. A measure of their success is that whereas they have maintained a 6 per cent increase in production per annum throughout the 1960s, their labour force declined by 2 per cent per annum in the same period. Most shipyards are on the west coast, at Uddevalla, Gothenburg, and Malmö, the three largest being Götaverken, Eriksberg, and Kockums, which among them account for 95 per cent of the tonnage launched annually. They all specialize in large tankers and bulk carriers, Kockums completing in 1968 one of the largest docks in the world, capable of constructing ships up to 700,000 tons. One of the most impressive displays of automation is at Götaverken's Arendal yard at Gothenburg, where sections weighing up to 300 tons of a vessel are prefabricated indoors and gradually pushed out on to the slips, the procedure being operated by only a few men at control panels. It is symptomatic of the Swedish approach to industry that Swedish shipyards must pay their own way even though the state in many other countries subsidizes shipbuilding quite substantially. Swedish shipyards often have to extend to their customers extensive credit and the only concession the state makes is to guarantee the credits. The money, however, must be raised in the normal way at market rates.

Good communications are essential in a country at once industrial and sparsely populated, and rapid changes have taken place here as elsewhere. The revolution of the nineteenth century came with the building of the railways from the 1850s onwards, which helped to make industrialization possible. Since then almost all railways have been electrified, the rest being diesel. There have been several closures of branch lines over the last few years to make State Railways more economic, but there are still 8,000 miles of track. Most of the rolling stock has been replaced in the last ten years, and Swedish trains are comfortable, clean, and usually very punctual. Despite their modernization and nationalization programme the railways continue to lose custom on their passenger service, although their freight service proves more attractive than road haulage, despite the increase in the number of large articulated lorries on the roads.

The twentieth-century revolution in communications started in the late 1940s when the motor-car came within the means of a large proportion of the population and roadbuilding began in earnest. Now one Swede in four owns a car, about 2 per cent of the gross national product is spent on roadbuilding, and there are 68,000 miles of road and 200 miles of motorway (scheduled to increase to over 900 miles by 1985). All trunk roads are tarmac except in Norrland, where some are still of gravel.

Domestic air travel, operated by Scandinavian Airlines System and its subsidiary AB Linjeflyg, has increased considerably too in the last few years, and in the north, with its vast distances between communities, the demand for taxi flights and helicopter services is growing.

Because of her relatively small population Sweden is spared many of the traffic problems of more densely populated countries, and in many parts of the country one can drive for hundreds of miles along an excellent tarmac surface without encountering any obstructions. Certain social problems have emerged, however. Largely because of high labour costs, public transport is extremely expensive to run in Sweden and as more people in rural areas acquire private cars and the number of passengers using public transport dwindles, the public services become too uneconomic and are terminated. In many places people with no private means of transport are dependent on an expensive taxi service or the goodwill of their more fortunate neighbours, and in the most isolated spots, with only a few elderly people who have never learnt to drive a vehicle, the situation causes some anxiety.

Internationally, Swedish streamlining and rationalization have led to an important development in her merchant fleet. Because of the high wages commanded by Swedish merchant seamen there is a growing tendency for Swedish shipping firms to invest in modern large ocean-going vessels, especially tankers, that operate in Australasia and South America, where a vessel can be at sea for long stretches and a minimum of time is spent in harbour. Shorter, less remunerative routes are increasingly being left for vessels of other nations. Passenger boats have been geared to the motorized society, the North Sea route now being served by several new car ferries plying between Gothenburg and Tilbury, Immingham and Hull. Passengers drive themselves on and off, most of them serve themselves at cafeterias on board, the boats are turned round very quickly, and labour costs are therefore kept down despite the high wages of the crew.

Power Supply

A plentiful supply of energy is a prerequisite of industry and in this Sweden is fortunate in having fast-moving rivers, especially in north Sweden, which have been harnessed to produce a cheap source of hydro-electric power. Although this is the still dominant source, covering about 35 per cent of Sweden's entire consumption, the use of oil is increasing rapidly and this has to be imported. Only about one-half of the potential hydro-electric power is exploited in Sweden so far, but harnessing the Norrland waterways is not as profitable or as easy as it was, partly because of the trend towards oil and partly because the population is beginning to object volubly to the destruction of the environment in the north. Even so, Swedes produce

5,350 kw-hours *per capita* of the population, a figure bettered by only Norway, Switzerland, and New Zealand. Most of the power is generated in the north and consumed in the south, and it is transmitted over a national network which covers a total of 6,200 miles, using 2,000-volt DC lines invented and produced by ASEA. Problems were caused in the past by exceptionally dry or severely cold weather, but these have been solved by co-operation within Scandinavia. Denmark has steam-power stations which are not affected by climatic conditions. She uses hydro-electric power from Sweden during the summer, while Sweden purchases power from Denmark in the winter if it proves necessary. Some large Swedish concerns are also supplied by Norwegian power-stations.

Oil is used in most of Sweden's thermal power-stations, which are usually placed on the coast or a waterway to facilitate oil deliveries. The largest thermal station has been built underground at Stenungsund. Other large stations have been built in Stockholm, Malmö, and Västerås.

Sweden's first atomic-energy station was opened at Agesta near Stockholm in 1963 and others are being constructed, but they are more or less research and development plants. The fuel used in these stations is uranium and there are uranium deposits in Sweden, but these are inadequate in both quantity and quality. In 1965 a uranium-mill at Ranstad in south-west Sweden was started, but so far the 120 tons per annum produced there costs twice the world market price. Before it can be used in light water-reactors, uranium has to be enriched and the plant needed for that operation is so costly that it is beyond Sweden's means. The United States and Britain so far lead in the sale of nuclear-reactor fuel, but the EEC's Euratom plans to build a plant for the use of all its members, a point that is not lost on those Swedes who advocate Swedish association with the EEC.

The building-up of Swedish industry was in the first place largely dependent on foreign capital, but now the situation has been reversed and direct investment by Sweden abroad has accelerated greatly since 1960. In order to meet stiffening competition in the international market Swedish firms have secured their position by setting up subsidiaries abroad. In 1960 a little over 200 Swedish firms had foreign subsidiaries, but by 1965 the number had risen to 450. It is, of course, the largest Swedish firms that predominate in these direct investments: SKF, L. M. Ericssons Telephone Co., Volvo, Svenska Tändsticks AB (Swedish matches), Atlas-Copco, Electrolux, Alfa-Laval, ASEA, and AGA in that order. Most of the subsidiaries are situated in Sweden's traditional export markets—mainly Europe, especially the EEC countries, with the emphasis on

West Germany and Italy. (Some Swedish wits have remarked *à propos* Swedish entry into the Common Market that they have already gone in via the back door.) Of the EFTA countries Sweden has invested most heavily in Britain. Recently, however, investments in the underdeveloped countries have increased–in the 1960s, for instance, investment in India went up considerably. The Grängesberg Co. is a part-owner of the Lamco joint venture in Liberia and Swedish shares in the project amount to about 30 per cent. In 1965 the total assets of Swedish subsidiaries abroad were said to be 8,669 million *kronor*.

Foreign investment has been a two-way process and over 500 foreign subsidiaries have been established in Sweden between 1955 and 1965. Philips, the Dutch firm, was attracted to Sweden as early as the 1920s and still retains its position as the largest subsidiary, but since 1960 a large number of British, American, and German manufacturers have formed subsidiaries, mainly in metal products, chemicals, textiles, and food-processing. Courtaulds Ltd bought 49 per cent of the shares in Svenska Rayon in 1963, while Unilever dominates the market in detergents. Switzerland staked a claim in Swedish business in 1962 when Nestlé bought out Findus, the frozen food company. The foreign share of total manufacturing in Sweden is well under 5 per cent.

Even such a brief survey of the Swedish industrial scene underlines the point that Sweden is now dependent on international trade. The great advance in her industries in the 1960s coincided with the setting-up of EFTA and the openings that free trade has offered, a fact that makes the question of membership of the EEC such a troubled one.

Because Sweden is associated with the welfare state there is a tendency also to consider her a country of state ownership, but strictly speaking she is one of the most capitalistic countries in Europe (although admittedly the state regulates industry in many ways). State ownership all in all amounted in 1968 to about 6 per cent, employing about 200,000 employees, and its total turnover was 16,000 million *kronor*, about 7 per cent of the gross national product. Since producers' and consumers' co-operatives own about 5 per cent, this means that between 89 and 90 per cent of Swedish industry is run by private enterprise.

Apart from operating postal services, communications, and transport the state is most concerned with the mining industry. In 1957 it bought 95 per cent of the shares of LKAB, the large iron-ore company in Lapland. The Swedish State Power Board produces 43 per cent of the total output of electricity, while the Swedish Forestry Service is responsible for the management of 18 per cent of Swedish forests. AB Statens Skogsindustrier (ASSI, i.e. the National Forest Industries) produces timber products, chemicals, paper, and wall-board. The state also owns minority shares in some shipbuilding firms and the paper and pulp industry. In 1968 ASEA and the state formed AB Asea-Atom to develop nuclear reactors and the following year the state took 50 per cent of the shares of the newly formed Uddcomb Sweden AB (the other shares being divided between Uddeholm and the American Engineering Inc.), for the manufacture of components for atomic power-stations and the chemical industry. State ownership has grown up over many years, has been effected for many reasons, often social, not commercial, and is not the result of any long-term policy. Uddevalla Shipyards, for instance, were acquired by the state in the 1950s because they were losing money and the whole area was dependent on them, while sawmills and paper-mills in the north of Sweden were bought in the 1930s because they were on the verge of bankruptcy and the whole area was threatened with unemployment. Recently, however, a Department of Industry has been set up which has formed a holding company called Statsföretag AB (State Enterprises Ltd) to administer a large part of the state-owned industries. Its two main aims are not necessarily compatible, for it wants industries under its control to expand and operate profitably; but it also wants them to participate fully in regional development and to operate for the good of the community. About twenty enterprises come under the aegis of state enterprises, commanding a total turnover of 2,500 million *kronor* and employing over 28,000 employees. The project caused many Swedish business-men great concern and aroused indignation at the Social Democrats' 'back-door socialism', while others watched the experiment with genuine interest. Krister Wickman, the first Minister of Industry (subsequently appointed Foreign Minister), and Gunnar Svärd, Manager of State Enterprises, have burnt their fingers on a number of occasions. The Kalmar Verkstads AB, a firm which was set up in an area needing employment to produce a new kind of mini-van made of plastic, sustained heavy losses, couldn't sell its product, and had to pay off its workers. Smaller losses but more sarcasm resulted from the failure of another venture, the Rationell Planering AB, for, as the name suggests, it was a management consultant firm aiming to help companies to make themselves more efficient. A large-scale failure which lost State Enterprises both money and face was the Durox Co., a building-materials firm bought in 1965 and sold again at a great loss in 1969. This ill-fated company attained notoriety when a newly-constructed plant was so badly planned (a most un-Swedish phenomenon) that the machinery would not function properly.

It is perhaps too early to judge the success or failure of the experiment, for it may yet prove profitable, and even alternatively, if it does little more than pay its way, it may nevertheless achieve its other object and help to solve the unemployment problem.

Labour Relations

The story of Swedish industry is a success story for those who pay homage to the gross national product. Smooth labour–management relations and collective bargaining have also played their part and help partly to explain the unimpeded progress in industry. The three large unions, LO (the Swedish Confederation of Trade Unions), the TCO (the Central Organization of Salaried Employees), and SACO (the Central Organization of Swedish Professional Workers), on the one hand, and the SAF (the Swedish Federation of Employers), on the other, sit round a table and reach agreements lasting for one to three years. These agreements are then binding for the specified period and if notice is not given two months before the agreement expires, then it remains legally in force. There is no outside interference in these negotiations, but if they break down without agreement having been reached, then by law a government-paid mediator has to be brought in. He cannot force a settlement on either side, but in practice he tends to set a time-limit on his services, which gives a sense of urgency to the negotiations and usually leads to a solution. If agreement is still not reached, a week's notice of a strike or lockout must be given. Once the contract has been drawn up, it is binding on the employers and on all members of the union concerned, and since the Swedish labour force is organized into such a small number of concentrated unions, Swedish industry is spared the 'leap-frogging' and 'who-does-what' inter-union strikes.

If there is a dispute concerning the interpretation of an agreement, either side can refer the matter to the Labour Court, which consists of seven members, two members each from SAF and LO and three drawn from outside, two of whom must have had experience as judges. Should the dispute involve white-collar workers, then one LO member will be replaced by a TCO member, and if a government employer is involved, one of the SAF members is replaced by a member appointed by the government employers. The court's function is not to arbitrate, but to adjudicate and to assess fines and damages, and its decision is final.

The system was evolved after the conference at Saltsjöbaden near Stockholm in 1938 (see above, p. 119) when, after a period of troubled labour relations, both sides realized that if they did not produce a constructive method voluntarily, then the government would feel obliged to bring in legislation. Since then Swedes have talked about

M

the 'spirit of Saltsjöbaden', a triumph of commonsense and compromise. The question at the back of everyone's mind now is whether this system, which has a splendid record, is going to prove adequate in the 1970s. To many ordinary workers LO has become a monolithic organization and its officials are so remote that they feel that they are caught up in a bureaucratic machine rather than a democratic process. It wasn't just in a geographical sense that the mine workers in Norrland who went on strike in 1970 felt very remote from their union representatives in Stockholm. And non-interference has been an accepted part of the negotiating machinery; but members of the TCO and SACO sense, rightly or wrongly, a conspiracy between the leaders of LO (which numbers the lower-paid workers among its members) and Prime Minister Olof Palme in the drive for 'equality'. The white-collar workers feel threatened, which is not a state of mind that readily leads to compromise in negotiations. There has already been one long-drawn-out national strike of white-collar workers in 1971 and there is a general feeling among many members of SACO that this strike was a prelude rather than a conclusion.

There is one branch of the economy that has not been consistently subjected to the test of economic competition and that is agriculture. In 1947 Sweden launched out on an agricultural policy that with slight modifications is still valid today. Although the aim is to make farms as efficient as possible, it is accepted that if Sweden is to remain virtually self-sufficient in food production, then some form of subsidy will be necessary. The accepted degree of self-sufficiency is currently at about 85 per cent and will be allowed to drop to 80 per cent in the next decade. To keep production to the requisite level and at the same time ensure a reasonable standard of living for farmers, a system of price protection is in operation. To improve efficiency, however, the state encourages small farmers to sell out or to turn their arable land into forest, and there has been, particularly in the last decade, a decline in the number of small farms and a corresponding increase in the size of farms being worked, which in turn has led to increased investment in farm machinery and in more specialization in one or two crops or in animal products. As in other industries, the result is that fewer people are producing more.

The Labour Market Board

The image of industrial efficiency has become slightly tarnished in Sweden, however, as more and more people begin to feel that too much is being sacrificed in the name of that great national divinity the GNP. The concentration of industry has drawn people from the sparsely populated north down to the cities in the south, the forestry industry has been so rationalized that many forestry workers have become redundant, and small farmers, particularly in the north, are encouraged to abandon their land in the interests of efficiency. Specialization in one or two crops has led to many farmers stream-lining their productivity by selling off their cattle. The result is that a strange desolation has descended over large parts of northern Sweden. Small plots of agricultural land wrested and kept from the forest by generations of hard-working peasants are now being over-grown again, while byres and barns stand empty and abandoned. Young people thinking of their future have had to leave their birth-place and go south, leaving behind only those who are too old to change their ways. Stig Claesson's tender novel *Vem älskar Yngve Frej* (Who Loves Yngve Frej), which portrays the forlorn, isolated life of the old generation abandoned in Norrland in the interests of progress, touched a very sensitive spot when it appeared in 1968. Four people, all of them over seventy, are the only remaining inhabi-tants of what had been a small but lively farming community, 'free men and women who had seen the community grow, develop, become depopulated, and then disappear'. They have, of course, the sops of the materialistic society, a telephone, radio, refrigerator, deep-freeze, and television but

> what can the TV show a free man or woman? Are these men and women to be compelled to be entertained by strange American singing personalities or just as strange Swedish ones? . . . They have done their bit but all their toil and labour has resulted only in silence . . . the silence descended. The forest waited. First the grass would grow tall and then the bushes. The alder and birch would grow high in the ditches and then the fir tree would wander in and cover over every trace of the work of generations. Not a trace would be seen.

The government has been aware for many years of the general problems involved in full employment and mobility of labour, and the allied tendency for the population to congregate in the large towns in the south. It set up in the 1950s the Labour Market Board (*Arbetsmarknadsstyrelsen*), the aim of which is not only to function as a national employment exchange, but also to give free vocational guidance and free retaining to assist in finding employment. It went much further in 1964 and adopted a regional development plan that would encourage industries by means of grants and loans to set up factories, etc., in the Northern Development Area, an area which covered about two-thirds of the area of Sweden, but has only 17 per cent of the total population and embraces roughly the whole of Norrland and part of west Sweden. In 1970 a transport subsidy was also instituted for the Northern Development Area. In order to remove the disparity in costs of running a business in the north and the south, firms operating in the Northern Area are given allowances for transporting finished and semi-manufactured goods to and from Norrland. In 1968 the sum of 1,500 million *kronor* was allotted to the Labour Market policy, which compares with only 150 million *kronor* in 1956. The government reasons that the best results will be achieved by selecting within the whole development area certain suitable potential growth-points where not just industry but social amenities generally will be built up, such as hospitals, schools, communications, libraries, etc.

The Labour Market Board has been granted funds to operate not just an employment agency with branches all over the country but a public service. A forestry or agricultural worker in Norrland, for instance, who has become redundant because of a thoroughgoing rationalization programme in his industry will be given vocational training in courses that may last from two weeks to two years, depending on the subject chosen, during which time he will receive his wages. If the training has to take place far from his home, he will also be given a travel allowance. The Board will then help him to find a post and if this involves his having to move house, he will be given a grant to cover expenses.

The government scheme has had many successes, has played a large part in maintaining full employment in Sweden, and has created several thousand new jobs in the development area. The Labour Market Board figures for 1966 showed that it had dealt with almost one million posts and had filled 80 per cent of them, had trained or retrained 40,000 workers, and issued 33,000 travel grants, all of which has played its part towards the progress of Swedish industry. One need not stay in Norrland long, however, to detect a smouldering resentment among a lot of people there. Norrland is a vast province, the growth-points designated by the government are very far apart (often on the coast), and many people are obliged to move from places they have been attached to all their lives. A few men leave their families in their country district, take employment further south, often living in barrack-type accommodation, and visit their homes whenever they can. The Labour Market Board is known sarcastically to these people as the 'travel bureau'. They say that Norrland has become Sweden's northern colony, a region from which south Sweden, 'the mother country', extracts great wealth in the form of timber, ore, and hydro-electric power, but pays the 'natives' very poorly in return. The trouble that arose over the threatened closure of Stekenjokk copper-mine in Jämtland in 1971 focused attention on the whole issue. The district is becoming increasingly depopulated, with local employment rationalized out of existence,

but it was confidently predicted that AB Statsföretag (State Enterprises) would invest in the mine which local workers are convinced
could be made into a paying proposition. The government, however,
examined the economics of the project and decided that it was not a
profitable long-term investment, and since their regional aid policy
includes the view that 'financial aid is to be granted on a once for all
basis so that a firm can operate on commercial principles without the
need for subsidies', they refused the necessary capital investment.
The ensuing criticism was acrid: it was pointed out that the Labour
Market Board would be spending millions of *kronor* on grants and
'charity' in the district, but that the same sum would not be channelled into a means of saving the people's community, livelihood, and
dignity. Matters came to a head in February 1971 when the miners
went on a hunger strike, and their action was so well publicized that
the government felt obliged to take action, promising at least temporary respite and relief work for the district.

An attempt to reverse the trend towards centralization has recently been made in Rute, in the island of Gotland (which, like
Norrland, also considers itself a 'colony'), where farms have been
abandoned and many people live on the summer tourists who stay
for only a short season. A 'village council' has been established there,
with the intention of influencing not just the central government but
local politicians too. The aim is to assume some control over the
region's resources by exploiting on a co-operative basis small industries peculiar to the district (in this case textiles and the quarrying of
limestone have been suggested). If the venture is successful, it may
well be applied to Norrland too.

Rationalization, centralization, and concentration of population
in certain areas remain a vexed question which is certainly not
peculiar to Sweden. It will be interesting to see if Sweden can produce a solution that could be applied to other countries with similar
problems.

Taxes

Sweden's efficient exploitation of her resources has made her a
very prosperous country in proportion to her population. Only one
four-hundredth of the world's population lives within her borders
and yet they export one-fortieth of the world's exports. The public
sector of the Swedish economy has expanded from 17 per cent in
1946 to well over 30 per cent of the gross national product and taxation is among the highest in the world. There is, of course, a lot of
complaining about tax levels, but Swedes of all political persuasions
appear to approve of the welfare state and appreciate that its benefits
must be paid for. Few people therefore advocate very radical changes

in the basic structure of the tax system, except those on the far Left who would like to see the rich taxed much more than they are at present. As it is, people commanding relatively modest salaries may well pay up to 50 per cent of their earnings in direct taxation, although there is an upper limit of 80 per cent to the amount that one has to pay. There is also a wealth tax levied annually on the net wealth of individuals, estates, and family trusts exceeding £8,000.

Indirect taxation has played an increasing role in recent years which is perhaps strange under a Socialist government that in principle disapproves of it. Value-added tax, which was introduced on 1 January 1969 at 10 per cent and now stands at 15 per cent, is the most important of the indirect taxes. Few things are exempt and not even food and books escape. Excise tax applies to alcohol, tobacco, and cars, and there is an 'energy tax' on sales of electricity, coal, coke, and fuel-oil to industrial consumers. Petrol has been singled out for a special tax, amounting to about 63 per cent of the retail price.

Social Welfare

The government current expenditure tables (1970–71) show clearly its priorities: social welfare heads the list with 28·3 per cent; then education 18·3 per cent; and then defence 12·8 per cent. Social benefits are impressively comprehensive and guide the citizens more or less from conception to demise. We have seen how the building-up of a social welfare state began in earnest in the 1930s and progressed to the point where the national supplementary pension scheme was finally accepted in 1959 and became effective in 1960. This supplementary pension will be paid to all those born after 1896 who have been gainfully employed and, together with the old-age pension, will be roughly equivalent to two-thirds of the annual income earned during the beneficiaries' fifteen highest-paid years. Social welfare changes since the introduction of this pension scheme have been slight, aiming at improving or expanding existing programmes and at simplifying the administration of the various welfare schemes.

An expectant mother receives free pre-natal care, including prophylactic medicines and dental treatment, courses in child-care and physical exercises at a special centre, free services of a trained midwife before and after the birth of the child, free confinement in a maternity hospital, and any travelling expenses incurred in excess of 4 or 5 *kronor*. Every mother receives a maternity grant slightly in excess of 1,000 *kronor* (£80; $208) and if she had been gainfully employed for a minimum of 270 days before the birth, she will also claim supplementary sickness benefit and her job will be guaranteed for six months. The child will have a free medical check-up periodically at a health centre until it starts school, after which the medical examinations will be done there.

For each child under sixteen the mother receives 900 *kronor* per annum (about £73; $190) paid in quarterly instalments and not subject to tax. Children start school at the age of seven, but there are day nurseries for children from the age of six months to six years. So far there are not nearly enough of these (the planners have said that they are to be given priority, especially as they are encouraging married women to go out to work) and in choosing which children to accept, importance is attached to whether or not the mother is gain-fully employed. For children of school age, holidays can be arranged in a children's camp or holiday home free or at a reduced cost, depending on the circumstances of the parents.

There are Child Welfare Officers to give advice and assistance in cases of children under eighteen and a Welfare Officer is always appointed for the children of unmarried mothers or of separated or divorced parents.

Young people intending to get married can receive advice from a Marriage Guidance Centre and can also be granted material assist-ance in the form of a home-furnishing loan, providing actual need can be shown. The upper limit is 6,000 *kronor* (£480; $1,248) and has to be repaid over eight years. This loan can also be procured by unmarried parents to help them to make a home for their children.

There is also a scheme for providing temporary home help to families where the housewife, because of serious illness, childbirth, or some similar cause, is unable to look after the home. There is a charge for this service, but people in low-income groups receive it free. The Social Welfare Service also includes holidays for house-wives if they belong to a low-income group. Housewives can choose from one of many holiday homes to which grants are made in order to keep the costs down. Their travelling expenses to and from the holiday home or resort are also paid and they can go off on their own for a complete break.

A vital part of the welfare system is the National Compulsory Health Insurance Scheme and Sickness Benefit. Contributions are paid in connection with income tax, and sickness benefits are related to income. Everyone receives free treatment at hospitals and clinics, and transport to the nearest hospital is free. Distances involved can be considerable, especially in the north, and some overnight expenses are also refunded. Should a doctor be asked to attend a patient at home, the patient must pay his fee and can then, by producing the receipt at the local health insurance office, reclaim three-quarters of it. Some essential medicines, such as insulin prescribed by a doctor, are free of charge, while with other prescriptions one has to pay the first 5 *kronor* oneself, is given a 50 per cent reduction on the next 20 *kronor*, and one hundred per cent reduction on anything over 25 *kronor*. This means that 15 *kronor* is the maximum paid for any prescription, a sum well in excess of £1 or $2.60.

Swedish hospitals are almost without exception modern, bright, well designed, and well equipped, and give the impression of having reached a different stage of medical history from that of the large Victorian brick edifices still encountered in some places in Britain. Swedish doctors take seven years to qualify and have a reputation for competence and conscientiousness. It is doubtful, however, whether the Swedes enjoy a better medical service than the British public. The new hospitals may be magnificent buildings, but there is such a shortage of staff in some parts of the country that they cannot be used to full capacity. This is particularly true in the summer months, when all the personnel have a minimum of four weeks holiday and senior physicians thirty-nine days, excluding public holidays and week-ends, which amounts in practice to about eight weeks. This has led to sections of hospitals having to close down for the holiday and to about one-third of all hospital beds being unused for the summer. Fortunately nature slightly ameliorates the situation, for fewer Swedes register medical ailments during the summer months.

As medicine becomes increasingly specialized, more and more doctors prefer to work in a well-equipped hospital, and the old family doctor is beginning to disappear from the medical scene. About half the patients are now treated at the out-patients' departments of the hospitals and the proportion will certainly increase in the future because the majority of the new generation of medical practitioners will opt for a hospital post. Doctors with private practices still exist. (Towards the end of 1965 there were approximately 8,500 doctors practising in Sweden and of these 1,200 were private and about one-quarter were over seventy years of age–the proportion has been slightly reduced since.) They are, however, in a sense at a disadvantage since they are not allowed to treat their patients in the city or county hospitals. In a country where the individual is very conscious of his right to lead his own life, they also expect to have their leisure time and few of them go out on calls, with the result that even those patients who do go to private doctors usually have to drive to the nearest hospital to be treated by the doctor on duty there if they are suddenly taken ill during the night, at the week-end, or on a public holiday.

Most complaints are levelled against the long waits involved in obtaining treatment unless one is classed as an emergency case. Even if one has made an appointment at the out-patients' department, one will often have to wait hours for attention and if one has organized one's ailments badly enough to require different forms of treatment in different parts of even the same hospital, one will have to join the queue in each separate case and be examined at each stage by a different doctor. Another cause of dissatisfaction is the impersonal attitude of many of the doctors, but it is difficult to see how a more personal relationship between doctor and patient can be established when the only point of contact is a brief interview and an examination in very clinical, antiseptic surroundings.

Medical service in the remote rural districts poses other problems. There the doctors will be medical county officers and will cover a large area, and have to make long trips to visit patients who are too ill to come to them. The north of Sweden has special problems in this respect and, of course, the more the process of depopulation continues, the worse the situation grows. Modern technology has helped in some ways, however – emergencies can, for instance, be transported by helicopter to the nearest hospital if necessary. The attractions of the densely populated areas, with their specialized hospitals, are such that about 12 per cent of the district medical officers' posts are unfilled and about 17 per cent of them are filled with people not licensed to practise.

It must be said that the government is acutely aware of the shortcomings of the system and that more doctors are being trained than ever before, while married women who are qualified nurses are being lured back into the profession; but prognostications suggest that even so, the situation will not improve in the foreseeable future. Ironically enough, this is partly because social welfare has made such successful progress and secured for the Swedish population almost the highest life expectancy in the world – and the older one grows the more medical attention one requires. People, moreover, are also more aware of their rights now and are no longer prepared to suffer illness humbly or stoically.

A disquieting feature of a highly-developed society is the increase of psychosomatic cases and Sweden is no exception. It is calculated that nearly half the hospital beds are occupied by mental cases and yet psychiatry and neurology are given scant attention in doctors' basic training. Too few then go on to specialize in this branch of medicine and less than half the hospital posts for psychiatrists are filled. F. Fleisher quotes the case of a large hospital intended for the care of psychopaths which was built in 1964 at a cost of over £3 million. 'Two years later, after failing to get even a skeleton staff, the government started to investigate the possibility of another use for the building'.[4] Fleisher also quotes a prominent Swedish senior physician in a county hospital as saying

> No matter how fine the life boats may be on the ocean liner, if there aren't enough of them, or if there aren't enough crew members to man them not all the passengers can be taken care of in times of need. This is the state of medical care in Sweden today. There are so many who are reaching after care but some have to be pushed back into the water and you have to hope that they can get along with a lifebelt.[5]

It is easy to get the situation out of proportion. The Swedes have, after all, access to some of the world's best-equipped and best-serviced hospitals, whatever their income and status in life, and anyone seriously ill will be given excellent attention. If a patient is only uncomfortably rather than dangerously ill, on the other hand, he may well find himself in the out-patients' department with plenty of time to meditate on the connection between the Latin word *patientem* and its connotations of suffering and patience.

Housing

Adequate accommodation must necessarily be part of a comprehensive welfare system and the Swedish government has exercised considerable control in both the building and allocation of housing since World War II. The housing situation in Stockholm, Gothenburg, Malmö, and other large towns in the 1920s and early '30s, when people were moving into the urban areas in large numbers, was a cause of great concern, the majority of working-class families living in sub-standard homes and overcrowded conditions.

Up to 1939 private enterprise accounted for 88 per cent of the housing production, but this figure has now dropped to 20 per cent, the rest being built by the state, local authorities, and non-profit-making co-operative groups. In their efforts to prevent exploitation in connection with this vital social amenity, the government introduced in 1942 strict rent controls. Accepted as a wartime measure, they have remained ever since and are blamed by many for the chronic housing shortage which seems to increase every year in the large cities.

As with the medical service, the public's expectations have risen manyfold in the last two decades and although Sweden was spared wartime destruction and has, moreover, stepped up her building programme so that she now completes more housing units than most countries in the world (12·5 per thousand inhabitants as

---

[4] F. Fleisher, *The New Sweden* (New York, 1967), p. 214.
[5] ibid., p. 208.

opposed to West Germany's 10 per thousand and Britain's 7·3), the fact remains that people in urban areas, especially in Stockholm, have their names on the housing list for years before finally getting accommodation. The shortage has led to a flourishing illegal trade in key money, with tenants subletting and making a healthy profit.

One reason for the acute shortage is the migration of so many forestry and agricultural workers to the towns. Another is the growing independence of individual members of the family who in the past would have stayed at home until they got married, but now want their own independent household even though perhaps living in quite close proximity to their families. There is also the contributing factor that as a consequence of higher living standards families who forty years ago would have lived in two rooms now expect and can afford five- or six-roomed flats.

The main reason, however, is that rigid government controls at a time when inflation is putting up incomes and prices have kept the price of accommodation artificially low. There is also now a generous government scheme of rent subsidies for families with one child or more under the age of sixteen. About 40 per cent of all families with children benefit by it. The amounts paid are on a sliding scale depending on the family income and the size of accommodation, but a family with an income of about 17,200 *kronor* (about £1,376; $3,578) receives a basic allowance of 720 *kronor* (about £58; $151) and the larger the family and the larger the accommodation, the higher the subsidy, which has helped to improve considerably the living standards of those families who have been on the waiting list long enough to get a flat, but has also helped to lengthen the housing queue considerably.

The government's use of building permits and loans as a weapon against unemployment has not helped the situation. It is easier to obtain planning permission and government loans to build in areas where the unemployment is high, but these areas are almost invariably the places with the shortest housing lists. It is in those areas that have been attracting workers, especially Stockholm, Gothenburg, and Malmö, that the worst housing shortages are registered.

Perhaps another reason for this shortage is the Swedes' refusal to accept anything but extremely high standards of housing. What in many countries would be considered as luxury is accepted as standard equipment in a Swedish home: central heating (usually oil-fired these days), double glazing, and parquet floors. When one moves into a new flat, the kitchen will almost certainly have been fitted with a brand-new electric cooker, a stainless-steel sink unit with twin bowls, a refrigerator, and nowadays often a deep-freeze. On each floor of the apartment block there will be a chute which will dispose of one's refuse and in the basement there will be a communal laundry-room with washing machines fitted. Careful observation and measurements of housewives' movements when working have led to standard Swedish kitchen equipment which eliminates a great deal of unnecessary drudgery. Surfaces are where one needs them, shelves and cupboards are the correct height, knobs and handles on cookers and cupboard-doors are carefully designed so that very small children are not able to manipulate them.

This careful planning has been typical of the whole approach to Swedish building and architecture generally since the 1930s and particularly since the war when whole new suburbs have been designed as an entity. One of the first of these suburbs to arouse interest on an international scale was Vällingby, some 12 miles from the centre of Stockholm, designed by Sven Backström and Leif Reinius. It has its own centre, with shops, post-office, banks, libraries, a civic centre, cinema, restaurant, etc. Many people commute by the fairly recently completed underground, but Vällingby also provides jobs for about 2,000 people. Since Vällingby was completed, other large-scale projects have been launched both outside Stockholm and the other major cities. Backström and Reinius went on to design Farsta, also near Stockholm, which was completed in 1960, while the most recently completed centre is Skärholmen. Great attention has been given to detail in all these designs. The sites are hilly and rather rugged, and against this background on different levels large well-appointed 14- or 15-storied tower blocks of glass and concrete rise up against the skyline. The architect has envisaged the centres of these new satellite towns as plazas where people can congregate and stroll without any danger from traffic. Each scheme is more ambitious and costlier than the last, employing the newest techniques in design and construction. Farsta, for instance, is heated centrally by an atomic energy plant, while Skärholmen includes among its amenities an hotel for old people and what is alleged to be the largest indoor car-park in Europe.

Architectural developments are not confined to the south of the country by any means. Luleå, for example, on the north-east coast not very far south of the Arctic Circle, boasts a centrally heated market area on different levels with escalators and conveyer pavements. With temperatures outside well below freezing-point thousands of customers can do their shopping in warm relaxed surroundings.

Opinions differ as to the merits of these new satellites. No one doubts that they are excellent examples of meticulous planning and efficiency, and that the designers have carefully considered the needs of the inhabitants and have tried to provide accordingly. Perhaps it is the cumulative effect of so much excellent planning that begins to depress the critics. Since 1947, when the Town Planning Act was passed, the authorities have exercised great power in this field. All areas have to submit a master plan to the state for approval and then there are regional plans with which the area plans have to harmonize. The result is an integrated architectural whole. David Jenkins writes that

> Swedish city planning has attracted great interest and even admiration abroad, not usually however, for its aesthetic qualities, but for its thoroughness. Hans Erland Heineman, a Swedish architect, answered the critics who complained of the drabness of the results: 'They demand a Brasilia, a Marina City, a Sydney Opera House, and this a field in which our city has perhaps not been able to supply the big sensations. In many ways, the Swedish architects of today seem to take a more analytical view of the planning of towns and buildings than their colleagues in other countries. This analytical view has given Sweden a body of architecture possessing unexampled consistency of quality . . .' Or, as some might put it, tiresome sameness.[6]

The sameness is not perhaps of design but of period, for in large sections of many urban areas there are no buildings predating World War II. Here, too, it is easy to exaggerate, for most towns still have their old sections, a particularly charming example being Stockholm's *Gamla Stan* which conjures up the memory of medieval merchants, Baroque noblemen, and Bellman and his bibulous Gustavian confrères. Nor should one forget that Sweden does not have the great conurbations of densely populated countries. A few minutes journey by underground even from the centre of the capital is all that is required to reach the country.

The tendency in urban areas in Sweden is to live in apartments rather than houses, and although, as already stated, these flats are usually of a very high quality, they are also small by British standards, which seems strange perhaps in a country where the density of population is 47 to the square mile as opposed to 588 in the United Kingdom. This should be considered in connection with the Swedes' strangely ambivalent attitude to town-dwelling generally. Despite the increasing urbanization which is particularly evident in the south of the country, and although Swedes are proud of their architectural and engineering feats and anxious to make their town apartments comfortable and pleasing to the eye, the fact remains that most Swedes reveal a puzzlingly antagonistic attitude towards urban areas where they live only as long as necessary. This appears

[6] D. Jenkins, *Sweden, The Progress Machine* (London, 1968), p. 255

to have a long history and British travellers to Sweden in the eighteenth and nineteenth centuries often commented on the town-
dwellers' habit of leaving their cities after the winter.

E. D. Clarke, for instance, who set off on a visit to Scandinavia in
1799, remarked that a characteristic of Stockholm's social life was
that it ceased with the arrival of summer.[7] Stockholmers considered
that after a long, arduous winter in town it was necessary to move to
their summer cottages to recuperate and enjoy the all too brief
summer in the country. One of Strindberg's Chamber Plays, *Oväder*
(The Storm), written a century later, shows the loneliness of an
ageing man alone in his flat in Stockholm in the summer when the
town is deserted.

The tendency to desert the town when possible has increased, and
now there are very few Swedes living in urban areas who have not
got access to a cottage, be it simple or sophisticated, near a stretch of
water, or a relation in the country who can be visited when the days
grow long. In the last few decades the Swedish summer 'grass
widower' has become a common phenomenon. At the commence-
ment of the school summer holidays early in June the whole family
moves out to its cottage and mother and children stay there for most
of the summer while father returns to his work in town, lives in the
town apartment during the week, but joins his family at the week-
end. There are very few children who return to school in August
without a glowing suntan, a sun-bleached forelock, and an aura of
abounding good health. Those who draw conclusions about national
characteristics from social environment would need to visit the Swede
not only in his well-appointed functional town flat but also in the
relaxed atmosphere of his other, more natural, home (in all senses of
the word) in the country or on a small island in the archipelago.
Sune Carlsson, a Swedish professor of business administration, put
the same point in a negative way in his remark to David Jenkins:
'We're just a bunch of farmers. We really don't know how to live in
cities'.[8] No doubt he goes too far, but public opinion polls certainly
show that the vast majority of people say they prefer not to live in
towns, although most of them do.

Education

The Swedish educational system illustrates certain essential
Swedish qualities: the desire to establish equal opportunity for all
members of society; the logical approach; and the readiness to pay
for a system considered necessary for the good of society.

Although, as we have seen, attendance at the primary school has

---

[7] E. D. Clarke, *Travels in various countries of Europe, Asia and Africa*, III (1824).
[8] Jenkins, op. cit., p. 253.

been compulsory since 1842 and interest in education has been a feature of Swedish society for many centuries, there were until the 1940s still many discrepancies in the system, with those who could afford it being assured of a better education than those who could not, and those in country districts often being less well served than those in the town. It was with a view to abolishing these anomalies that a Schools Commission was set up in 1946. Its recommendations, submitted in 1948, for a nine-year comprehensive school were not unanimous, but the *Riksdag* accepted them and in 1950 proposed in principle a nine-year compulsory comprehensive school to replace most of the existing primary and secondary schools, but on an experimental basis with different schools in different areas participating. In 1957, by which time one-third of the population was involved in the experiment, an Educational Drafting Committee was set up to assess the results and, after considering them, to draw up the final structure of the nine-year school. By 1961 the committee put forward its proposals concerning the nine-year *grundskolan* (i.e., basic school) and although grave misgivings were expressed by certain members of the *Riksdag*, the proposals were accepted unanimously in 1962.

The *Riksdag* also passed the first Schools Act, which grants to everyone in Sweden the right to attend school free of charge and the obligation to attend for a minimum period from the ages of seven to sixteen. Swedish schools in the past had been rather disciplinarian, with a strong emphasis on examinations, on the assimilation of facts, and with a tendency to accept the infallibility of the authorities. One of the main aims of the 1962 reforms was to alter this attitude and to lay particular stress on the development of a child's personality.

The universal system which has been evolved by dint of this experimenting is that all children must attend the nine-year comprehensive school from the age of seven. There are three levels of three years each and no streaming. In the Lower School the emphasis is on the basic skills of reading, writing, and arithmetic plus music, physical education, religious instruction, and some form of handicrafts. Pupils also start learning English in the third year of the Lower School, that is, when they are nine years of age, and it remains a compulsory subject throughout the rest of their training at the comprehensive school, seven years in all. The emphasis is on the spoken language with an extensive use of the direct method and language laboratory courses, which has led many of the old guard to despair at children's inability to understand the grammar and structure of language or to build up a large vocabulary. On the other hand, there are very few young Swedes today who cannot hold their own in a conversation in English and who have not acquired an impressive pronunciation. The Middle School continues with the basic subjects and adds history, geography, nature study, and civics.

In the Upper School (classes seven to nine, i.e., age groups fourteen to sixteen) an element of choice is introduced, although 30 of the 35 periods a week are taken up with general subjects which include physics, chemistry, and biology. The alternative subjects are economics, art, technology, and a second foreign language (either French or German). The authorities are not allowed to enforce their will at any stage and it is the pupils and their parents 'after information has been provided by the school' according to the Schools Act who choose the optional subjects, and the school cannot deprive a pupil of the right to take the subject of his choice. In class eight, visits are arranged to various places of employment so that pupils can gain some knowledge of what is involved and then in the final year of the Upper School practical, vocational guidance is given, and every pupil must 'work' for a fortnight at a factory, an office, or some other place.

When a pupil has completed the nine years of schooling, he is given a final report showing what courses he has followed and the final marks obtained in each, and in theory these marks entitle him to continue at the *gymnasium* if he wishes, although in practice certain minimum requirements have been stipulated before pupils can carry on with some *gymnasia* courses.

After the comprehensive school those who wish to continue their education can continue at the *gymnasium*, a sort of sixth form. Until 1964 there were three kinds of *gymnasia*, the general, technical, and commercial, but in that year the *Riksdag* voted to fuse them and by 1966 the new *gymnasium* had emerged. The old general *gymnasium* had been something of a hothouse for the careful nurturing of candidates for higher education, with the emphasis on the more academic subjects, such as classical languages and history. The new institution has adapted its courses more consciously to the needs of a modern society, giving preference to such subjects as technology, economics, modern languages, and civics. It offers three-year courses in five different fields, namely the liberal arts, social studies, economics, natural sciences, and technology, and a pupil completing any one of these is entitled to a place at a university or college, assuming there is a place available. There is also a two-year *gymnasium*, with courses in social sciences and economic and technological subjects, but these do not lead to university entrance. Approximately half the *gymnasium* pupils opt for the two-year course.

The *studentexamen*, the final examination at the *gymnasium* which had entitled the successful candidate to wear the white student cap, was abolished in 1968. It had long been considered a symbol of privilege and was viewed very sourly by the Social Democrats, who in their youth had been deprived of educational opportunities whatever their potential. This passing was therefore hailed by many as a triumph in the struggle for equality, although others missed the air of festivity the student cap could bestow on university junketing and the traditional heralding of spring on Walpurgis Night.

Now that the basic nine-year comprehensive school has been fully introduced, it is possible to discern definite trends. One of the most startling is that almost 90 per cent of the pupils completing the nine-year course are opting to continue their education at the *gymnasium* level. Obviously in the future those arranging further training for school-leavers will soon have to assume that their beginners have had an eleven- or twelve-year basic education.

The changes in education have amounted to a minor revolution in society and have engendered an enormous activity in school-building. About 18 per cent of the national budget is directed towards education and educational research. Of that sum 64 per cent comes direct from the state and the remainder from the various administrative districts, and many municipalities spend over half their budgets on education. This perhaps explains the striking number of new schools in Sweden, their up-to-date equipment, and the wealth of free textbooks as well as free lunches for all and free medical care for the pupils. The children's allowance of 75 *kronor* a month (about £6; $15.60) is extended beyond sixteen if a child opts to continue at school, and if in a country district there is no appropriate school, then the pupil is granted a lodgings and travel allowance. Pupils who have attained the age of nineteen during their course are also awarded a study grant of 75 *kronor* a month without any form of means test.

Private schools have never played a large part in the Swedish educational system, where first the Church and then the public authorities have assumed responsibility, and most of the few still remaining are finding themselves virtually starved out. There are some ten private boarding schools still operating and they offer courses mainly at the Upper School and *gymnasium* level. In 1970 four of these became 'National boarding schools' by a ruling of the *Riksdag* and receive a state grant, but in return they are expected to accept pupils who need to get away from their home environment and the children of Swedes living abroad.

The great increase in the number of children staying on at school has had repercussions on the universities. In 1950 about 15,000 students were at universities or equivalent institutions, but by 1970 this figure was 120,000 and it is still rising. The universities of Uppsala and Lund (founded in 1477 and 1668 respectively) were for

N

centuries the only traditional seats of learning in Sweden; then in the nineteenth century Stockholm and Gothenburg university colleges were established, although they were not actually granted their charter until the twentieth century. In 1963 Umeå University was founded, and since then university colleges have been established in Linköping, Örebro (a branch of Uppsala University), Växjö (Lund University), and Karlstad (Gothenburg University), while Falun, Gävle, Härnösand, Jönköping, Kalmar, Kristianstad, and Luleå now all boast Colleges of Education, and Solna, Södertälje, Norrköping, Borås, Västerås, Gävle, and Luleå have training colleges for nursery school teachers. All these institutions are now run by the state.

Sweden does not have the grant system which university students enjoy in Great Britain, but students can take out an interest-free loan of up to 8,000 Swedish *kronor* per annum which is repayable over a number of years after the student has qualified and started earning a salary. Students also receive a monthly allowance of approximately £12 or $31.20 and a special allowance if they have children to support. There are a number of extremely comfortable student hostels in university towns, comprising bed-sitting rooms and on every floor a communal kitchen at one end of the corridor and a communal bathroom with showers at the other. These buildings often also include small self-contained apartments for married students. The educational 'explosion' has led to a shortage of accommodation, which is acute in the large towns, especially Stockholm.

Nowhere will one hear harsher criticism of the new educational system than at the universities. The great explosion has led to a flood of applicants and whereas in some faculties (Science, Medicine, Dentistry, for instance) there is a restricted entrance, there is traditionally no restriction in the Arts faculties on students who have the necessary entrance qualifications. The result is an unsatisfactory staff–student ratio and students in many Arts subjects, especially the popular ones like English and Scandinavian Literature, have not infrequently taken their initial degree without having had any contact with the professors in the subjects. Similarly it is proving impossible for many university teachers to combine teaching and research, and since promotion in academic circles is still based on a publish-or-perish system, many academics arrange for unpaid sabbatical leave in order to keep abreast of their subjects.

There is in Sweden a profound respect for education and this reveals itself in the many forms of adult education arranged by local authorities and numerous public and private institutions. The most particularly Scandinavian of them are the Folk High Schools, which were first established in the mid-nineteenth century and originated in

Denmark, the brainchild of N. F. S. Grundtvig, the Danish Romantic writer, theologian, and educationalist. They are informal, often
idealistic, residential colleges supported by a variety of organizations
such as the Co-operative Society, trade unions, certain religious
organizations, temperance movements, etc., and are attended by
adults who want to fill the gap in their general education. In the past
they have tended to cater for those who for various reasons, often
financial, had to leave school when only fifteen, take up employment, and now want to widen their cultural horizons. The emphasis
has changed recently and now many of the students take courses
concerned with the organization or associations that support the
Folk High School.

There are also numerous correspondence courses including those
organized by state-run adult *gymnasia*. Extremely active too is the
Arbetarnas Bildningsförbund (the Workers' Educational Association),
which with the help of state subsidies organizes classes all over the
country. It is calculated that about one million Swedish adults (out
of a total population of 8 million) enrol for some form of evening
class, modern languages proving the most popular.

The changes in Swedish education in this century, but especially
in the last two decades, have been on a vast scale and there are many
Swedes who deprecate the extent to which the old disciplines have
been swept away and who predict a drastic falling-away of the high
standards of the past. There are also many teachers who insist that in
practice the new informal attitude has not so much removed harmful
fears and inhibitions in the child as created an acute problem in
classroom discipline. Conversely the system has many enthusiastic
supporters who feel that for the first time all Swedish children, whatever their background, are being given the opportunity to develop
their talents, and who insist that a welfare state which prides itself on
bestowing on every citizen the right to live a full life must have such a
universally comprehensive system. Educationalists in many highly
developed countries are watching with keen interest to see what the
results will be in the long run.

The State and the Arts

The Ministry of Education is also responsible for culture and a
notable change has become discernible very recently in its attitude
to what was becoming the Cinderella of the welfare state. The
approach has been as typically logical and pragmatic as one comes
to expect of Swedish politicians. The Social Democrats are anxious
to achieve equality and had directed their energies and financial
resources to the elimination of the more obvious class barriers,
mainly by distributing wealth more evenly and improving the

educational system. By the early 1960s it was becoming obvious that 'culture'–the theatre, opera, museums, concerts, and serious literature–was still largely the prerogative of the middle and upper classes, and there developed a feeling that this form of class distinction should also be removed by subsidizing and popularizing the arts. Three arguments could be put to the more materialistic members of the party for the justification of these subsidies: with the working week being reduced and holidays lengthened a leisure problem could easily arise; the arts could help citizens in some ways to adapt themselves more easily to the rapidly changing society; and in a country with a small population there would not be sufficient demand to support artists adequately.

In the preface to his report *The State and Culture in Sweden 1970* Ingvar Carlsson, Minister of Education and Cultural Affairs, writes:

> it must be admitted that the cultural sector was long excluded from reformatory work. In the late fifties and above all in the sixties, responsible politicians in Sweden–as in other countries of similar structure–became aware of the fact that the cultural sector was lagging behind . . . in my opinion it is justifiable that the basic problems of security and social justice, as well as the creation of a modern educational system should be given priority, in view of the limited economic resources.[9]

Now that the educational programme was launched, it was to be 'culture's' turn.

Cultural subsidies were no novel notion, of course, and there is a long tradition of patronage of the arts in Sweden, whether by royalty, or nobility, or the state, a point made by N. Elvander in his *Rôle of the State in Sweden's Cultural Life* (1965). 'Ancient monuments and antiquities', which include runic stones and churches, have been preserved by the state since 1666; a Royal Academy of Fine Arts was established in 1735 to train Swedish painters, sculptors, and architects; and, as we have seen, the Gustavian era saw the foundation of the Swedish Academy, the Royal Opera, and the Royal Dramatic Theatre. In the nineteenth century patronage was partly carried on by the *Riksdag* and partly taken over by the new industrialists. The National Museum of Fine Arts was founded in 1844 and shortly afterwards the *Riksdag* elected to support Swedish artists by buying indigenous works for the museum. In 1863 the *Riksdag* gave a grant to the Swedish Academy for the foundation of scholarships to outstanding authors. By the 1920s, when the Social Democrats had come to political prominence, the view was fostered that the state should

[9] *The State and Culture in Sweden*, published by the Swedish Institute (Stockholm, 1970).

encourage cultural activities and the National Museum received greatly increased grants with the pious hope that it would actively help to propagate the arts. Education was always dear to the hearts of these pioneer Social Democrats and they encouraged the setting-up of public libraries and in later years pioneered the system of the library bus and the library boat for the remote areas in the country and off the coasts of Sweden.

The depression in the early 1930s had a deleterious effect on the cultural situation and caused practising artists to despair. If the new social system was to abolish personal wealth and thereby many of the artists' customers and patrons, but if the state was not willing to assume the role of patron, what then was the position of the arts to be in the welfare state? In 1937 a form of compromise was reached when the *Riksdag* agreed to designate a minimum of one per cent of state construction costs to the acquisition of works of art for public buildings; and to assign part of the profits of the state lottery to the arts, especially the theatre and classical music.

The war brought this to an end and although in the immediate post-war period a fixed sum was stipulated for works of art for public buildings and the government introduced a system whereby writers received a small remuneration when their books were borrowed from public libraries, the decade after the war was a lean one for the arts in many respects and led to creative and executive artists stating their grievances and their demands with such fervour that by 1959 the Ministry of Education promised to take immediate action. Some measures followed almost immediately, such as the doubling of money available for the purchase of works of art for public buildings, better scholarships for creative artists, and an increase in the amount to authors in connection with public library loans.

Artists began to call themselves 'cultural workers' and demanded equal rights with other workers in the equitable welfare society. The point was underlined on May Day (1 May) in 1962 when a contin-gent of 'cultural workers' joined the traditional workers' parade, including many well-known actors, dancers, writers, and musicians. F. Fleisher quotes part of a speech made on that occasion by Ingrid Thulin the actress, who on the strength of talented performances in several Ingmar Bergman films enjoys an international reputation. She maintained that the welfare state must be able to afford a rich and varied cultural life.

It is not certain that doubling the standard of living is the same as doubling happiness. At times we may forget that the goal of our efforts and endeavours isn't only to produce more products, create more leisure time and greater leisure problems . . . Material prosperity must also be used for excursions into the realm of the spirit.[10]

It was all grist to the mill and helped accelerate the course that the government had already embarked upon. A Department of Cultural Affairs was set up within the Ministry of Education in 1963 and has initiated several schemes.

Professional orchestras that were formed earlier this century in Stockholm, Gothenburg, Malmö, Hälsingborg, Norrköping, and Gävle and were struggling financially now basically have their activities paid for by public funds in the form of grants from the state and local government.

There is an Academy of Music which, apart from its own aims of furthering musical life and guaranteeing musical standards at the music conservatoires in Sweden, also now administers for the state a fund set aside for music scholarships and publications.

A Nationwide Concert Foundation has been instituted with its head office in Stockholm and regional offices in Kristianstad for south-west Sweden, Gothenburg for west Sweden, and Luleå for north Norrland. Its aim is 'to promote musical life by arranging and sponsoring concerts, providing information and study material, promoting musical education and contacts with musical life abroad and undertaking any other activities aimed at increasing the general interest in music'. In practice it has developed a school concert programme covering large parts of the country; general concerts for young people and adults throughout the country (over 600 concerts a year); so called 'internal concerts', in hospitals, prisons, trade union meetings, etc. The Foundation prepares information on the music and sends it to schools in advance of the concerts, and encourages a personal contact between the audience and the musician. It also assists amateur orchestras with training and the opportunity to work with professional musicians and conductors. The Foundation (in effect the state) covers the travelling expenses and accommodation of the musicians on tour and half their fee, and claims one-half of the receipts from the actual concerts.

Opera, ballet, and drama had all been supported in some measure in the past, and now increased state grants are given annually to the Royal Opera-House in Stockholm, the Opera-House in Gothenburg, the Royal Dramatic Theatre, to ten municipal theatres, and to a National Touring Theatre. The charming eighteenth-century Drottningholm Court Theatre is also subsidized quite heavily.

The Swedish film industry had enjoyed a large measure of fame in the first part of this century but went through a critical period as an

[10] Fleisher, op. cit., p. 288.

increasingly large proportion of the population acquired TV-sets; box-office receipts fell drastically as a consequence and the industry seemed doomed. Matters came to a head when Harry Schein wrote his pamphlet *Can we afford Culture* in 1962, in which he not only complained about the 25 per cent entertainment tax on the cinema, but also put forward a practical proposal to help save the film industry. He suggested that the tax should be reduced to 10 per cent and should not go into the state coffers, but should be used to stimulate film-making, the backing of artistic films which would otherwise be considered too large a financial gamble, training people with talent, and advertising Swedish films abroad. The result has been the setting-up of a Swedish Film Institute headed by Schein which uses the 10 per cent tax to support Swedish film producers, to award Swedish feature films of quality, to help cover losses sustained by Swedish producers of films that have won international awards, to train directors, cameramen, and technicians, and to stimulate interest in quality films by arranging 'film festivals'–in effect sending a series of foreign films on tour in the provinces and compensating local cinema managers for all financial losses sustained. The Institute has been subjected to criticism recently for having grown too powerful and becoming too obviously the arbiter of good taste in cinematic art, but it must also be given the credit for the emergence of such film directors as Jörn Donner, Jan Troell, Bo Widerberg, Vilgot Sjöman, and Mai Zetterling.

Since its inception, broadcasting has been the monopoly of the Swedish Broadcasting Corporation, which operates very much on the same lines as the British Broadcasting Corporation. For many years it offered little choice, but in 1955 a second radio programme was started and in 1966 the *Riksdag* voted the setting-up of a second TV channel. The authorities have assiduously avoided any form of advertising on either radio or television, being anxious to escape what they consider to be the awful excesses of American commercial television. In that they have doubtless been successful, but few deny that Swedish television is extremely dull, especially during the summer months when the producers' ardour is dampened by the knowledge that those Swedes who can will have returned to nature for the season. There have been a few notable programmes, particularly good dramatizations, for instance, of Strindberg's novels *Hemsöborna* (The Islanders of Hemsö) and *Röda rummet* (The Red Room), but a large amount of transmission time is taken up with heavy-handed discussions, old films, and pedestrian American TV programmes. In a wider context, however, Swedish radio plays a leading role in the cultural life of Sweden, its music and drama departments particularly helping to set a high standard.

Performing artists in Sweden enjoy considerable security by most international standards. Once a young Swede has gained entrance to a ballet or drama school or a music academy, he will be given an excellent training and will have a good chance of a contract guaranteeing a regular salary for the whole year with one of the state-subsidized theatres or orchestras.

Creative artists complain that their situation is much more precarious, but they admit that it has improved recently. Most controversial of the new systems recently introduced are the life pensions for Sweden's more prominent artists, which guarantee the artist an annual income of about £2,500 ($6,500), but grant him nothing if his income reaches that figure unaided. Since almost all the hundred people singled out for the award are established artists (Ingmar Bergman, Birgit Nilsson, Pär Lagerkvist, for instance) who have already struggled through the difficult period and are earning in excess of the stipulated amount, the result is a magnanimous gesture which is costing the state almost nothing. However, a grant system has been considerably widened in scope recently, allowing over 150 artists to receive about £1,000 ($2,600) per annum for three years regardless of their other income.

Authors writing in Swedish have a very small potential market and very few can live on earnings derived from their creative fiction. The government has improved their lot by raising the sum paid for each volume borrowed at a public library to 6 öre, 2 öre of which go direct to the writer concerned and 4 of which are added to a writer's fund, run by the authors themselves, for the award of travel grants and five-year grants amounting to almost £1,000 per annum. Even so, most authors have to eke out their income by working as journalists, teachers, etc.

It is difficult to gauge whether government support has led to a healthier situation in the arts today. David Jenkins, an American who has lived in Sweden for some time, finds that on the whole 'the artistic sophistication of Sweden seems to have increased over the years' but that on the other hand 'evidence of progress is apparent primarily among intellectual leaders. The gap between the artists (and those involved in the effort to bring art to the masses) and the masses themselves seems large'.[11]

It is early yet to pass judgement, but at least so far the fears that state subsidies might lead to state-controlled mediocrity have proved unfounded – Ingmar Bergman, Max von Sydow, Widerberg, Troell, Birgit Nilsson, Berit Lindholm, Elisabeth Söderström, and a hopeful corps of rising artists in the world of drama, opera, ballet, and literature testify to that. Whether the spiritual striving

[11] Jenkins, op. cit., pp. 235f.

of the individual artist will in future be so stifled by organized welfare that the source of his inspiration will run dry remains to be seen.

'Organization Sweden'

Over the last half-century the Swedish ability to organize has become so evident that the Swedes themselves often call their country 'Organization Sweden'. Almost every citizen from school age upwards is a member of at least one, and often several, organizations with interests ranging from the spiritual to the wholly practical. It starts at an early age, for schools have their Student Councils, on which sit usually one or two representatives from each class; after which there are academic associations, professional organizations, trade unions, the employers' confederation, a Farmers' Association, forestry associations, a Retail Association, a National Tenants' Association, a General Export Association, associations to protect the environment, to promote temperance and religious doctrines, to protect the motorist, to cover different aspects of the arts, travel, sport–and literally thousands of others. The Swedes are not 'clubbable' by nature and the aim of the organization will in principle not be to offer social entertainment but to further the interests of the members in respect of the subject forming the hub of the organization.

Gradually these numerous organizations have become part of the system of running the country. When the government is considering legislation on an important issue, it sets up first a commission to examine the question from different angles and to sound out opinion. An official of one of the appropriate organizations will almost certainly be asked to join the commission, and any associations whose members are likely to be immediately affected by the legislation will be invited to contribute. The commission may well sit for two years or more, compiling comments and suggestions for emendations, and will eventually present to the government a compromise on the original proposal, which then not infrequently goes through the *Riksdag* without a division, the debating having in a sense already taken place outside parliament. The system has much to recommend it, since it does ensure that a cross-section of opinion has been sounded out and many of the people most nearly affected have been at least indirectly approached; but it has obvious dangers.

Gunnar Heckscher was drawing attention to one of them when he criticized the 'Harpsund Democracy' which he saw as a threat to true parliamentary democracy in the late 1950s and early 1960s (cf. above, p. 160). Nils Elvander, in his study *Intresseorganisationerna i dagens Sverige,* to some extent draws the same conclusions, maintaining that too much stability in Swedish politics and a tendency to see co-operation and compromise as virtues in themselves could in the long run become disadvantageous and could isolate important aspects of society from public discussion, debate, and control. Professor Heckscher was leader of the Conservative Party at the time, while Dr Elvander is a Social Democrat, which helps to emphasize that their opinions are not just a matter of party politics.

The tendency has grown for interest-groups to negotiate directly with the government department concerned and to bypass the *Riksdag* and the opposition. One of the drawbacks of the system of proportional representation used by Sweden is that electors vote almost exclusively for the party and not the individual candidate, and there is no tradition of contacting one's local member of parliament. When one considers that the alternative for a citizen wanting legislation modified in some way is to approach the government administration via his 'organization', the dangers to parliamentary democracy become apparent. There is also added difficulty for the individual who has no organization to help him agitate and who can easily feel smothered by the bureaucratic procedure.

On the other hand, if there has been a miscarriage of justice or a case of officialdom having caused unnecessary hardship, Swedish society has put an effective means of redress into the citizen's hands. The 1809 Constitution drawn up after the dethronement of Gustav IV Adolf included the establishment of a *Justitieombudsman*, an official who was to hold a watching brief on the government and the way it conducted its affairs. Since then this *Ombudsman* (the word simply means 'representative' in Swedish, the *Ombudsman* in Sweden being known as *Justitieombudsman* or JO), who is still appointed by the *Riksdag* and is an expert in legal matters, has extended his field of activities and protects the people against public officialdom.

Theoretically the *Ombudsman* has very limited powers, for he cannot revoke a decision taken by courts or the administration, but can only recommend prosecution or petition the *Riksdag* to revise rulings. In practice he is given every facility to investigate complaints, he has access to all government and legal documents, and in a country like Sweden where there is a strong desire to conform, he has a potent weapon: he can criticize publicly, one of the worst fates that can befall a public servant. The *Ombudsman* submits an annual report, distributed to all government agencies, which gives an account of the major cases dealt with by his office. No official has any desire to figure in the report, a fact that indirectly bestows considerable power on the *Ombudsman*.

Private citizens can petition him, and about 1,200 people a year do so, but he can also initiate investigations himself if he finds it necessary. He reads the newspapers carefully and keeps his eyes open when, in following up other complaints, he inspects hospitals, prisons, and other similar institutions. About 200 cases a year are investigated on his own initiative. As many as 80 per cent of the complaints taken up by his office prove to be unfounded, which means that the number of cases that he has to rectify is very small, but the amount of unfair practice prevented by the very existence of his office is, of course, incalculable. His investigations cover a wide field and he found, for instance, against the staff of a mental institution in 1966; in 1963 against the Stockholm police for their handling of a murder investigation; in 1966 against the head of the National Medical Board for acting as a private consultant without first obtaining permission to do so from the government, and against a court of law for not allowing costs in a particular case; and in 1967 against a civil servant for refusing information to the press.

This last point indicates another means society has of protecting itself against bureaucracy. All government documents except those concerned with state security are available for the inspection of the public. Few people want to avail themselves of this right, but the newspapers cover all government offices through *Tidningarnas Telegrambyrå* (T.T.; i.e., the Swedish News Agency) and draw important items to the attention of their readers. F. Fleisher[12] quotes the Wennerström affair as a good example of how the system can function to the benefit of the public. Stig Wennerström, a colonel in the Swedish Air Force, was arrested in 1963 on charges of espionage, and a commission was appointed to examine the extent of his activities. Journalists asked to see the reports submitted to the commission by the Prime Minister and some of his cabinet colleagues, but they were refused. Representatives of leading Swedish newspapers appealed to the King-in-Council, maintaining that the government was contravening the Freedom of the Press Act which is part of the constitution, and this led to the appointment of four leading legal experts to decide whether there had in fact been a breach of the Act. Their final decision was that the release of most of the information contained in the reports would not jeopardize the security of the state, and with minor omissions the material was therefore made public. It made sensational reading, for it revealed that despite warnings from the secret police, Wennerström had been allowed to retain a position of great importance to national defence and had been able to sell vital information to the Russians over a long period. The most important point to emerge, however, is that the freedom of a responsible press helps to keep Sweden relatively free from corruption, mismanagement, and graft in high office.

[12] op. cit., p. 162.

For the very articulate and for those with enough initiative to complain to the correct authorities, the citizen is therefore well guarded against the potential evils of bureaucracy. Among the more diffident or the more eccentric members of society, however, those who do not like to raise their voices or join organizations, there can arise an undefined feeling of frustration. Their lives are organized for them and many vital decisions are taken out of their hands by a swelling volume of well-meaning public officials. This is the obverse of Organization Sweden.

The Perennial Problems

It has become fashionable since the war to consider Sweden to be a model welfare state, and those who believe in such a phenomenon sing its praises, while those who do not, point to the lurid accounts of Swedish immorality, the lack of religion, the high incidence of alcoholism and suicide, and with obvious *Schadenfreude* utter a *vanitas vanitatis*. Many moral strictures have certainly been removed in Sweden in this century, but it is difficult to assess whether this has led to a serious deterioration of moral standards or simply to less hypocrisy.

The hegemony of the State Lutheran Church began to wane by the end of the nineteenth century with the growth of industrialization, the population movement into urban areas, and the subsequent anonymity of the large towns. The Church also lost many followers with the rise of Social Democracy, for she was fused in the revolutionaries' mind with the Establishment–a view which the intransigence of the clergy did little to counteract at the turn of the century, when a measure of understanding on their part might well have bridged the gap between Christianity and socialism. The decline in the Church's authority has continued until by today Sweden enjoys the reputation of being the most secularized country in western Europe.

The Church herself has divided on many issues. Since the 1950s, for instance, there has been a great argument about women's demands to enter the ministry. The first woman was ordained in 1959, and there are now over a dozen female Lutheran pastors in Sweden, but some bishops and many other clergymen are still not reconciled to the innovation. There is also disagreement within the Church about the attitude she ought to adopt towards the 'new morality'. The Church officially approves only of sexual relations solemnized by marriage and birth control only by married couples, but many clergymen privately, and sometimes publicly, state that it is high time that the ecclesiastical authorities adopted a much more realistic view of present-day Swedish conditions. Carl-Gustaf Boëthius, who

edits *Vår Kyrka* (Our Church), a semi-official State Church maga-
zine, said on a television programme in 1964 that he considered it
silly to insist that all pre-marital sexual intercourse is immoral and
that for some unmarried couples who had been courting for several
years sexual relations would probably be positively beneficial. If he
wanted to spark off a national debate he had chosen the right
medium. Over a quarter of the State Lutheran pastors in the country
demanded his resignation, some defended him, but the official reaction was that he was wrong but entitled to speak his mind.

On the whole the Swedes tend to think of the Church as part of the
bureaucratic machine, as indeed in some respects she is. The bishops
and certain other high-ranking clergymen are appointed by the
Cabinet (who are bound to be better Socialists than Christians),
while the parish priests feed necessary statistics on births, deaths,
current addresses, etc., into the state machine. Except for the first
Sunday in Advent, Christmas, and Easter, church services are poorly
attended, the latest survey showing that only about one Swede in ten
goes to church as frequently as once a month, and one rarely hears
discussions on religious matters or dogma in Sweden.

Even so, it would be rash to conclude that the Swedes are irreli-
gious. All Swedes are nominally born into the State Church, but
since 1952 it has been a simple matter to opt out and by doing so to
become exempt from a very small church tax. Less than one per cent
of the population has seceded, which may simply be imputed to
passive indifference, but oddly enough about 90 per cent of the
population are confirmed and some 95 per cent of those who marry
choose to do so in church. When it was recently suggested that religious instruction should be discontinued in schools, the clergy felt
obliged to take action and sounded out public opinion. Their survey
showed that an overwhelming majority of parents wanted religious
instruction to remain on the school syllabus, and the Minister of
Education felt obliged to leave the subject where it was. Other
surveys show the same ill-defined but firm desire to retain a traditional form of religion. In 1956 about 84 per cent of those who were
asked confessed to a belief in God, although only half of them said
they were specifically Christians, while in 1965 over 60 per cent said
that if the Church were to be divorced from the state, they would
apply for membership anyway. Newspapers and periodicals often
carry articles with an anti-religious and anti-ecclesiastical bias,
written by intellectuals who disprove logically the need for the
Church, and few Swedes would be bold enough to disagree with a
logical argument in public. When asked about spiritual matters in
circumstances more nearly approximating the secrecy of the polling
booth, however, the majority of Swedes seem neither more nor less

religious than most modern nations. They can rarely accept strict dogma or the authority of the clergy, but the majority do accept the existence of God and believe in some form of after-life.

Apart from the State Lutheran Church there are also a number of Free Church organizations, mostly revivalist movements of British or American origin, the largest and most influential being the Pente-costalists, with some 90,000 members, the Swedish Missionary Society with over 90,000 members, the Baptists with 50,000, and the Salvation Army with 40,000 members. Although in terms of numbers their combined membership is little over 4 per cent of the entire population, their influence is much greater, for they have been in the forefront of popular education programmes and study circles, and include several members of the *Riksdag* among their number.

Since the Reformation the Catholic Church has played an insignificant part in the spiritual life of the country and is traditionally viewed with great suspicion by the Swedes. During the reigns of Johan III and his Catholic son, Sigismund of Poland, there seemed at least a possibility of a revival of Catholicism in Sweden, but under Karl IX in the early seventeenth century legislation became increasingly restrictive. By 1667 the presence of Catholics was forbidden completely and for the next century and a half chaplains at foreign embassies were the only Catholic priests allowed in the country. A measure of religious tolerance was introduced during the reign of Gustav III, but of more significance in the revival of Catholicism in Sweden was the marriage in 1823 of the Crown Prince Oscar (later Oscar I) and Princess Joséphine, daughter of Eugène de Beauharnais, duke of Leuchtenberg, and a Catholic. St Eugenia church in Stockholm, consecrated in 1837, was the first Catholic church to be built in Scandinavia since the Reformation. A slight move towards Catholicism began then, but it was very gradual and between the two World Wars there were still only eleven Catholic priests and five parishes in the whole of the country; and at the end of World War II there were only about 5,000 Swedish Catholics. This number has grown considerably since then (currently standing at about 33,000) mostly because of the influx of immigrants from Catholic countries who have been attracted to Sweden by high wages and good working conditions. Not all the new members are foreigners, however, and throughout the 1960s about one hundred Swedes a year, mainly intellectuals, have joined the Catholic ranks. Since 1962 there has been a Catholic bishop in Stockholm, Dr John E. Taylor, OMI, who was born in America. Despite the slight trend towards Catholicism it is difficult to imagine that this religious denomination will ever gain more than a tiny proportion of the population.

As for the 'new morality', it is doubtful how new it is. Admittedly there has been in the past an aura of respectability about the middle and upper classes, and they would be the people most likely to make their views heard. In 1774 the young Nathaniel Wraxall visited Sweden, where, as he tells us in his *Cursory remarks made in a tour through some of the Northern parts of Europe* published the following year, he visited the Jennings, a noble Swedish family of English extraction, at their Forsmark estate and met the charming Charlotte, Mrs Jennings's nineteen-year-old niece, with whom he conversed in French. On taking his leave Wraxall embraced Mrs Jennings and with pleasant anticipation prepared to do likewise with Miss Charlotte. She, however, laid her hands on her chaste breast and warded him off with the words 'Monsieur, il faut souvenir que je suis Suédoise'. When in 1839 Almquist published his prose work *Det går an* (translation title: *Sara Videbeck*), which contains a reasoned case for free love between Sara Videbeck and her beloved Sergeant Albert, he caused a national scandal and seriously damaged his career. For Strindberg's Miss Julie suicide was her only recourse after having degraded her honour by lying with Jean (although admittedly she had perhaps sinned against the social rather than the moral code, Jean being only a valet); while Fröding was persecuted beyond the bounds of sanity after his detailed description of the sexual act in his poem 'En morgondröm' (A Morning Dream) included in the cycle *Stänk och flikar* (Splashes and Rags; 1896). Even in the late 1920s and early 1930s Swedish authors influenced by Freud and D. H. Lawrence found themselves indignantly and severely criticized for their eroticism.

One can just as easily quote chapter and verse to show, however, that many people took a lot of licence in the past. Bellman's *Fredmans Epistlar*, which bridge the Age of Liberty and the Gustavian Era, abound in licentious acts; the Gustavian poet Kellgren, in his poem 'Sinnenas Förening', describes the sexual act with great verve and in other poems too he makes it obvious that his relations with his beloved Chloë were more than chivalrous. Mary Wollstonecraft found in Sweden a 'total lack of chastity in the lower class of women'. There was in fact for centuries a tradition of sexual relations before marriage in rural society; the illegitimacy rate was high; and even among couples who had every intention of marrying each other it was common practice to wait until the woman was pregnant. In some isolated districts the couples probably had in any case to wait several weeks for a change in the weather conditions before being able to reach the pastor and legitimize their issue.

What seems to have happened in recent years in this, as in so many other spheres, is a rationalizing of the situation. Since people were having extra-marital intercourse, then it was reasoned that it would be beneficial to all concerned to remove the social stigma, to teach young people enough about sex to prevent unwanted children from being conceived, or if children were born to unmarried mothers, to afford as much practical assistance as possible.

As recently as 1938 providing information on contraceptive methods was an indictable offence, yet by 1944 sex education was introduced into schools and by 1956 it had become a compulsory subject. In that year the National Board of Education issued its illustrated textbook for teachers, *Handledning i sexualundervisning* (Sex Instruction in Swedish Schools), which explains the need for sex education and the kind of sex instruction that should be given to children at different ages. This instruction is dovetailed with the new comprehensive system so that the seven- to eleven-year-olds in the Lower School are told plainly and simply where they came from, the part their fathers played, how they developed in the womb, and how they are dependent on their parents in their homes. The Middle School (11–14-year-olds) deals objectively with information on the sexual organs, puberty, menstruation, conception, pregnancy, etc. The Upper School (14–16-year-olds) goes on to discuss sex and youth, bringing in moral and social concepts, sexual abnormalities, social welfare relating to maternity, and child care. Those who go on with their schooling after the comprehensive school continue their sex education too, being given a recapitulation of the material previously presented, but now with emphasis on contraceptive techniques and the dangers of venereal diseases.

This kind of instruction was not introduced without a storm of protest from many. One hundred and forty Swedish doctors publicly asked for the teaching of 'firmer sexual norms' and they were supported by several religious groups armed with a petition containing 200,000 signatures. In typical Swedish fashion a Commission was set up to examine the whole question of sex education in schools and the teachers' manual, and it is still sitting. Some of its recommendations have already filtered through, however, and have led to certain emendations, but not in the direction hoped for by the protesters. As Birgitta Linnér points out, the recommendations indicate that the official attitude

has come around to recognizing the fact that Sweden is a pluralistic society. For example, one of the passages from the original handbook reads as follows: 'The teacher must uphold the view that continence during adolescence is the only course the school can recommend with good conscience. Pupils should be made to understand that it is better to establish a home at an early age, even if under modest circumstances, than to enter without further scruples into an intimate liaison'. In the amended version this has been changed to read: 'It is important for the students to realize that laws and norms vary from time to time, from people to people, and that within one and the same country, different groups may have different views on sex relations . . .'[13]

In practice sexual instruction in schools has not gone so smoothly as the official curriculum would suggest, and experts complain irritably that this is largely because teachers have not been trained properly to deal with the subject, many of them are embarrassed by it, and either ignore it or try to cram it into the end of the term when it is not properly assimilated. Needless to say, remedial measures are being taken. The National Association for Sex Education (*Riksförbundet för sexuell upplysning*, RFSU) arranges university seminars and extension courses for teachers, offering expert lectures and discussions on both medical and psychological aspects of sex, especially as experienced by teenagers.

Of course, sexual instruction is not confined to the schools. Several books on the subject have appeared recently, and Swedish Radio and TV have broadcast programmes aimed especially at giving teenagers adequate information on sexual relations and morality. The tendency seems to be towards an increasing acceptance of the fact that teenagers have sexual intercourse. *Vägen till mognad* (The Road to Maturity) by Lis Asklund and Torsten Wickbom, published in 1966 in connection with a TV schools series, states that in Sweden 'the opinion has become more and more general that the woman and the man have the same right to sexual experience before marriage'. The RFSU publication *Samspel* (Harmonious Relationship), which appeared the following year, more or less takes as its point of departure that sexual experience among teenagers is the rule, not the exception; and *Sexualliv och samlevnad* (Sex Life and Living Together) by Linnér and Westholm, which appeared in 1968, is, in the words of B. Linnér, 'the first textbook to follow the new basic philosophy for sex education programmes in secondary schools . . . and consistently applies a pluralistic view to ethical matters'.[14]

Surveys show that there is justification for assuming sexual experience among Swedish teenagers. An investigation into the sexual habits of 500 people with an average age of eighteen carried out in Örebro in 1964 by H. Lindroth and B. Rundberg showed that 57 per cent of the boys had experienced intercourse (for the first time usually when sixteen) and 46 per cent of the girls (for the first time at

[13] B. Linnér, *Society and Sex* (Stockholm, 1971), p. 10.
[14] ibid., p. 16.

seventeen). Professor G. Karlsson's study the following year of
students at six different institutions and with an average age of
twenty-two for the men and twenty-one for the women showed that
from 62 to 86 per cent had had sexual experience. A more recent and
much wider survey, *Sex Life in Sweden*, published by the Ministry of
Education and Cultural Affairs in 1969 – a Swedish Kinsey Report –
reports on a representative sample of the population between eighteen and sixty years of age. Ninety-five per cent had had sexual
intercourse, the average age for the introduction being 16·6 for the
men and 17·2 for the women. Ninety per cent had had pre-marital
sexual relations.

The RFSU is an independent organization whose members include both individuals and associations (trade unions, political
organizations, youth clubs, etc.). It aims at spreading knowledge
about sexual matters and tolerance in sexual morals and behaviour,
at planned parenthood, and affording practical assistance so that the
population can enjoy both harmonious sex relations and parenthood.
It accepts sexual relations as the norm, but believes that every child
conceived should be wanted, and so deals with propaganda for
birth control. It runs a counselling service for people with sexual
problems, displays posters bearing such legends as 'Children? Yes –
but when we want them', and through its chain of thirty-two shops,
through the post, and in automatic vending machines it sells contra-
ceptives, using the profits to help with its other activities.

There would seem, therefore, to be justification for the criticisms
levelled against Swedish sexual morals. The relentless logic of the
reformers in this field, as in so many others, is proving that the
restraints of the past were often based on prejudice, something to
which the modern Swede dare not admit. Most parents who would
previously have forbidden their children, especially their daughters,
pre-marital sexual relations have bowed to the new philosophy,
schools explain it all, student hostels have no segregation, hotel
receptionists do not raise their eyebrows if Mr Pettersson and Miss
Svensson want a double room, and travel agents mind their
own business if unmarried couples want to go on a holiday tour
together.

A closer look at the statistics, however, suggests that the situation
has probably not changed in practice. The Swedes are rather a
sensuous nation, although presumably no more so now than before,
but a revealing factor in the 1969 report on *Sex Life in Sweden* is that
most people (87 per cent of the men and 91 per cent of the women),
even if accepting the habit of pre-marital relations, feel that faithful-
ness in marriage is essential. In the previous eleven months 90 per
cent of all the married Swedes in the survey had been faithful to

their marriage partners. Perhaps one of the main differences between Sweden and many other countries is therefore the frankness
with which the matter is treated.

The same *laissez-faire* attitude is adopted generally towards censorship and pornography, and it is perfectly legal to sell over the
counter publications as lascivious as one likes. When newsagents and
tobacconists started to go so far that their display of pornography
offended those with no desire to buy, however, then it was felt that
they were encroaching on the civil liberties of others, and in February 1971 the *Riksdag* passed a law allowing pornography for private use, but forbidding it to be exposed in shop windows. The
citizen thus has the right to take it or ignore it as he personally
chooses.

Connected with the morality question and the subject of even
more intense current debate is the 'woman question'. It is generally
acknowledged that Swedish women are physically extremely attractive and that natural blondes are the rule rather than the exception.
What also strikes visitors to Sweden is how capable and practical
Swedish women are, tackling with energy, commonsense, and not a
little self-confidence what has to be done and often making a much
more vital impression than their menfolk. Nor is this only a modern
phenomenon. The Icelandic sagas convey the obvious respect
afforded to many Norse women, such as Aud the Deepminded who
scorned her relation's invitation to visit him because he had sent too
small a retinue to fetch her, and Hallgerd who could have saved her
husband Gunnar's life by a lock of her hair, but refused it because he
had once boxed her ears. One of the most successful rulers in Scandinavia in the Middle Ages was Queen Margareta, during whose
lifetime the Kalmar Union was a political reality, and one of the
outstanding spiritual leaders of that age was St Bridget, who exercised authority over monks as well as nuns–and perhaps even over
the king himself. There is often a forceful woman at the centre of
Almquist's prose works; the men in Selma Lagerlöf's novels usually
owe their salvation to a strong-willed, righteous heroine; and Strindberg himself, that renowned misogynist, not infrequently shows his
hero battling in vain against a female vampire. Even in Swedish
children's books it is often the little girl who occupies the central
position, Pippi Långstrump (Longstocking) being perhaps the best
example.

Despite these obvious examples of female strength of personality,
the fact remains that Swedish women had allowed themselves by the
first half of the nineteenth century to be placed in as subjugated a
position as women in other European countries, with few legal rights
and no hopes of any career except marriage. The move towards

emancipation could be said to have begun in 1828 when Fredrika Bremer, its first pioneer, published some short articles drawing attention to the plight of women in society. She devoted her life and her writings to the liberation of women and their right to be treated as individuals rather than appendages to their male guardians, a theme taken up by many Scandinavian writers in the late nineteenth century, notably by Ibsen and Bjørnson. Many reforms followed: in 1873 women were allowed to sit academic examinations; in 1884 unmarried women were declared legally of age at twenty-one; by 1919 women had full suffrage; in 1920 a Marriage Code gave equal responsibility to partners in marriage; in 1923 the *Riksdag* granted women the same rights as men in the civil service and by 1947 equal pay in governmental service; in 1949 the new 'parental code' afforded to both parents legal authority over their dependent children; by 1959 the last official sign of legal discrimination was removed when women were allowed to become ordained ministers of the State Church.

This was not synonymous with real equality, however, although most visitors to Sweden by that time were struck by the independence of Swedish women, free to live their own lives, go where they pleased unhampered by the unwritten rules about male escorts and women's traditional passivity. One can see Swedish women performing some jobs usually considered to be the male's prerogative, such as driving omnibuses, underground trains, and taxis, and some engineering firms also employ women at their production lines, Volvo being a case in point.

The 1960s saw a surge forward in women's bid for true equality and the movement was all the more powerful for coinciding with two essential developments, one social and one economic. The new educational system has meant that all children up to the age of sixteen are given the same education regardless of sex. Until recently there was still a division of the sexes over what the timetables simply called 'handicraft', for it was taken for granted that the boys would want to do woodwork and the girls needlework and cookery; but this distinction is being erased and in many schools boys are choosing to learn to cope with childcare, while girls are turning their hands to carpentry. The economic factor was a shortage of labour in industry, which has caused both big business and government alike to entice married women on to the labour market. The leaders of the women's cause have viewed recent developments with some annoyance, for they say that women are more or less being exploited in the way the Negro was in the United States. They have been given the unskilled, poorly-paid jobs in industry with few incentives and few chances of promotion. When industry is expanding, they will be lured into full- or part-time work, but if there are signs of a recession, they will be the first to be dismissed.

Two publications which appeared in the 1960s brought the whole question very much to the fore. *Kvinnors liv och arbete* (Women's Life and Work), a collection of essays published in 1962, is concerned with women's position on the labour market and the prejudices that preclude them from many forms of employment and restrict their progress in others. *Kvinnor och människor* (Women and Human Beings; 1964) by Eva Moberg, Vilhelm Moberg's daughter, is deliberately provocative, and succeeded in causing a violent fluttering in the dovecote. Up to this point there had been a lot of discussion about woman's two roles, as a career woman and as a housewife and mother, but Eva Moberg took the view that it was time to consider man's role in the same context. There was, she maintained, no reason why a man should be allowed to concentrate all his energies on his career and ignore the housekeeping and the children, and yet a woman should be expected to lead a schizophrenic life, spending part of her time on her career and another section on motherhood. There was, she insisted, only *one* role, the human role, and that should be fulfilled by both men and women, husband and wife being mutually responsible for running the home and bringing up the children. Once the guffaws and the indignant spluttering had died down, some of her views began to percolate and have contributed to the change of attitude that is discernible in society.

In 1960 LO (Confederation of Trade Unions) and SAF (Employers' Confederation) agreed on the introduction of equal pay for the same work in industry, and over the next five years special rates for women were phased out. Also in the 1960s all the political parties introduced into their programmes the promise to examine the question of equal rights for women; the three main unions, LO, TCO, and SACO, stated their intention of aiming for equality of the sexes; and SAF, LO, and TCO set up jointly the Swedish Women's Labour Market Committee for the continuous study of questions affecting sex equality at work.

So far, however, women are still very much in the minority in the more specialized spheres. There have been only two women ambassadors, neither of whom are career diplomats; political party candidates are overwhelmingly male; and only four women have aspired to ministerial level. In the professions generally the situation is more or less the same, with male doctors, lawyers, physicists, engineers, etc., far outnumbering the females. Doubtless the new educational system will make some difference as its effects have time to work through society; and Eva Moberg and other gifted intellectuals, both male and female, will keep the matter in the foreground in public debates in Sweden for many years to come.

A problem that continues to defy attempts at improvement is alcoholism in Sweden. One can deduce from many sources that it is a phenomenon of many centuries' standing. We know, for instance, that Swedish food in the Middle Ages and during the Vasa period was mostly salted and that most citizens in all walks of life sated their consequent thirst by consuming large amounts of beer. Bellman's Stockholm at the end of the Age of Liberty was noted for its gin-shops and their dissolute customers, while Gustav III forfeited the support of many of his peasants when he forbade the use of private grain distilleries throughout the country. The potato was regarded with great suspicion and no enthusiasm even by the starving sections of the population at the turn of the eighteenth century until it was realized that it could be made into an excellent potato snaps, when it became popular. Drunkenness was manifest in most rural districts in the nineteenth century, as can be seen from the accounts of Wieselgren's struggles against it, while the situation in the towns worsened as increasing industrialization drew more workers into urban areas. Selma Lagerlöf's Salvation Army girl whose life was devoted to saving the souls of drunken workmen had many long-suffering sisters in reality in Sweden as elsewhere.

The trade unions were among the organizations which early in the twentieth century realized that if the workers' conditions were to be improved, some positive action would have to be taken against alcoholism. Their most notable success was among the Stockholm stevedores at the turn of the century who were allowed to drink during working hours and could obtain alcohol at the docks on credit extended by their employers. Many of them were rarely completely sober and when their wages were paid out, they would often barely cover drinking debts. Union officials were instrumental in having many of the public houses closed, and by exhorting and harassing their fellow-members addicted to alcohol, finally succeeded in raising their standard of living and saving their reputation.

The temperance movement campaigned extensively in the first decade of this century, and by 1914 a plan for the rationing of spirits evolved by Dr Ivan Bratt was introduced in Stockholm. By 1917 the Bratt System had been extended to the whole country and the state-controlled *Systembolaget* (Central Wine and Spirit Co.) was set up, establishing a nationwide monopoly in the sale of alcohol. A national referendum on total prohibition was arranged, but the result was so indecisive that Branting, who was Prime Minister at that time, did not feel justified in introducing such drastic measures;

but the rationing system was drastic enough. Only income-earners over twenty-five were eligible for a *motbok* (the ration book), married women did not qualify, nor did people living in old-age homes; it was almost a certificate of good behaviour which was withdrawn if the holder was charged with drunkenness, had defrauded the Inland Revenue, or was on national assistance. Alcohol was served in restaurants only with meals and there were no bars.

The system did not abolish the abuse of alcohol, since those desperate enough could obtain it on the black market if all else failed; but it increased strong feelings of guilt where drinking was concerned. By 1955 it was decided to abolish the *motbok* and the restrictions bound up with the purchase of alcohol. At the same time *Systembolaget* launched a campaign to persuade people to buy more wine and less of the much more potent snaps, which was the main cause of drunkenness. Their campaign has been partially successful –more wine is now bought, but sales of spirits have dropped only marginally.

Since the state monopoly buys in large quantities, it is given very good service by French, German, and Spanish wine-merchants, and it offers a good selection of very reliable table wines. Little more can be said in praise of what they offer. They have only 275 shops in the whole of the country and residents in some sparsely populated areas are several hours' drive from their nearest 'Systemet'. *Systembolaget*'s object is to discourage their customers and one can assume that they select their unsmiling personnel accordingly. A curiously oppressive mood descends on customers as they enter the shop, cheerful comments are assiduously avoided, and if a red light goes on by the side of the cash-register, the customer will be required to show his means of identification. There is a blacklist of alcoholics who are refused any kind of alcohol. Purchases are placed into anonymous bags, presumably to avoid encouraging the people met subsequently outside; but actually there are few things more recognizable than these anonymous bags and most customers can be seen shamefacedly plunging them into their brief-cases out of sight.

The sight of a drunken man on the street, not uncommon in certain parts of most Swedish towns, causes an almost neurotic reaction from those around him, some muttering in annoyance that it ought not to be allowed and others looking acutely embarrassed. Since there are no English-type pubs or relaxing cafés in the French style, it is difficult to see where else those addicted to alcohol can go unless they can afford to frequent expensive licensed restaurants. Certainly no criminal is as quickly bundled out of sight by the police. It is strange that a nation so aware of the rights of minority groups and of the problems of many emotionally deprived people feels so little sympathy for the drunkard.

When it comes to dealing with drunken driving Swedish common-sense reasserts itself. A very small amount of alcohol in the blood-stream (less than half the permitted maximum in the United Kingdom) leads to a stiff prison sentence, and police road-blocks are set up quite frequently in the evenings to make random checks. A convicted driver can arrange to serve his sentence at a convenient time, often opting to spend his summer vacation paying off his debt to society.

As with alcoholism, so with suicide, improved living standards have done little to ameliorate the situation, and perhaps the two conditions are related, for they both seem to stem from a desire to find an outlet for a deep feeling of inadequacy. According to a study by an American psychoanalyst, Herbert Hendin, published in 1964 under the title *Suicide and Scandinavia*, Swedish suicide victims are most often men of thirty-five or over who feel they have failed to live up to their own high expectations. It is perhaps worth recording that whereas according to figures issued by the World Health Organization Sweden's suicide rate is ninth in the world, her rates for crimes of violence are very low. David Jenkins, himself an American, writes that whereas the Swedish suicide rate is about 18 per 100,000, it is 10 per 100,000 in the United States. 'Sweden's record gives no reason for jubilation, to be sure, but if a suicide rate almost double that of the United States reflects deep social sicknesses, then the murder rate in the United States (five times that of Sweden) should be even more indicative of moral failings'.[15] Violent death of any sort is distressing, but if it is committed, then presumably it is better for the community as a whole if it is self-inflicted.

The Literary Scene

As we saw in an earlier chapter, new frontiers were opening in the 1930s in Swedish literature, with gifted working-class authors such as Harry Martinson, Jan Fridegård, Eyvind Johnson, and Vilhelm Moberg enriching literature with descriptions and intimate impressions of a social world hitherto unsung. It was also a time of experimenting, with lyric poets, notably Gunnar Ekelöf and Artur Lundkvist, introducing their readers to surrealism, psycho-analysis, and other new ideas that had excited them in their own reading of foreign literature. Swedish isolation during World War II had its effect on Swedish letters, reflected in the *Angst* and pessimism of the

[15] op. cit., p. 17.

Fyrtiotalisterna, the Forties Group, with Stig Dagerman, Erik Lindegren, and Karl Vennberg setting the mood.

Since those war years the Swedish literary scene has changed considerably, and although the established authors, Lagerkvist, Martinson, Johnson, etc., have continued their dedicated probing of the human condition and produced some of their finest work, many new names and theories have also so crowded the stage that it is difficult to grasp the main themes. One can, however, discern certain patterns.

The best indication that the icy depression of the Forties Group was beginning to thaw came in 1946 when Lars Gyllensten (1921–   ) and a fellow-medical student published their collection of poems entitled *Camera Obscura.* It was given serious reviews by the critics, but was later revealed as a conscious parody of the pessimistic *Angst*-ridden and sometimes incomprehensible verse of the Forties Group. Over the next few years there was a return to a more idyllic world, with prose-writers finding inspiration in their quiet native provinces and poets seeing beauty in simple, everyday scenes and objects. Per Wästberg's (1933–   ) first novel, *Pojke med såpbubblor* (Boy with Soap Bubbles; 1949), seemed a deliberate attempt to bring resignation and fantasy back into the world of literature, dealing as it does with a sensitive, imaginative boy who gazes into soap bubbles and sees visions there. Sara Lidman (1923–   ), a farmer's daughter from Västerbotten in northern Sweden, set her first novel, *Tjärdalen* (The Tar Pit; 1953), in a small, remote community which becomes a microcosm of our world of love, responsibility, and guilt.

The north of Sweden is also the region frequently chosen by Per Olof Sundman (1922–   ) for the setting of his novels, which he keeps as unemotional and as factual as possible. His method is to describe characters' actions and conversation without comment, so that the reader draws his own conclusions. The method at its best is surprisingly evocative and causes the reader long after he has finished reading the book to ponder over the situation and the characters. *Undersökningen* (The Investigation; 1958), for instance, is a factual, objective account of a local official's investigation into allegations that the manager of the large local industrial plant is a drunkard. The emotions of neither the official nor the manager are reported, nor do we know at the end of the book whether the allegations were wholly justified, but we find ourselves speculating on these matters and on the character of the two men, the ethics of the situation, and the social system that created the situation in the first place.

The deliberately objective, documentary novel has been taken further by Per Olof Enquist (1934–), who wrote *Hess* (1966), a novel about Rudolf Hess, and in 1968 *Legionärerna*, a report rather than a novel about the Balts whom Sweden handed over to the Russians at the end of the war.

Tomas Tranströmer's (1931–) first collection of poems, *17 dikter* (17 Poems; 1954), restores stillness and a muted happiness to Swedish lyric poetry. He achieves a simplicity which offers a measure of security and an implicit belief in a benign supernatural being even in a world that is threatened.

There has been a great deal of experimenting in Swedish lyric poetry over the last two decades. Exponents of the 'new simplicity', so beautifully exemplified by Tranströmer and Göran Palm (1931–), have taken the form as far as they can, aiming at the 'democratization' of poetry, using simple, indeed banal, language to record everyday, commonplace experiences. Jarl Hammarberg (1940–), for instance, combines in his casual, colloquial verse bits of posters, graffiti, signs, slogans, public announcements, and so on, fitted together, often ironically, to capture the atmosphere of everyday life.

Some poets have favoured *poésie concrète*, verbal experimenting where form and content are one. It is no coincidence that Bengt-Emil Johnson (1936–), one of the best-known exponents of this kind of poetry, is also a trained musician, for *poésie concrète* contains variations on words reminiscent of variations on musical phrases. Indeed *poésie concrète* seeks to combine all the modern art forms, for the visual layout on the page is important, while some of the systematic juggling with language produces sounds akin to modern music. Lars Bäckström makes the point in his essay on modern Swedish poetry,

> a constant and intentional breaking down of barriers and merging of different kinds of art is pursued by these experimenters; that they should also be pictorial artists producing picture-poems is part of the same tendency towards the freest possible combination of all the arts (a tendency known to the world at large from the American happening movement).[16]

All these poets stress the importance of freedom and insist that the great thing is to communicate. It must be admitted that since what many of them have produced is a mutilation of language appreciated by a minority of the population, they cannot be deemed to have succeeded in their attempts at 'democratic' poetry which communicates. But the experimenting itself is a healthy, vital sign, which reflects a society that is also experimenting in many fields.

[16] Lars Bäckström, in *Sweden Writes* (Stockholm, 1965), p. 169.

A most significant feature in the past decade has been Swedish writers' involvement with political affairs. It is almost as though having declared themselves 'cultural workers' they were determined to prove that they have a definite active role to play in society both nationally and internationally, striking blows for freedom and the individual's rights both at home and abroad. Sara Lidman left her sheltered Västerbotten and travelled to Africa and Asia, afterwards writing the two novels *Jag och min son* (I and My Son; 1961) and *Med fem diamanter* (With Five Diamonds; 1964). The first is set in South Africa and is concerned with a white man's betrayal of the black population; the second in Kenya and depicts a coloured man whose life is fashioned by the whims of white people. In 1966 she wrote *Samtal i Hanoi* (Conversations in Hanoi) which takes the form of a diary and, despite its deliberate restraint, conveys the committed radical's indignation at the Vietnam situation and her great sympathy for the suffering Vietnamese. Two years later, in 1968, Sara Lidman directed her indignation at events nearer home. Her documentary *Gruva* (Mine) reveals how little true industrial democracy there is at the state-owned mine at Kiruna after forty years of a Social Democratic government. The book led to a public outcry and played its part in the sudden strike that broke out at the mine a few months later.

Per Wästberg left his little white boy blowing soap bubbles and also went to Africa, where he too gathered material for indignant prose works, *Förbjudet område* (Forbidden Area) and *På svarta listan* (On the Black List), both of which appeared in 1960.

Jan Myrdal, son of Alva and Gunnar Myrdal, has gone politically well to the Left of his Socialist parents and after travelling widely in Central Asia, China, and Afghanistan, has made his reputation with such works as *Rapport från en kinesisk by* (Report from a Chinese Village; 1963) and *Samtida berättelser av en europeisk intellektuell* (Contemporary Confessions of a European Intellectual; 1964). His radical articles in *Aftonbladet* (a Socialist evening paper) have played a considerable part in forming fashionable Swedish popular opinion.

The problems still existing in Swedish society are also taken up by modern Swedish authors, their method ranging from indignation to gentle irony. Stig Claesson's *Vem älskar Yngve Frej* (Who Loves Yngve Frej; 1968), a gentle, amusing, but sad novel, criticizes effectively trends in society that are leading to the depopulation of large tracts of northern Sweden. Lars Gyllensten, one of the most significant Swedish writers active today, examines in his novels the relation between ideals and reality, socialism in theory and practice, the existence of a God and yet man's freedom to fashion his own life, the danger of living without norms and yet the equal danger of holding too firmly to convictions. Gyllensten wrote his own Ten Commandments in 1965, which taken as a whole add up to a code for a humanist always searching but rarely passing judgement. The code has special reference to the modern scene in many parts of the world. The Third Commandment reads, for instance, 'Thou shalt reflect that comfort agrees as well with other people as it does with you'; the Fourth Commandment admonishes us to 'take care of those who cannot take care of themselves'; while the Sixth Commandment runs 'Thou shalt not spread venereal diseases, or bring unwanted children into the world, or expose other people to sexual violence. Also, you should play your part in keeping the birth-rate as low as possible, because altogether too many children are born'.[17]

Göran Sonnevi (1939–   ), a Marxist poet, protests against the injustices and atrocities in many parts of the world, and indeed first made his mark with a poem 'On the war in Vietnam'. His method is to present the horror of the war in a cold, controlled language and to contrast it with the smug safety of Sweden. Sonnevi also takes Sweden to task in his poem 'Example' for exploiting workers in underdeveloped countries:

> It's been said to me
> that ALFA LAVAL invests
> in South Africa's
> black labour!
> The suspicion that this is true
> makes me in part furious
> in part helplessly sunk
> Paralysis, laziness,
> blunt despair
> go together with the
> thickening November winter . . .[18]

A further noticeable feature of Swedish literature today is the closing-down or restricting of some of the fine, old literary and cultural journals, such as *Bonniers Litterära Magasin* and *Konstrevy*, and the mushrooming of small magazines and newspapers, often in brochure or stencil form, almost invariably politically well to the Left and often aggressively determined to get across a 'message'. It is not necessarily a healthy sign, indicating the hectic and sometimes artificial atmosphere of the literary scene, but offering little con-

---

[17] G. Simpson's translation included in *Sweden Writes*, p. 226.
[18] R. Fulton's translation in *Lines Review*, No. 35 (December 1970).

fidence to those who like to see at least some element of continuity in cultural affairs.

Swedish authors are subjected to a source of frustration not experienced by English-speaking writers–a small potential readership. A few major authors have been well translated and have made their mark on the international scene long after they have become established at home, but the majority of Swedish creative writers, especially those producing the most fascinating experimental verse, will never have the satisfaction of leading a European literary trend, no matter how gifted and avant-garde they may be. At the present time, when Swedish poets are throwing up so many interesting ideas, the language barrier is causing a loss to the outside world as well as to the poets concerned.

In his novel *Paradis för oss* (This Paradise; 1952) Frank Burns, Gunnar Hägglöf's pseudonym, introduces a Swedish professor of history who says to an English visitor:

Has it not struck you, Mr Bancroft, that Sweden is really quite a new country? . . . One must remember that only 80-odd years ago Sweden was a poor and quite forgotten country in a corner of Europe, with a small upper class of landowners and officials and under them the large majority of the population, the peasants in the country districts. Then the tide turned. The industrial revolution reached us too. We acquired a large industry and became affluent. Since then we have rebuilt the whole of Swedish society. Sweden today is effective, and has become rationalistic and materialistic. All this has not taken more than a few decades. Just look at our towns! Where in Europe can you see so many new houses, so many new schools, hospitals, and cinemas as here? And look at the Swedish countryside! I assure you, I no longer recognise my childhood district and yet I'm not much more than 60 years old.

The statement is a half-truth. The rationalistic, materialistic Swedes have created for themselves a modern country with more new apartments, telephones, refrigerators, motor-cars, and boats per head of the population than anywhere else in Europe. They have not attempted to build a paradise, whatever irony Frank Burns may have intended with the title of his book, but have taken as their prime object every citizen's right to self-fulfilment and in their methodical way have gone from one issue to another, making the necessary adjustments on their road towards that object.

Kathleen Nott, who lived for some years in the Stockholm area, writes that 'Sweden seems to me to be the most comfortable country in Europe – and the least cosy'.[19] The Swede Jörgen Eriksson reveals something of the same sentiment when he exhorts his fellow-Swedes 'by all means eliminate material scruffiness, get rid of ugly and formless objects. But when the stage props are given a star role then the play's usually a pretty thin affair – if not tragically absurd'.[20] Swedes have a well-developed sense of visual beauty, and wherever one goes in Sweden one is struck by the loving care that has gone into decorating and adorning the home, offices, banks, shops, even supermarkets, hotels and restaurants, and indeed most public buildings. The beautiful clear lines of Swedish glass, ceramics, and furniture, immediately distinguishable and distinguished, are not restricted to the world of the rich but are found almost everywhere in Sweden. There is a certain air of self-consciousness about it all, and the visitor to Stockholm will be taken to admire the beautiful murals and mosaics in the new underground stations and the display of the latest designs from Kosta, Orrefors, Gustavsberg, and realizes that a Victorian monstrosity in such surroundings would be a positive affront. One has the feeling, however, that the Stockholmer is perhaps enjoying displaying the aesthetic objects round him more than actually living with them.

The rather self-conscious air and the lack of cosiness are perhaps partially related to two central facts: Sweden is a small country in terms of population and the move to the towns is of recent origin. Behind the smugness and the justifiable pride in their undoubted achievements, the Swedes, especially those living in the capital, seem to have a constant need for assurance that they are doing well and are becoming very internationally-minded. Strangely enough, few things are more parochial than their internationalism. They exhibited a great interest in the United Nations during Dag Hammarskjöld's term of office as Secretary-General and one could often detect a proprietary note in Swedish news reports from the United Nations at that time. The Middle East has become a popular subject with the news media in Sweden and many of their reports begin with 'Ambassador Jarring . . .' A lot of time is spent compiling foreigners' views of Sweden, and the leading national daily newspapers with all their sterling journalistic qualities occasionally comment on criticism of Sweden by often quite obscure foreign visitors in a manner reminiscent of the *Aberdeen Press and Journal*, a Scottish newspaper known for its quaint local patriotism, when it interviews summer tourists.

The small population, together with a high degree of literacy, also leads to a conformity of views that is quite marked. An article in

[19] K. Nott, *A Clean Well-lighted Place* (London, 1961), p. 126.
[20] Quoted P. Britten Austin, in *On Being Swedish* (London, 1968), p. 111.

a leading newspaper will often lead to a so-called 'public debate', with all the newspapers and other mass media having their say and the public generally discussing the issue. There is always a great inclination to accept the views of the 'experts' who have been consulted, however, and in Paul Britten Austin's words, 'in a foreigner's eyes "debate" seems the wrong term. It is usually, indeed, very lop-sided. Intellectual life is to an extraordinary degree a prey to fashion, even more so than in Britain and the United States'.[21] One rarely comes across an article or hears a public speech which strongly defends old-fashioned views and roundly condemns new-fangled ideas. This is not to say that people holding reactionary views do not exist, but that it is not fashionable to express them volubly. The Jan Myrdals and Sara Lidmans hold the stage and only in general elections and anonymous surveys does it become obvious that just under half the adult population are not Socialists, Marxists, or Maoists.

The fact that so many people with a peasant background have recently moved to urban areas has also led to conformity. Urban manners and customs must be carefully adhered to and the newest modern conveniences and appliances quickly mastered so that the former peasant does not stand out as being too bucolic. This may also partly explain the reserved attitude assumed by Swedish city-dwellers when in public. One does not proffer information, encroach upon others' privacy, or attempt to establish contact unless asked to do so. The Swedish city-dweller is embarrassed at being caught at a disadvantage; he wants to be able to be prepared for visitors, to have things properly organized, and to avoid improvisation.

Frank Burns's history professor was only stating a half-truth, however. Sweden is a modern country, but she has enjoyed a degree of stability denied almost every other country in the world. Her political institutions, the acceptance of the *Riksdag*'s authority, of the rights of the citizen, of the whole pattern of democracy, have their roots in the earliest times, and all reveal the lasting effects of a relatively gentle evolution. Unimpeded progress has been possible because Sweden has escaped the turmoil that has held back so many other countries. She has never been invaded since the Germanic tribes wandered in, close on the tracks of the receding ice, and although settlers have come to Sweden throughout the centuries (Finnish immigrants in Norrbotten, Hälsingland, Dalarna, and Värmland; Jews, Walloons, and, in the last three decades, immigrants from other Scandinavian countries, from Germany, Italy, Poland, Hungary, Yugoslavia, Greece, and Turkey), they have

[21] P. Britten Austin, *The Swedes: How They Live and Work* (Newton Abbot, 1970), p. 132.

done so in small numbers, adding variety to the population but never creating a minority problem. The only minority ethnic group in Sweden, the Lapps, preceded the Germanic tribes, and far from giving rise to ethnic problems, ask simply to be left unmolested in the country's most inaccessible terrain in northern Sweden to tend their reindeer herds.

The Swedish people themselves are fashioned by their history, and although now the majority of Swedes live in urban areas, dress well, live well, and travel abroad to a sunny beach almost annually, they retain, as we saw earlier, their close ties with nature and abandon with great alacrity their town comforts for a more primitive cottage or a boat.

The links with rural society are never far from the surface. Swedish designs in ceramics, glass, and textiles have their origins and often their source of inspiration in folk tradition; the rich Swedish lyric tradition in poetry owes much to the poet's response to a peaceful, unspoilt Swedish landscape, while when one analyses the indignation expressed fiercely in some Swedish prose, one finds that the cause is rooted in an antagonism towards the urban areas and their harmful effects on the rural environment.

The numerous public holidays are still grouped round traditional festivals, some of them older than Christianity. The Swedish Christmas season is celebrated more elaborately than in Britain and is an amalgam of pagan and Christian customs, commencing with the display of an Advent calendar and a visit to church on the first Sunday in Advent; then incorporating the Lucia festival on 13 December, a combination of a Christian celebration of a saint's day and a pagan custom of marking the passing of the longest night; reaching its climax on Christmas Eve with exchange of presents and Christmas Day with an over-indulgence in food and drink associated with the Viking period; and being rounded off with Twelfth Night, also a public holiday.

Further links with the past are preserved on 13 March, when the *Vasalopp* (the Vasa Race), the largest ski-race in the world, is run. Most Swedes are skilful skiers and every year over 5,000 of them enter this gruelling national event, a long-distance ski-run which ends at Mora, the point from which men of Dalarna set off to overtake the young Gustav Vasa in 1520 and to offer their support in the bid to expel the Danes and their tyrant king. Similarly on Midsummer Eve throughout the Swedish countryside maypoles, symbols of fertility, are raised, village fiddlers and accordionists play traditional folk-music, and Swedes enjoy their *fête champêtre*, dancing in the silvery, romantic light of the midnight twilight. The folk tradition is particularly strong in the province of Dalarna, where many of the local people quite unselfconsciously still wear their national costume.

In August there is again an open-air celebration, this one heralding the season of the crayfish, a delicacy which one apparently needs to be Swedish in order to appreciate fully. These events and the relaxed smiling participants are an essential part of Swedish life, although they are often ignored or forgotten in accounts of modern Swedish society.

The Swedes have taken great strides forward in the last few decades, have preserved a democratic tradition, and built up a humane welfare state. They have not been able to shed all their old problems, they have created several new ones, and they have no illusions about the ultimate emergence of the ideal state. Their active, pragmatic approach to life and their willingness to experiment are at once their strength and their weakness, for by dealing effectively with tangible social problems they not infrequently create intangible emotional ones. Moreover, the more success they have in pragmatic matters, the more impossible it seems to be for them to accept with a shrug of the shoulders that some emotional tangles cannot be unravelled. Frank Burns introduces into *Paradis för oss* a M. Bourdet, a very Gallic Frenchman who is frankly puzzled by the Swedes. 'The other day', says M. Bourdet

I read in a Swedish newspaper a long article by a lawyer and a doctor, who were discussing the problems of jealousy. The doctor seemed to think that jealousy comes from some kind of disturbance of the inner secretion and the lawyer maintained that it could be explained by far too restrictive divorce laws, but both were in agreement that with a little more sexual instruction and a few extra hormones and a more liberal divorce law it would doubtless be possible to abolish completely such a deformity as jealousy.

It is something of a parody, but it puts its finger on an essential Swedish trait.

As a nation, however, the Swedes have a genuine desire to eradicate social injustice, and even those who criticize Sweden adversely would almost invariably admit that it is a fair and a fair-minded country, characterized by freedom and beauty. The freedom extends to most spheres–political freedom, freedom of movement and of choice. In such a sparsely populated country there is room to breathe, to move, and to find seclusion easily and speedily. In a country where the rights of every citizen are respected there also exists the freedom to develop one's talents no matter how humble one's origins.

P

Foreign visitors, and indeed many Swedes, may carp at some imperfections, but when one brings these critics back to the salient points, that Sweden is an equitable, uncorrupt society where everyone is adequately educated, clothed, fed, and accommodated, and is, moreover, given spiritual freedom and human dignity, then they admit that the Swedes have just cause for national pride.

Swedish Rulers

Erik Segersäll (the Victorious) d. before 994

Olof Skötkonung *c.* 994–1022

Anund Jakob *c.* 1022–50

Emund *c.* 1050–60

Stenkil *c.* 1060–66

Halsten and Inge *c.* 1080–1110

Filip and Inge *c.* 1110–22

Ragnvald d. *c.* 1130

Sverker the Elder *c.* 1130–56

Erik (IX; St Erik) *c.* 1156–60

Karl (VII) Sverkersson 1161–67

Knut Eriksson 1167–96

Sverker the Younger Karlsson 1196–1208

Erik (X) Knutsson 1208–16

Johan (I) Sverkersson 1216–22

Erik (XI) Eriksson 1222–29, 1234–50

Knut Långe 1229–34

Birger Jarl (Regent) 1250–66

Valdemar 1250–75

Magnus Ladulås 1275–90

Torgils Knutsson (Regent) 1290–98

Birger Magnusson 1290–1318

Magnus Eriksson 1319–65

Erik (XII) 1357–59

Håkon 1362–71

Albrekt of Mecklenburg 1363–89

Margareta (Regent) 1389–1412

Erik (XIII) of Pomerania 1396–1439

Engelbrekt (Regent) 1435–36

Karl Knutsson (Regent) 1436–40

Kristoffer of Bavaria 1440–48

Karl (VIII) Knutsson 1448–57, 1464–65, 1467–70

Sten Sture the Elder (Regent) 1470–97, 1501–03

Hans (Johan II) 1497–1501

Svante Sture (Regent) 1504–12

Sten Sture the Younger (Regent) 1512–20

Kristian II 1520–21

Gustav I (Regent) 1521–23; (King) 1523–60

Erik XIV 1560–68

Johan III 1568–92

Sigismund 1592–99

Karl IX (Regent) until 1604; (King) 1604–11

Gustav II Adolf (Gustavus Adolphus) 1611–32

Kristina 1632–54

Karl X Gustav (Charles X) 1654–60

Karl XI 1660–97

Karl XII (Charles XII) 1697–1718

Ulrika Eleonora 1719–20

Fredrik I of Hessen 1720–51

Adolf Fredrik 1751–71

Gustav III 1771–92

Gustav IV Adolf 1792–1809

Karl XIII 1809–18

Karl XIV Johan (Bernadotte) 1818–44

Oscar I 1844–59

Karl XV 1859–72

Oscar II 1872–1907

Gustav V 1907–50

Gustav VI Adolf 1950–

Swedish Prime Ministers in the Twentieth Century

1900–02	F. V. von Otter
1902–05	E. G. Boström
1905	J. Ramstedt
1905	Ch. Lundeberg
1905–06	K. Staaff (Liberal)
1906–11	A. Lindman (Conservative)
1911–14	K. Staaff (Liberal)
1914–17	Hj. Hammarskjöld
1917	C. Swartz (Conservative)
1917–20	N. Edén (Liberal)
1920	Hj. Branting (Social Democrat)
1920–21	L. De Geer
1921	O. v. Sydow
1921–23	Hj. Branting (Social Democrat)
1923–24	E. Trygger (Conservative)
1924–25	Hj. Branting (Social Democrat)
1925–26	R. Sandler (Social Democrat)
1926–28	C. G. Ekman (Liberal)
1928–30	A. Lindman (Conservative)
1930–32	C. G. Ekman (Liberal)
1932	F. Hamrin (Liberal)
1932–36	P. A. Hansson (Social Democrat)
1936	A. Pehrsson (Agrarian)
1936–46	P. A. Hansson (Social Democrat)
1946–69	T. Erlander (Social Democrat)
1969–	O. Palme (Social Democrat)

Appendix C

Sweden's Top Manufacturers in 1969

Company	Activities	Turnover Mill. SKr	Exports Mill. SKr	Number employed
1. AB Volvo	Machinery and transport equipment	4,400	2,071	34,000
2. AB Svenska Kullagerfabriken (SKF)	Basic metals and metal products	4,227	930	64,100
3. Allmänna Svenska Elektriska AB (ASEA)	Electrical machinery	3,333	1,342	34,900
4. SAAB AB	Machinery and transport equipment	3,080	838	26,600
5. L. M. Ericsson Telephone Company	Telecommunications equipment	2,907	847	53,600
6. The Grängesberg Company	Mining, basic metals, metal products, plastics, building and construction	2,840	796	25,100
7. AB Skånska Cementgjuteriet	Building and construction	2,510	100	21,000
8. Svenska Tändsticks AB (STAB)	Paper and paper products, chemicals and chemical products, machinery	1,909	395	32,500
9. BPA Byggproduktion AB	Building and construction	1,646	—	17,200
10. Stora Kopparbergs Bergslags AB	Forestry, utilities, wood products, paper and paper products, chemicals and chemical products, machinery, plastics	1,622	530	13,300
11. AB Electrolux	Metal products and machinery	1,583	1,044	27,900

12. Svenska Cellulosa AB (SCA)	Forestry, utilities, wood products, paper and paper products, chemicals and chemical products, plastics	1,370	1,010	11,400
13. Sandvikens Jernverks AB	Mining, basic metals, metal products	1,339	1,155	10,300
14. Alfa-Laval AB	Metal products and machinery	1,330	353	14,600
15. Atlas Copco AB	Metal products and machinery	1,280	1,126	12,000
16. AB Svenska Metallverken	Basic metals, metal products, plastics	1,272	346	8,400
17. Uddeholms AB	Forestry, utilities, mining, paper and paper products, chemicals and chemical products, basic metals	1,152	617	14,000
18. Luossavaara-Kiirunavaara AB (LKAB)	Mining	1,148	1,136	6,900
19. Mo och Domsjö AB	Wood products, paper and paper products, chemicals and chemical products	1,119	895	7,600
20. Boliden AB	Mining, chemicals and chemical products, basic metals	1,107	—	6,500
21. AGA AB	Chemicals and chemical products, metal products, machinery	954	51	14,500
22. AB Bofors	Basic metals, metal products, transport equipment	946	229	8,700
23. Scan econ. association	Food manufacturing	934	78	2,200
24. AB Cementa	Wood products, non-metallic mineral products, metal products, plastics	913	110	11,300
25. Facit AB	Furniture and fixtures, machinery	879	582	13,200
26. Fagersta Bruks AB	Mining, basic metals and metal products	774	688	8,700

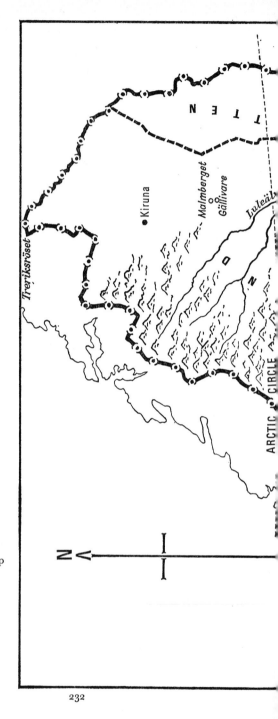

1 Sweden
General Map

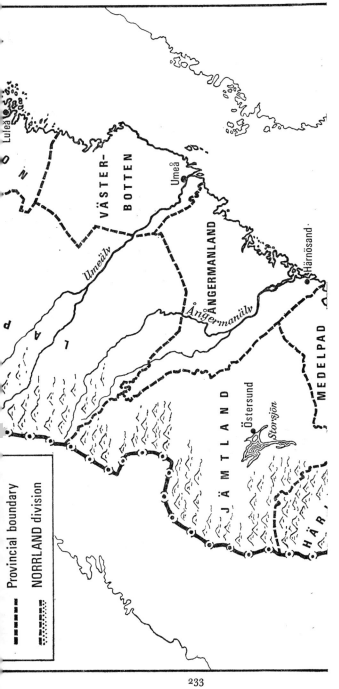

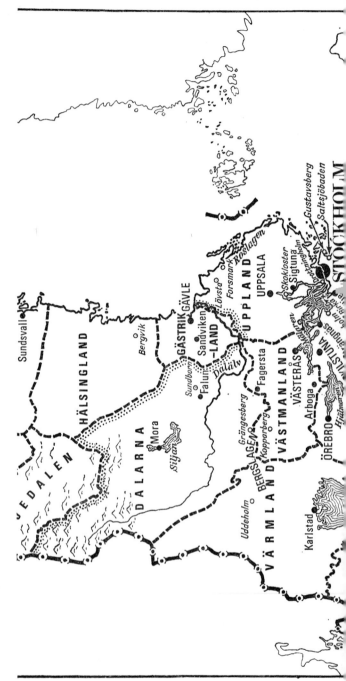

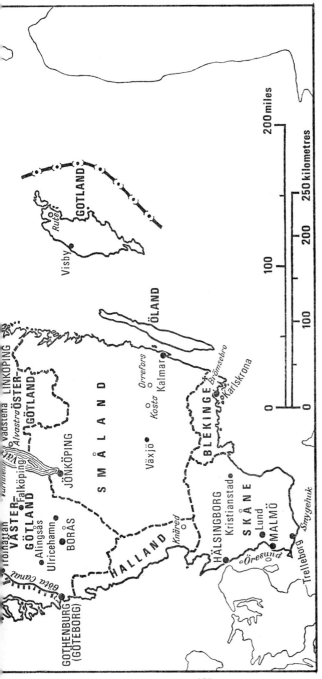

2 Sweden and northern Europe

A Selective Bibliography

Books in English on Sweden are listed in N. Afzelius's *Books in English on Sweden* (Stockholm, 1951); *About Sweden 1900–1963*, a bibliographical outline by B. Holmbäck published in *Sweden Illustrated*, XV (Stockholm, 1968); *Suecana Extranea 1963–1966*, published by the Swedish Institute (Stockholm, 1969); and *Suecana Extranea* published twice a year by The Royal Library, Stockholm, and listing items published from 1967 onwards. I have listed where possible the English rather than the Swedish version of a work and given the date of the latest edition.

Works covering all periods

I. Andersson, *A History of Sweden* (translated by C. Hannay, London, 1965); S. Oakley, *The Story of Sweden* (London, 1966. Contains useful selective bibliography); S. Carlsson and J. Rosén, *Svensk historia* I and II (3rd ed., Stockholm, 1970. Contains excellent extensive bibliographies); *Sveriges historia genom tiderna* (ed. H. Maiander; Stockholm, 1947); C. Grimberg, *Svenska folkets underbara öden* (new revised ed., Stockholm, 1963); J. Rosén *et al.*, *Den svenska utrikespolitikens historia* (Stockholm, 1952–); G. Hägglöff, *Britain and Sweden. From the Vikings to the Common Market* (Stockholm, 1966); M. Roberts, *Essays in Swedish History* (London, 1967); A. C. O'Dell, *The Scandinavian World* (London, 1963); W. R. Mead, *An Economic Geography of the Scandinavian States and Finland* (reprinted London, 1968); E. Heckscher, *An Economic History of Sweden* (Cambridge, Mass., 1954); K. Samuelsson, *From Great Power to Welfare State* (London, 1968); R. Murray, *A Brief History of the Church of Sweden* (Stockholm, 1961); E. Bredsdorff, B. Mortensen, & R. Popperwell, *An Introduction to Scandinavian Literature from the Earliest Time to Our Day* (Cambridge, 1951); A. Gustafson, *A History of Swedish Literature* (Minneapolis, 1961. Contains good bibliography and lists of English translations of Swedish literature); G. Bergman, *A Short History of the Swedish Language* (Stockholm, 1947); H. Cornell, *Den svenska konstens historia* (2nd ed., Stockholm, 1966. Comprises Swedish painting, sculpture, and architecture from the Viking period to the end of the nineteenth century).

237

Chapter 1

V. Moberg, *Min svenska historia* I and II (Stockholm, 1970–71. A most readable but highly subjective history); M. Stenberger, *Sweden* (London, 1962); idem, *Det forntida Sverige* (Stockholm, 1964); idem, *Sten, brons, järn* (Stockholm, 1969); J. Brønsted, *The Vikings* (London, 1960); P. G. Foote and D. W. Wilson, *The Viking Achievement* (London, 1970); D. W. Wilson, *The Vikings and Their Origins* (London, 1970); S. B. F. Jansson, *The Runes of Sweden* (Stockholm, 1962); S. U. Palme, *Kristendomens genombrott i Sverige* (Stockholm, 1962); E. Lönnroth, *Sverige och Kalmarunionen* (Stockholm, 1934); idem, *Från svensk medeltid* (Stockholm, 1964); S. U. Palme, *Sten Sture den äldre* (Stockholm, 1950); E. Peacy, *St Birgitta of Sweden* (London, 1934).

Chapter 2

M. Roberts, *The Early Vasas. A History of Sweden 1523–1611* (Cambridge, 1968); J. Lisk, *The Struggle for Supremacy in the Baltic 1600–1725* (London, 1967); I. Svalenius, *Gustav Vasa* (Stockholm, 1963); K. B. Westman, *Reformationens genombrottsår i Sverige* (Stockholm, 1918); C. J. I. Bergendoff, *Olaus Petri and the Ecclesiastical Transformation in Sweden 1521–1552* (New York, 1928); I. Andersson, *Erik XIV. En biografi* (Stockholm, 1963); M. Roberts, *Sweden as a Great Power 1611–1697. Government, Society, Foreign Policy* (London, 1968); idem, *Gustavus Adolphus. A History of Sweden 1611–1632* (London 1953–58); N. Ahnlund, *Gustav Adolph the Great* (Princeton, 1940); C. V. Wedgwood, *The Thirty Years War* (London, 1938); N. Ahnlund, *Axel Oxenstierna intill Gustav Adolfs död* (Stockholm, 1940); J. Rosén, *Scandinavia and the Baltic* (in *New Cambridge Modern History*, V, 1644–88, Cambridge, 1961); S. Stolpe, *Christina of Sweden* (London, 1966); C. Weibull, *Christina of Sweden* (Stockholm, 1966); R. Fåhraeus, *Magnus Gabriel De La Gardie* (Stockholm, 1936); F. G. Bengtsson, *The Life of Charles XII* (translated by N. Walford, Stockholm, 1960); R. M. Hatton, *Charles XII of Sweden* (London, 1968); Voltaire, *Histoire de Charles XII* (1731); O. Haintz, *Karl XII* (Berlin, 1958).

Chapter 3

B. J. Hovde, *The Scandinavian Countries 1720–1865* (New York, 1948); C. G. Malmström, *Sveriges politiska historia från Konung Karl XII:s död till statshvälfningen 1772* (Stockholm, 1893–1901); L. Thanner, *Revolutionen i Sverige efter Karl XII:s död* (Stockholm, 1953);

K. Hagberg, *Carl Linnaeus* (London, 1952); G. Trobridge, *Sweden-borg, life and teaching* (4th ed., New York, 1962); R. N. Bain, *Gustavus III and his Contemporaries* (London, 1894); C. T. Odhner, *Sveriges politiska historia under Gustaf III:s regering* (Stockholm, 1885–1905); B. Hennings, *Gustav III som kronprins* (Stockholm, 1935); *idem, Gustav III* (Stockholm, 1957); *idem, Fyra gustavianska studier* (Stockholm, 1967); S. Carlsson, *Sverige och Storbritannien 1787–1790* (Lund, 1944); P. Britten Austin, *The Life and Songs of C. M. Bellman* (Malmö and London, 1967); G. Hilleström, *The Drottningholm Theatre – Past and Present* (Stockholm, 1956); S. Carlsson, *Gustaf IV Adolf* (Stockholm, 1946); F. D. Scott, *Bernadotte and the Fall of Napoleon* (Cambridge, Mass., 1935); D. P. Barton, *The Amazing Career of Bernadotte* (London, 1929); R. E. Lindgren, *Norway–Sweden. Union, Disunion and Scandinavian Integration* (Princeton, 1959); A. Söderhjelm, *Oscar I* (Stockholm, 1944); C. Hallendoff, *Från Karl XV:s dagar* (Stockholm, 1924); S. Eriksson, *Karl XV* (Stockholm, 1954).

Chapter 4

A. Montgomery, *The Rise of Modern Industry in Sweden* (London, 1939); *idem, Industrialismens genombrott i Sverige* (Stockholm, 1947); K. Samuelsson, *Hur vår moderna industri vuxit fram* (Stockholm, 1963); L. Jörberg, *The Industrial Revolution in Scandinavia 1850–1914* (*Fontana Economic History of Europe*, Volume 4, Chapter 8, London, 1970); F. E. Janson, *The Background of Swedish Immigration 1840–1930* (Chicago, 1931); D. V. Verney, *Parliamentary Reform in Sweden 1866–1921* (Oxford, 1957); J. Westerståhl, *Svenska fackförenings-srörelsen* (Stockholm, 1945); King Oscar II, *Mina memoarer* (Stockholm, 1960–63); Z. Höglund, *Hj. Branting och hans livsgärning* (Stockholm, 1929); L. Furhoff and H. Hederberg, *Dagspressen i Sverige* (Stockholm, 1968); L. Kihlberg, *Karl Staaff* (Stockholm, 1962–63); I. Anderson, *Arvid Lindman och hans tid* (Stockholm, 1956); K. Hildebrand, *Gustaf V som människa och regent* (Stockholm, 1945–48); G. Ahlström, *Det moderna genombrottet i Nordens litteratur* (Stockholm, 1947); B. M. E. Mortensen and B. W. Downs, *Strindberg. An Introduction to his life and work* (2nd ed., Cambridge, 1965); W. A. Berendsohn, *S. Lagerlöf, her life and work* (London, 1968).

Chapter 5

E. Håstad, *Sveriges historia under 1900–talet* (Stockholm, 1966); S. Hadenius, H. Wieslander, and B. Molin, *Sverige efter 1900. En modern politisk historia* (Stockholm, 1969); O. A. Rustow, *The Politics of Compromise* (Princeton, 1955); J. Barres, *The Åland Islands Question* (New Haven, 1968); Å. Elmér, *Från Fattigsverige till välfärdsstaten* (Stockholm, 1969); H. Tingsten, *Den svenska socialdemokratiens idéutveckling* (Stockholm, 1941); M. W. Childs, *Sweden, The Middle Way* (Yale, 1947); R. Shaplen, *Kreuger, Genius and Swindler* (New York, 1960); E. Wigforss, *Minnen* (Stockholm, 1950–54); F. Ström, *Memoarer I and II* (Stockholm, 1942); Ö. Undén, *Minnesanteckningar* (Stockholm, 1966); H. Tingsten, *Mitt Liv* (Stockholm, 1961–64); I. Anderson, *Åsyna vittne. Människor och händelser i press och politik 1914–1940* (Stockholm, 1968); A. and G. Myrdal, *Kris i befolkningsfrågan* (Stockholm, 1934); H. Tingsten, *The Debate on the Foreign Policy of Sweden 1918–1939* (London, 1949); S. S. Jones, *The Scandinavian States and the League of Nations* (Princeton, 1939); I. Scobbie, *Pär Lagerkvist. An Introduction* (Stockholm, 1962); G. Orton, *Eyvind Johnson* (New York, 1971).

Chapter 6

W. N. Medlicott and A. H. Hicks, *The War and the Neutrals* (ed. A. and V. M. Toynbee, London, 1956); W. N. Medlicott, *An Economic Blockade* (*History of the Second World War*; London, 1952–59); T. K. Derry, *The Campaign in Norway* (ibid.); G. Hägglöf, *Svensk krigshandelspolitik under andra världskriget* (Stockholm, 1958); J. H. Wuorenen, *Finland and World War II 1939–1940* (New York, 1948); J. Jacobson, *The Diplomacy of the Winter War* (Cambridge, Mass., 1961); Å. Thulstrup, *Svensk utrikespolitik under andra världskriget* (Stockholm, 1950); I. Anderson, *Från det nära förflutna. Människor och händelser 1940–1955* (Stockholm, 1969); C. Wahlgren, *På skilda fronter. Upplevelser som officer och tidningsman* (Malmö, 1970).

Chapters 7 and 8

The Swedish Institute, Box 7072, Stockholm, S-10382 operates a valuable information service, commissioning and distributing publications in English on many aspects of modern Swedish life and culture. K. Nott, *A Clean Well-lighted Place. A Private View of Sweden* (London, 1961); D. Connery, *The Scandinavians* (London, 1966); F. Fleisher, *The New Sweden. The Challenge of a Disciplined Democracy* (New York, 1967); D. Jenkins, *Sweden. The Progress Machine* (London, 1968); P. Britten Austin, *On Being Swedish* (London, 1968); idem, *The Swedes. How they Live and Work* (Newton Abbot, 1970); P. Meurling, *Tage Erlander* (Stockholm, 1953); *Sweden in Europe* (Royal Ministry for Foreign Affairs, Stockholm, 1971); G. Hildén, *Vi och EEC*

(Stockholm, 1971); *Scandinavia and European Integration* (Proceedings of Conference held at Aberdeen University, 1971); F. Wendt, *The Nordic Council and Co-operation in Scandinavia* (Copenhagen, 1959); V. Slettin, *Five Northern Countries Pull Together* (published by the Nordic Council, Copenhagen, 1967); N. Andrén, *Power Balances and Non-Alignment: A Perspective of Swedish Foreign Policy* (Stockholm, 1967); O. Nyman, *Parlamentarismen i Sverige* (Stockholm, 1950); N. Andrén, *Modern Swedish Government* (Stockholm, 1968); N. Elder, *Government in Sweden* (Oxford, 1970); B. E. Grimlund and L. Ricknell, *Den nya riksdagen* (Stockholm, 1970); P. Vinde, *Swedish Government Administration* (Stockholm, 1971); D. V. Verney, *Public Enterprise in Sweden* (Liverpool, 1959); G. Arpi, *Sveriges nutida näringsliv* (Stockholm, 1967); M. Norgren (ed.), *Industry in Sweden* (Stockholm, 1968); M. and C. Norgren, *Industrial Sweden* (Stockholm, 1971); *Modern Swedish Labour Market Policy* (published by National Labour Market Board, Stockholm, 1966); *Detta djävla Norrland. 20 författare möter glesbygden* (Stockholm, 1971); T. L. Johnston, *Collective Bargaining in Sweden* (London, 1962); B. Carlson, *Trade Unions in Sweden* (Stockholm, 1969); K. J. Höjer, *Den svenska socialpolitiken* (Stockholm, 1965); Å. Elmér, *Svensk socialpolitik* (Stockholm, 1966); B. Molin, *Tjänstepensionsfrågan* (Summary in English: *The Supplementary Pension Question. A Study in Swedish Party Politics*, Gothenburg, 1965); *Social Benefits in Sweden* (Swedish Institute, Stockholm, 1970); K. Åström, *City Planning in Sweden* (Stockholm, 1967); J. Orring, *School in Sweden* (Stockholm, 1968); S. Thorsell and M. Kärre, *Before School Starts* (Stockholm, 1969); B. Stenholm, *Education in Sweden* (Stockholm, 1970); F. Fleisher, *Folk High Schools in Sweden* (Stockholm, 1968); *The State and Culture in Sweden* (published by Swedish Ministry of Education & Cultural Affairs, Stockholm, 1970); N. P. Sundgren, *The New Swedish Cinema* (Stockholm, 1970); P. Cowie, *Sweden. Guide to work of 170 Swedish directors etc. in Swedish Cinema* (London, 1970); N. Elvander, *Intresseorganisationerna i dagens Sverige* (Stockholm, 1966); D. C. Rowat (ed.), *The Ombudsman. Citizens' Defender* (London, 1965); L. Gustafsson, *The Public Dialogue in Sweden. Current Issues of Social, Esthetic and Moral Debate* (Stockholm, 1964); B. Linnér, *Society and Sex* (Stockholm, 1971); L. Wahlström, *Den svenska kvinnorörelsen* (Stockholm, 1933); J. Rössel, *Kvinnorna och kvinnorörelser i Sverige 1850–1950* (Stockholm, 1950); M. B. Sandlund, *The Status of Women in Sweden* (Report to the United Nations, Stockholm, 1968); H. Hendin, *Suicide and Scandinavia. A psychoanalytic study of culture and character* (New York & London, 1964); E. Hj. Linder, *Fem decennier av 1900 talet I and II (Ny illustrerad svensk litteraturhistoria*, Stockholm, 1964); L. Bäckström (ed.), *Sweden Writes. Contemporary Swedish Poetry and*

Prose, Views on Art, Literature and Society (Stockholm, 1965); *Sweden Number* of *The Literary Review* (New Jersey, Winter 1965–66); *Sweden in Literature. Adam International Review*, Nos. 304–6 (London 1966); Å. Runnquist, *Moderna svenska författare* (Stockholm, 1967); *Scandinavian Writing Today*. Times Literary Supplement No. 3628 (10 September 1971).

Index

(The Swedish letters å, ä, and ö have been treated as a, a, and o)

243

Printed in Great Britain by
Richard Clay (The Chaucer Press) Ltd.
Bungay, Suffolk